# STUDY GUIDE

## Terence J. Bazzett

State University of New York at Geneseo

to accompany

BRYAN KOLB

IAN Q. WHISHAW

# AN INTRODUCTION TO BRAIN AND BEHAVIOR

WORTH PUBLISHERS

**Study Guide**
by Terence J. Bazzett
to accompany
Kolb/Whishaw: **An Introduction to Brain and Behavior**

ISBN: 0–7167–5103–8

Printing: 5  4  3  2
Year:  04  03


Printed in the United States of America




Worth Publishers
41 Madison Avenue
New York, NY  10010
www.worthpublishers.com

# Contents

# To the Student

Worried about doing well in this course? Relax. By opening this study guide you've taken an important step toward improving your grade. Now take the next step and spend a minute or two reading through the information below.

I've been teaching brain and behavior courses for more than 15 years, and in that time I've observed the way my successful students prepare for quizzes, exams, and presentations. I've tried to incorporate that knowledge into the design of this study guide. My goal was to create a relatively simple tool that could enhance a student's performance without requiring an excessive amount of time or effort.

Each chapter of this study guide contains the following elements. For each item, I've offered a few suggestions for its effective use.

*Summary:* After you've read the chapter and listened to the lectures, read the summary quickly. It's okay to skim through this summary, as long as you're comfortable with your understanding of the key terms. If any of the terms look unfamiliar, you may wish to revisit your text to make sure you have a clear sense of how the term fits into the chapter.

*Key Terms* and *Key Names:* Take special note of key terms used by your professor in lectures and put stars by them in your study guide. If you're not completely clear on the meaning, look it up in the text and write a brief description next to the term. Some professors stress key names, whereas others may not refer to them at all. If your professor does not emphasize these names, do not labor to memorize them. Instead focus on terms. As a way to study for an exam try selecting a relatively large number of terms listed in this guide and stressed by your professor. Take a stack of 3 × 5-inch cards and randomly choose terms, writing about five on each card until you have a stack of cards containing terms that you think will appear on the upcoming exam. Get together with a few classmates and try a game that follows the rules of the word game Taboo. In general, this is how you play: One student selects a card and then tries to get his or her teammate to say the word by describing associated terms, concepts, and so on. Keep in mind that the person viewing the card can't use any form of the word to be guessed (no rhyming words either; these are "taboo"). Teammates then switch so that both get a chance to read and guess words. To determine a winning team, keep track of the number of correct terms and the amount of time to guess them. The most words in the shortest amount of time wins. This may sound corny, but if the alternative is sitting home alone trying to memorize terms, you may find this game of "bioboo" (as my students call it) less tedious, even a little enjoyable.

*Practice Test:* Don't panic if you don't get them all correct! This guide is very general and takes information from throughout each chapter without bias. Your professor will likely be much more specific about some topics, and may skip others completely. Missing a question that your professor has not covered and will not be using for a test is not cause for alarm. Essay questions are even more general than the multiple-choice questions, but I've tried to select topics that tend to interest a majority of professors. For each multiple-choice and essay question, I've given you a page number from your text where you will find the information needed to support the correct answer (though sometimes that information runs on for a page or two). Matching questions do not have page numbers listed for answers since many of them incorporate information from throughout the chapter. You can certainly look through and find the correct answers, but you can also just trust me on those. When I teach this course, diagram questions are among my favorite to use on tests. If your professor emphasizes drawings and diagrams, like I do, pay particular attention to this section of the Practice Test.

*CD-ROM:* The CD that comes with the textbook is top of the line. Great graphics, lots of accurate information, animations, video clips, and so on. The easiest studying you can do to prepare for an exam is browsing through this CD. You might want to save it for the end of your study time, when you're burned out on reading and writing. Regardless of when you use it, you should check out the CD exercises as a novel and effective approach to exam preparation.

*The Web:* I've put in just a few of the many sites that correspond to some main topics in each chapter. Should your professor require a written project, these Web sites might jump-start your research. I've also tried to find some sites with particularly nice photos, videos, animations, and so on. One note of caution: Be sure to read the site addresses very carefully. Some have the www prefix, some do not. Some contain long strings of letters and numbers. Most are worth the trouble if you're interested in the topic. Unfortunately, it is possible that some of these sites will be defunct by the time you try them. Sorry, there's nothing we can do about that until the next edition of this guide is printed.

*Crossword Puzzles:* I love puzzles and I felt that there should be something particularly enjoyable in this guide, so I've included a relatively simple crossword puzzle for each chapter. These puzzles are actually "simple" only in terms of the number of words. Recalling these words (and correctly spelling them) can be very tricky. There is always the answer key if you get stuck. But before going to the answer key, try looking through the list of key terms. Most of the answers for these puzzles can be found in that list.

Good luck with your class.

## Acknowledgment

I would like to thank Dr. Elaine Hull for her contributions to this and all of my works.

Good teachers answer students' questions.
Great teachers answer students' questions, and inspire them to ask more.

Thanks for the inspiration, Elaine.

# Foundations of Behavioral Neuroscience CD-ROM

Below are tree structures showing you the major headings for the five components of the CD-ROM that came with your textbook. When you see the codes indicated on the right presented in the study guide, you should locate that content material on the CD-ROM and complete the activities. The graphics, text, audio, and video components of this learning device will greatly aid your understanding of the concepts presented in the textbook.

This CD-ROM also contains multiple-choice study questions for each chapter of the text to aid in test preparation.

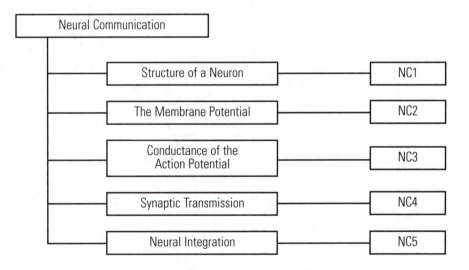

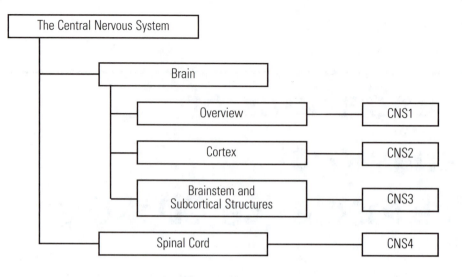

The Central Nervous System

Brain

Overview — CNS1

Cortex — CNS2

Brainstem and Subcortical Structures — CNS3

Spinal Cord — CNS4

Research Methods

Benefits of Animal Research

EEG — RM1

Electrical Stimulation — RM2

Stereotaxic Apparatus — RM3

Microelectrode — RM4

Histology — RM5

Confocal Microscope — RM6

CT — RM7

MRI — RM8

PET — RM9

Optical Imaging — RM10

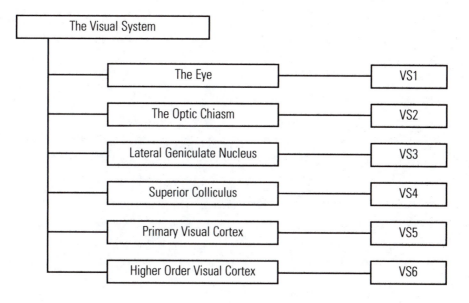

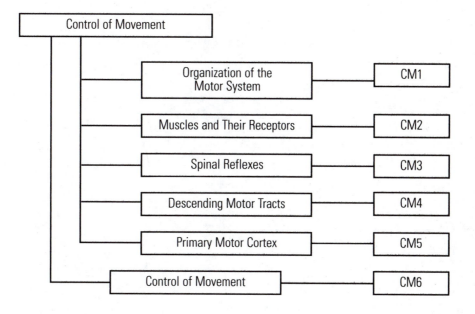

# STUDY GUIDE

# 1  What Are the Origins of Brain and Behavior?

## CHAPTER SUMMARY

Those who study neuroscience have long struggled to understand the relationship between *brain* and *behavior*, two inextricably linked yet vastly different entities. The brain may be described as an organ, as tissue or matter. Behavior, on the other hand, is far less tangible, described as an observable action but lacking in physical substance. The problem for researchers and philosophers alike has been to adequately explain how brain and behavior are related. This chapter sets the stage for the rest of the text by describing the brain, describing behavior, and then discussing theories of how the two are related.

The term *brain*, as used in the brain/behavior problem described above, generally refers to the entire *nervous system* which includes not only the brain but also the *spinal cord* and *peripheral nerves*, all of which play essential roles in the generation of behavior. The nervous system is an elaborate series of *nerve cells* that carry information to and from the brain and periphery via the spinal cord. Nerve cells that make up the brain and spinal cord collectively are referred to as the central nervous system, while all other nerve cells are considered to be part of the peripheral nervous system. Cells traversing these two systems include *sensory* and *motor neurons*, some of which make up the *autonomic nervous system* responsible for regulation of many internal organs and vital functions such as digestion, heart rate, blood pressure, and the like.

The term *behavior* used in the brain/behavior problem described above may be simply described as movement of an organism having both cause and function. Such movements may include both inherited and learned behaviors. Regarding the relationship between brain and behavior, a positive correlation has been noted between complexity of the nervous system and range of behaviors exhibited across species.

Theories of how brain and behavior are linked date back thousands of years, with early theories described as addressing the mind/brain problem ("mind" describing the psyche or soul responsible for our behavior). *Aristotle* was among the first to philosophize about the relationship between mind and brain, suggesting that human behavior is a product of the *psyche*, a nonmaterial entity that operates independent of material body organs, including the brain. This philosophy formed the basis for the theory of *mentalism*. Mentalism remained relatively unchallenged until the 1500s, when *René Descartes* proposed that the mind, though separate from the brain, is somehow linked to this physical organ. This theory, proposing a nonphysical mind that was dependent upon the brain for receiving information and for controlling physical human behavior, formed the basis for the theory of *dualism*. More specifically, Descartes's theory of dualism placed the mind within the *pineal gland* and put forth the hypothesis that pineal control over *ventricular fluid* was the basis of behavior. Dualism gained support through observations of individuals who seemingly lost aspects of their basic personality (their mind) following damage to the brain. Dualism dominated the scientific approach to the study of brain and behavior until the mid-nineteenth century, when *Alfred Wallace* and *Charles Darwin* independently arrived at the same idea that all living things are related. Darwin advanced this theory by proposing the *theory of natural selection* as a means by which functional diversity can lead to an array of physical features as well as behaviors. *Gregor Mendel* lent support to Darwin's theory of natural selection by demonstrating that such functional diversity can evolve from *heritable factors* (which we now know are *genes*). Darwin's theory suggested that all species shared common behaviors as well as common organs (including the brain). His theories further suggested that the brain, and subsequently behavior, were built up over time through *evolution*. These theories formed the basis for our current perception that behavior is controlled by the brain, termed simply *the brain theory*.

Although the nervous system (brain) is required for behavior, it is not essential for life. In fact, most living organisms lack a nervous system. Thus, nerve cells give animals the unique ability to create purposeful movement. Such movements range from those produced by the simplest *nerve net* (found in jellyfish), to a *segmented nervous system* (in flat worms), to a collection of neurons called *ganglia* (in clams and snails), to the most complex system of *chordates* containing a spinal cord and brain (in you). The size and complexity of the nervous system in chordates vary widely, but in general the evolutionarily most advanced species tend to have the largest *cerebral cortex* and *cerebellum* relative to the rest of the brain.

Humans belong to the *primate order* within a family called *Hominidae*. Present-day humans (*Homo sapiens*) are believed to represent a single descendent of numerous *hominid* (human-like animals) ancestors. Among the early hominids were *Homo habilis* (handy human), *Homo erectus* (upright human), and *Neanderthals*. The relatively large brain of Homo sapiens is believed to have evolved through *encephalization*, which is a process of increasing size and complexity of the cerebral cortex, which allows more complex behavior. Encephalization through evolution has resulted in a human brain that is larger in size (relative to body size) than any other animal. When considering that greater brain mass is required for increasingly sophisticated actions, this puts humans at the top of the scale for capacity to engage in complex behaviors.

Enlargement of the human brain is thought to be a response to changes in climate and food sources, and subsequently the need to develop strategies to adapt to these changes. For example, humans likely evolved into fruit gatherers, requiring more sensory and motor skills than grazing animals. Enlargement may also have been promoted by increased cerebral blood flow. Increased blood flow is associated with enhanced ability to cool the brain and presumably enhanced capacity for tissue growth and cell proliferation. *Neoteny* is the theory that humans represent a primate that expresses juvenile features of earlier ancestors, including a larger *cranium* (allowing for greater brain mass) relative to body size and prolific nerve cell growth (as seen during development) over a longer period of time.

Within the human species, it is difficult to determine what brain factors (e.g., weight, volume) if any correlate directly to intellectual capacity. Part of this problem results from an imprecise definition of what constitutes *intelligence*. In addition, brain size seems to correlate somewhat to body size, adding an additional extraneous variable to this task. Much of what we consider intelligent or complex behavior also seems to result from learning within our culture rather than ability inherent in brain cells.

## KEY TERMS

*The following is a list of important terms introduced in Chapter 1. Give the definition of each term in the space provided.*

### *Defining Brain and Behavior*

Brain


Hemispheres


Gyri


Cerebral cortex


Temporal lobe


Frontal lobe


Parietal lobe


Occipital lobe


### *Nervous System Structure*

Nerve cell


Spinal cord

Central nervous system

Peripheral nervous system

Nervous system

Sensory pathways

Motor pathways

Autonomic nervous system

**Brain and Behavior**

Psyche

Mentalism

Pineal body

Ventricles

Mind–body problem

Dualism

Materialism

Natural selection

Genes

Brain theory

**Evolution of Brain and Behavior**

Nerve net

Bilaterally symmetrical

Segmented

Ganglia

Chordates

Cerebellum

Primate order

**Human Evolution**

Hominids

Australopithecus

Homo habilis

Homo erectus

Neanderthals

Homo sapiens

Encephalization

Principle of proper mass

Encephalization Quotient, EQ

Neoteny

Radiator hypothesis

Species-typical

Culture

Dyslexia

# KEY NAMES

*The following is a list of important names introduced in Chapter 1. Explain the importance of each person in the space provided.*

Fred Linge

Aristotle


René Descartes


Alfred Russell Wallace


Charles Darwin


Gregor Mendel


Donald O. Hebb


H. J. Jerison


## PRACTICE TEST

## Multiple-Choice Questions

*Answer each of the following multiple-choice questions with the best possible answer based on information from your text.*

1. When trying to define brain, behavior, and the relationship of the two, you could say . . .
   A.  both represent physical objects
   B.  both represent theoretical concepts
   C.  the brain is conceptual whereas behavior is physical
   D.  the brain is physical whereas behavior is conceptual
   E.  the two are most likely unrelated

2. Which of the following is not a name for one of the lobes of the cerebral cortex?
   A.  Cortical
   B.  Temporal
   C.  Frontal
   D.  Parietal
   E.  Occipital

3. The cerebral cortex is best described as which of the following?
   A. A term for the brain
   B. A term for the outer surface of the brain
   C. A term for the part of the brain that is responsible for behavior
   D. A term for the inner core of the brain
   E. A term for the spinal cord

4. What is the term commonly given to the brain and spinal cord collectively?
   A. The nervous system
   B. The sensory pathway
   C. The motor pathway
   D. The peripheral nervous system
   E. The central nervous system

5. Donald O. Hebb proposed that the brain needs ongoing sensory and motor experiences to maintain intellectual activity. As evidence he cites an experiment in which subjects deprived of all sensory input and motor output exhibited which of the following?
   A. Significantly increased time spent sleeping
   B. Inability to remember the experience
   C. A level of brain function similar to a coma
   D. An extremely unpleasant sensation, sometimes including hallucinations
   E. An extremely pleasant sensation, similar to that of meditation

6. The common crossbill inherits both the adaptive beak and the adaptive behavior for extracting seeds from pinecones. By comparison, the roof rat . . .
   A. inherits the adaptive behavior and adaptive crossed incisor teeth
   B. inherits only the adaptive behavior
   C. learns the adaptive behavior from a parent
   D. learns the adaptive behavior from watching the crossbill
   E. cannot extract seeds from these pinecones

7. Aristotle was among the first to philosophize about the "mind," suggesting that it was . . .
   A. the same as the brain
   B. the equivalent to what religious groups called the "soul"
   C. located in the heart
   D. cooled by the blood
   E. material in structure

8. Following Aristotle were the theories of René Descartes that the brain and mind represented separate entities—one material and one nonmaterial, respectively. This theory formed the basis for which of the following philosophical positions?
   A. Mentalism
   B. Materialism
   C. Dualism
   D. Evolution
   E. All of the above

9. Descartes was also among the first to suggest that the brain drove body function through mechanical means. What form of energy did he suggest was the basis for movement?
   A. Thermal energy produced by heat from the brain
   B. Electrical energy produced by individual cells in the brain
   C. Hydraulic energy produced by movement of fluid from the brain
   D. Chemical energy produced by chemicals in the brain
   E. None of the above; Descartes did not believe the brain played a role in physical movement

10. The perspective of materialism disregards the need to consider which of the following?
   A. Behavior
   B. The brain
   C. The mind
   D. Evolution
   E. All of the above

11. Phineas Gage was one of the first substantial case studies supporting the concept that particular behaviors are localized to specific brain regions. What region of Gage's brain was damaged to produce his particular behavioral deficits?
   A. Frontal lobe
   B. Temporal lobe
   C. Parietal lobe
   D. Occipital lobe
   E. Cerebellum

12. From the theories of Charles Darwin, and related research since his time, modern researchers believe which of the following regarding human emotions?
   A. Emotions are inherited rather than learned
   B. Human emotions are similar to emotions expressed by other animals
   C. Emotions are common to all human cultures worldwide
   D. Both the brain and behaviors (including emotions) have evolved together over time
   E. All of the above

13. Taxonomy is the field of biology concerned with naming and classifying species. Currently taxonomists have identified approximately what percentage of species currently thought to inhabit the earth?
   A. Over 95%
   B. Approximately 75%
   C. Approximately 50%
   D. Approximately 25%
   E. Less than 5%

14. The phyla that contains clams, snails, and octopuses represents the simplest nervous system that contains a collection of neurons termed a . . .
   A. ganglia
   B. brain
   C. spinal cord
   D. central nervous system
   E. None of the above; the nervous system in these animals lacks any organization

15. The family of hominids, to which humans belong, also includes which of the following?
    A. Gorillas
    B. Chimpanzees
    C. Neanderthals
    D. Orangutans
    E. All of the above
    F. None of the above

16. Which of the following species from the human lineage has the largest encephalization quotient (EQ)?
    A. Monkey
    B. Chimpanzee
    C. Homo sapien
    D. Homo erectus
    E. Homo habilis

17. The principle of proper mass, in general, states that . . .
    A. larger brains are associated with larger animals
    B. larger animals tend to have more complex behaviors
    C. larger animals tend to have less complex behaviors
    D. larger brains are needed for increasingly complex behavior
    E. brain size is not related to complexity of behavior

18. Neoteny is one theory to explain why humans have developed such complex and large brains relative to other primates. Which of the following is true according to this theory?
    A. Adult humans have a greater capacity for neural development than do other adult primates
    B. Adult humans have some physical features that resemble those of juveniles from other primates
    C. Adult humans have some behavior patterns that resemble those of juveniles from other primates
    D. All of the above
    E. None of the above

19. In attempting to correlate brain size to capacity for intellect, researchers measured the brain of Albert Einstein and found that it was . . .
    A. of average size
    B. approximately 5% smaller than an average brain
    C. approximately 5% larger than an average brain
    D. approximately 10% larger than an average brain
    E. approximately 20% larger than an average brain

20. Researchers suggest that learning disabilities (and thus the capacity to learn) are directly linked to physiological functions. Supporting this idea, several features of dyslexia have been noted in addition to difficulty mastering language-related tasks. Which of the following is *not* a physical correlate to dyslexia?
    A. Dyslexia appears to be more prevalent in boys than girls
    B. Abnormal neural growth in the language center of dyslexics may be related to the disability
    C. Testosterone may be a factor contributing to the disability
    D. Dyslexics tend to have vision problems in addition to the learning disability
    E. Dyslexic children often have difficulty learning to write as well as read

## Short Answer Questions

*Answer each of the following questions with a brief but complete written answer based on information from your text.*

1. Briefly describe the function of the autonomic nervous system.

2. Humans have the most complex nervous system of any animal, and thus the greatest capacity for learning new adaptive behaviors. However, humans still retain some inherited patterns of responding. Briefly explain why such basic behaviors are still present in humans.

3. René Descartes put forth the theory of dualism, suggesting that the brain and the mind are separate yet closely related features of all humans. Currently, researchers suggest a similar relationship between the brain and behavior. Briefly explain how Descartes's original proposal of dualism differs from our current perspective on brain and behavior.

4. Phineas Gage, after his tragic brain injury, became a case study supporting the idea that higher level functioning (human behavior) is controlled by particular regions of the brain. Briefly describe the type of injury Gage suffered, the location of the injury, and the behavioral changes that were apparent following this injury.

5. Briefly describe the concept of natural selection, and give an example of how this process could lead to development of an increasingly complex nervous system.

6. Large-brained animals (animals with complex behaviors) have the appearance of a wrinkled or folded brain surface called the cortex. Briefly explain the folded appearance of the cortex and how these folds may be related to complex behavior patterns.

7. One theory of why humans have such large and complex brains is that this is an evolutionary adaptation to environment changes over the past several million years. Briefly explain why a brain might evolve greater complexity in response to changes in the animal's environment.

8. Briefly explain the "radiator hypothesis" of the evolution of human brain growth.

9. In attempting to correlate brain size to intelligence, researchers have found that the brain of an average human female weighs approximately 10% less than the brain of an average human male. Give a brief explanation of what this finding likely suggests.

10. It is unlikely that the human brain has (through evolution) developed the specific capacities to do such things as design modern computers. However, this is unquestionably a behavior in which humans (and thus their brains) engage. Does this observation refute the concept that the brain has evolved to undertake complex behaviors? Explain your answer.

# Matching Questions

*Complete each of the following matching questions based on information from your text.*

1. Match the following lobes to the appropriate regions of the brain pictured below:

   A. Frontal
   B. Occipital
   C. Parietal
   D. Temporal

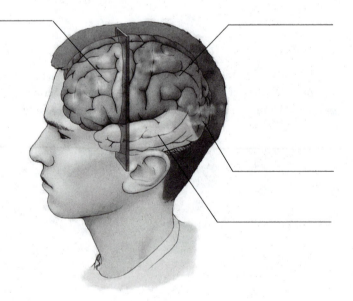

2. Match each of the following historical names with their area of contribution to our current understanding of the relationship between the brain and behavior.

    A.  Mendel               ___  Materialism
    B.  Aristotle              ___  Animal instincts
    C.  Descartes           ___  Dualism
    D.  Harlow               ___  Genes
    E.  Darwin               ___  Mentalism

3. Match each of the following names to their correct feature.

    A.  Homo erectus     ___  Most recently evolved species
    B.  Homo habilis      ___  Co-existed with early modern-day humans
    C.  Neanderthal       ___  First to walk upright
    D.  Homo sapiens     ___  Known for their use of tools

4. Rank order from 1 (lowest) to 5 (highest) of the encephalization quotients (EQs) of the following animals.

    ___  Rat
    ___  Homo sapiens
    ___  Elephant
    ___  Chimpanzee
    ___  Dolphin

# CD-ROM Exercises

1. Visit module CNS2 of your CD to visualize the frontal, parietal, temporal, and occipital lobes of the brain. Rotate the brain to conceptualize the arrangement of these lobes from different perspectives. Also view the lobes in a sagittal section of the brain.

2. Visit module CNS1 of your CD to visualize the sensory pathways in the brain. Use the menu to see connections for olfaction, somatosensation, audition, and vision.

3. Visit module CNS3 of your CD to visualize the cerebellum. Note the location of this structure relative to the spinal cord. Rotate the cerebellum to conceptualize its shape and substructures.

# The Web

*Consider using the following Web sites for additional information on some of the topics from this chapter:*

1. The Brain Project (philosophy of mind and brain): www.culture.com.au/brain_proj/

2. The Brain Injury Association Inc. (closed-head injuries): www.biausa.org/

3. Philosophy of Mind: www.liv.ac.uk/~bdainton/mind2b.html

4. Charles Darwin: www.sc.edu/library/spcoll/nathist/darwin/darwin.html

5. Evolution of the brain: www.neurophys.wisc.edu/brain/evolution

The easiest way to get to these sites is to link to them through the student Web site at www.worthpublishers.com/kolb. This site also has further study aids and practice quizzes.

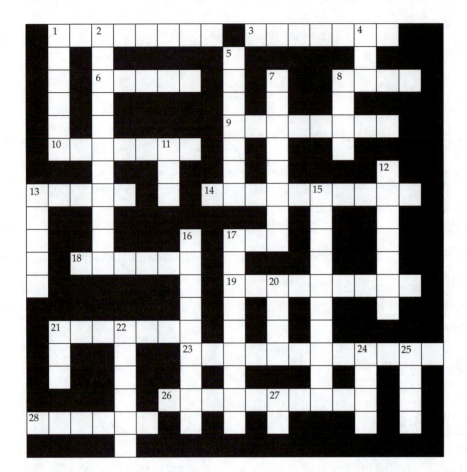

# CROSSWORD PUZZLE

## Across

1. An action produced by the brain
3. Darwin's _____ Selection
6. Peripheral nerves may be sensory or . . .
8. Singular form of 13 across
9. Brain lobe near your ear
10. Modern human primate family; with 24 down
13. 22 down studied these in his plants
14. Name for half a brain
17. The brain and spinal cord: abbr.
18. We call it "mind," Aristotle called it . . .
19. The lobe in the back of your brain
21. The order for chimps and gorillas
23. For a while they co-existed with 10 across
26. The "little brain" in the back
28. Outer layer of the brain, for short

## Down

1. Organs associated with minds
2. 14 across plural . . . two per brain
4. Another for the order in 21 across
5. Group behaviors, or a way to make yogurt
7. Human-like animals
8. Series of folds in 28 across
11. Simple nervous system, or a fishing aid
12. Lobe in the front of your brain
13. Singular of 8 down
15. In nervous system terms, it's either central or . . .
16. Nervous system organization as in a flatworm
17. Our phylum; named from the notochord
20. 17 down animals have this spinal component
21. Not the CNS
22. He did research with pea plants
24. See 10 across
25. Parietal is one of them
27. Encephalization Quotient, abbr.

# How Is the Brain Organized?

## CHAPTER SUMMARY

In Chapter 1 you learned that in simple terms, the function of the brain is to produce behavior. Chapter 2 expands on this concept to include, along with behavior, the brain functions of creating a *sensory reality* and creating *knowledge*. To understand how the brain accomplishes these tasks it is useful to know how the brain is organized. The language, or *nomenclature*, used to describe the brain is important because names given to brain structures may describe aspects of function, location, or physical features of those structures. This nomenclature is at times confusing, due in part to the fact that the brain has been studied for centuries by many cultures; as a result, contributions to the scientific literature span time and languages. In general, the relative location of structures is usually defined using the terms *medial* (middle), *lateral* (side), *dorsal* (top), *ventral* (bottom), *anterior* (front), and *posterior* (back). The terms *superior* and *inferior* are sometimes used to describe dorsal and ventral, respectively. Sometimes the terms *rostral* and *caudal* are used to describe anterior and posterior, respectively. In addition, the direction in which information moves from one structure to another is generally termed *afferent* (information coming into a structure) and *efferent* (information leaving a structure).

Upon visual inspection, it becomes clear that the brain is wrapped in connective tissue. There are actually three layers of tissue. A tough, fibrous outermost layer is called the *dura mater*. Beneath the dura mater are the *arachnoid layer* and the *pia mater*. These two layers are thinner and less durable than the dura mater and tend to follow all the contours of the brain's uneven surface. *Cerebral spinal fluid (CSF)* circulates between the arachnoid and pia mater layers, providing a cushion for the brain.

Gross observation of the brain reveals a *cerebrum* (divided evenly into two *hemispheres*) and a *cerebellum*. The outer layer of these structures appears very convoluted (wrinkled). As discussed in Chapter 1, this wrinkling allows more surface area to be compressed into the confines of the skull. The wrinkles also have names. *Gyri* are raised surfaces, whereas *sulci* are the indentations. Very deep sulci are called *fissures*. The area where the brain connects to the spinal cord is called the *brainstem*, and it is at this level that protruding cranial nerves can be seen. Finally, an elaborate system of blood vessels covers the entire brain.

When the brain is cut into sections, several gross features can be clearly identified. Hollow, fluid-filled cavities called the *ventricles* can be seen in several areas. It is within these ventricles that CSF is produced. The *corpus callosum*, a large band of white matter connecting the two hemispheres, can also be clearly identified. Beyond these few large structures, it is difficult to identify brain structures with the naked eye. Inspection with a microscope, however, reveals a wide array of cell types and connections in the brain tissue. In fact, the human brain is composed of about 80 billion *neurons* and 100 billion *glial cells*. Neurons can be distinguished from glia by the presence of *axons* (nerve fibers) that connect neurons. Glial cells lack this distinctive feature. Because it is so extensive, the nervous system is often subdivided into parts based on location and function. For example, the *central nervous system (CNS)* refers to the brain and spinal cord. The *peripheral nervous system (PNS)* is considered all neurons outside of the CNS. The *cranial nervous system* includes the brain and cranial nerves.

The brain may be subdivided into several distinct regions, each containing numerous structures. The *brainstem* or *hindbrain* region is composed of deep internal structures that sit atop the spinal cord and are responsible for motor, sensory, and integrative functions. These structures are the *medulla, reticular formation, cerebellum,* and *pons*. The medulla controls vital functions such as breathing, heart rate, and blood pressure. The reticular formation is responsible for waking and sleeping. The cerebellum is responsible for rapid complex movements. The pons is made up of fibers connecting the cerebellum to the rest of the brainstem and acting as a bridge for information exchange.

The *midbrain* region, located anterior and dorsal from the hindbrain, consists of the *superior* and *inferior colliculi* (collectively called the *tectum*) and the *tegmentum*. The superior colliculus processes information about location of visual stimuli. The inferior colliculus has a similar function for auditory information. Likely, the function of the tectum is to localize all types of sensory input. The tegmentum is responsible for some aspects of movement. The tegmentum contains the *substantia nigra*, a structure particularly important for initiating movement. The *diencephalon* (a midbrain region) consists of two structures called the *thalamus* and the *hypothalamus*. Each of these two structures is made up of over 20 smaller nuclei, with each of these nuclei likely influencing different behavioral functions. For example, the hypothalamus controls temperature regulation, feeding, sleeping, emotions, and sexual behaviors (to name a few). The hypothalamus also directly controls the *pituitary gland*. The thalamus receives a large amount of incoming sensory information and likely acts as a way station, or switchboard, for processing and directing this information to appropriate brain regions.

The forebrain consists of three principle structures: the *cortex*, the *basal ganglia*, and the *limbic* system. The cortex includes the outer convoluted structure seen upon gross inspection. In the human brain, the cortex comprises approximately 80 percent of the total weight of the brain. It is believed that the cortex is involved in the highest level processing of sensory information, including thinking or cognition. Neurons from the cortex innervate nearly every structure in the brain, and likely influence nearly every aspect of behavior. In general the cortex is divided into four regions or *lobes*. These lobes (mentioned in Chapter 1) are the *frontal* (anterior-most region), *occipital* (posterior-most region), *parietal* (dorsal region between frontal and occipital) and *temporal* (ventral region between frontal and occipital). The cortex can also be divided into five distinct layers, each responsible for a different aspect of information processing. The five primary structures that make up the basal ganglia are the *caudate nucleus, putamen, globus pallidus, substantia nigra,* and *subthlamic nucleus*. Collectively, these structures play a vital role in control of movement. Parkinson's, Huntington's, and Tourette's disease all have a basis in malfunction in this system and all result in disrupted movement. The limbic system includes the *amygdala, hippocampus,* and the *cingulate cortex*. The limbic system controls many aspects of emotional and sexual behavior, as well as some aspects of learning and memory formation.

The *spinal nervous system* is composed of the *spinal cord*, encased within the bony *vertebrate* that make up the backbone. The spinal cord is segmented, with nerves running to and from particular body regions (or dermatomes). These nerve fibers carrying information from the body enter the spinal cord through the dorsal region (termed the *dorsal root*). Fibers sending information to the body exit the spinal cord from the *ventral root*. When sliced into sections, a distinctive region of cell bodies within the spinal cord appears gray, while regions of nerve fibers entering and exiting the cord appear white. In general the spinal cord conveys information to and from the brain, but some simple reflexive behaviors function independently of brain activity and are mediated by cells within the spinal cord.

The *internal nervous system* is commonly termed the *autonomic nervous system*, which controls internal organs and glands. The autonomic nervous system is actually composed of two opposing systems termed the *sympathetic* and the *parasympathetic nervous systems*. When activated the sympathetic nervous system arouses the body, stimulating increased heart rate and blood pressure while decreasing digestive function. In contrast, parasympathetic nervous system arousal causes an increase in digestion and a decrease in heart rate and blood pressure.

There are several principles that can be applied to any division of the nervous system. First, the concept of *summation* suggests that the nervous systems are constantly being bombarded with information from our environment. For a system to make sense of all of this information, sensory signals must be condensed through some process of summation, or the weighing of excitatory and inhibitory input. Second, most neurons are likely designated as processing either sensory or motor signals. Although this is obvious in neurons receiving input from the environment or those sending signals to muscles, even within intermediate regions receiving and transmitting a very large number of signals (like the cortex), researchers have designated motor and sensory regions and layers. Third, a peculiar feature of our nervous system is that sensory and motor processes associated with the left side of our body are controlled by the right hemisphere of our brain, and vice versa.

Regarding the two hemispheres of the brain, it has been noted that primary control of a few behaviors is localized to a single hemisphere. Language in humans is considered a primary function of the left hemisphere, with far less influence coming from the right. Conversely, spatial concepts are generally processed in the right hemisphere.

It is also important to realize that behaviors may result not only from excitation of a particular area, but also from active inhibition of an area. We intuitively understand that damage to a structure can result in loss of behavior; but also, some regions actively stop behaviors from occurring. In Huntington's disease, for example, degeneration of parts of the basal ganglia results in abnormal motor behaviors that include flaying limb movements. Similarly, Tourette's disease causes degeneration of a part of the basal ganglia that results in facial tics and uncontrollable vocalizations, including swear words in some cases. Such diseases represent loss of a structure normally exerting inhibitory influence over expression of behaviors.

Finally, it seems that the nervous system is composed of several systems that process information in parallel. However, because these systems are so intimately linked it is difficult to establish independent features of each. Despite this difficulty, the approach taken by neuroscientists is that each aspect of behavior may be localized to some region (or regions) of the nervous system.

# KEY TERMS

*The following is a list of important terms introduced in Chapter 2. Give the definition of each term in the space provided.*

### Nomenclature

Dorsal

Ventral

Medial

Lateral

Anterior

Posterior

Rostral

Caudal

Superior

Inferior

Afferent

Efferent

### Brain Structure and Components (surface)

Meninges


Dura mater


Arachnoid layer


Pia mater


Cerebrospinal fluid (CSF)


Cerebrum


Cortex


Cerebellum


Gyri


Sulci


Fissures


Hemispheres


Brainstem

Cranial nerves

Stroke

**Brain Structure and Components (internal)**

Frontal section

Sagittal

Ventricles

Corpus callosum

Subcortical regions

Nuclei

**Cells and Fibers**

Axons

Nerve tract

**Neuroanatomy and Brain Function**

Central nervous system (CNS)

Peripheral nervous system (PNS)

Cranial nervous system

Internal nervous system

Forebrain

Hindbrain

Midbrain

Diencephalon

Reticular formation

Pons

Medulla

Tectum

Superior colliculus

Inferior colliculus

Tegmentum

Substantia nigra

Hypothalamus

Thalamus

Pituitary gland

Limbic system

Basal ganglia

Neocortex

Limbic cortex

Frontal lobe

Parietal lobe

Temporal lobe

Occipital lobe

Cytoarchitectonic maps

Top-down processing

Caudate nucleus

Putamen

Globus pallidus

Giles de la Tourette's disease

Amygdala

Hippocampus

Cingulate cortex

**Spinal Nervous System**

Dermatome

Dorsal root

Ventral root

Gray matter

Law of Bell and Magendie

**Internal Nervous System**

Autonomic nervous system

Sympathetic system

Parasympathetic system

*Functional Organization of the Brain*

Synapses

Summation

Contralateral

Lateralized

Visual field

Excitation

Inhibition

Parallel System

Hierarchical System

Focal symptoms

Cingulate gyrus

Olfactory System


Olfactory bulb


Pyriform cortex


## KEY NAME

*The following is an important name introduced in Chapter 2. Explain the importance of this person in the space provided.*

John Hughlings-Jackson


## PRACTICE TEST

## Multiple-Choice Questions

*Answer each of the following multiple-choice questions with the best possible answer based on information from your text.*

1. Based on the name, where would you expect to find the superior colliculus, relative to the inferior colliculus?
   A. Superior colliculus would be located dorsal from the inferior colliculus
   B. Superior colliculus would be located ventral from the inferior colliculus
   C. Superior colliculus would be located medial from the inferior colliculus
   D. Superior colliculus would be located lateral from the inferior colliculus
   E. Location cannot be determined from the name.

2. Which of the following best describes the term *afferent* as it refers to neural information?
   A. Active
   B. Inactive
   C. Coming into a region of the nervous system
   D. Going out of a region of the nervous system
   E. Coming before a behavior

3. The meninges is a three-layered structure encasing the brain and composed primarily of connective tissue. Which of the following is the Latin name for the tough outermost layer?
   A. Pia mater
   B. Dura mater
   C. Arachnoid layer
   D. Meninges externalis
   E. None of the above

4. Both the cerebrum and the cerebellum have very wrinkled surfaces. Which of the following terms is *not* used to describe these convolutions?
   A. Gyri
   B. Sulci
   C. Denti
   D. Fissures
   E. All of the above are used to identify the convolutions on the external surface of the brain

5. Which of the following is produced within the ventricles in the brain?
   A. Neural impulses
   B. Electrical impulses
   C. Cerebral spinal fluid
   D. Blood plasma
   E. Oxygen

6. A collection of nerve fibers (axons) found outside of the CNS is simply referred to as "nerves." However, when such a fiber bundle is located within the CNS, it is generally referred to as a . . .
   A. ganglion
   B. nucleus
   C. tract
   D. structure
   E. cord

7. How many cranial nerves have been identified protruding from the brainstem?
   A. 12
   B. 12 pairs
   C. 21
   D. 21 pairs
   E. The total number of cranial nerves has not yet been determined

8. The diencephalon is . . .
   A. also referred to as the "between brain"
   B. found in the brainstem
   C. found between the hindbrain and the midbrain
   D. contains a structure called the hypothalamus
   E. All of the above are true of the diencephalon

9. Which of the following is true of the cerebellum?
   A. It is well developed in animals that move slowly and steadily
   B. It is located ventral from the pons and medulla
   C. It is one of the smallest structures in the brain
   D. It is shaped like a carrot
   E. None of the above are true of the cerebellum

10. If the medulla were severely damaged, which of the following would most likely occur?
    A. The animal would show disrupted movement
    B. The animal would show disrupted memory
    C. The animal would show disrupted waking and sleep patterns
    D. The animal would show disrupted emotional behavior patterns
    E. The animal would likely die

11. Located in the tectum are the superior and inferior colliculi. The superior colliculus receives a great deal of sensory input from the visual system. It is not surprising that the adjacent inferior colliculus . . .
    A. also receives a great deal of sensory input from the visual system
    B. receives a great deal of sensory input from the auditory system
    C. controls most eye movements
    D. controls visual aspects of dreams
    E. controls pupil dilation

12. The substantia nigra is a nucleus located within the tegmentum. Which of the following best describes the function of the substantia nigra?
    A. It is involved in memory
    B. It is involved in sexual behavior
    C. It is involved in the initiation of movement
    D. It is involved in vital respiratory and cardiovascular functions
    E. It is involved in sleep behavior

13. Which of the following is the most distinctive functional feature of the thalamus?
    A. It controls all aspects of movement
    B. It acts as a gateway for all sensory input being sent to the cortex
    C. It has inhibitory control over nearly every other structure in the brain
    D. It processes input for all sensory systems except the visual system
    E. It produces cerebral spinal fluid

14. The cortex is unique in several features. Which of the below describes a unique feature of the cortex?
    A. It is involved in mental processes such as perception and planning
    B. It comprises the majority of brain volume in humans
    C. It can be subdivided into several distinct layers, each with a unique function
    D. It can be subdivided into several regions called lobes, each with a unique function
    E. All of the above describe the cortex

15. Giles de la Tourette's disease is believed to be primarily a result of basal ganglia dysfunction. Which of the below might be a symptom of Tourette's disease?
    A. Difficulty breathing
    B. Loss of balance
    C. Extreme weight loss
    D. Extreme weight gain
    E. Involuntary cursing

16. The limbic system includes the amygdala, cingulate cortex, and hippocampus. When would you be most likely to utilize your hippocampus?
    A. When watching television
    B. When listening to the radio
    C. When studying for an exam
    D. When walking on a path through the woods
    E. When sleeping

17. Which of the following is *not* one of the five groups of vertebrate found in humans?
    A. Basal
    B. Thoracic
    C. Lumbar
    D. Sacral
    E. Cervical
    F. Coccygenual

18. Which of the following is *not* true of the sympathetic nervous system?
    A. Activation increases heart rate
    B. Activation increases digestion
    C. It acts to arouse the body
    D. It works in opposition to the parasympathetic nervous system
    E. Initiation of this system arises from the spinal cord

19. Which of the following most accurately describes the structure of the cortex as it relates to sensory and motor functions?
    A. There are certain regions of the cortex designated for sensory functions
    B. There are certain layers of the cortex designated for sensory functions
    C. There are certain regions of the cortex designated for motor functions
    D. There are certain layers of the cortex designated for motor functions
    E. All of the above are true

20. Damage to a brain structure in your right hemisphere that controls motor function would likely lead to disruption of movement in which of the following?
    A. The right side of your body
    B. The left side of your body
    C. Both sides of your body
    D. Neither side of your body, since motor control is primarily a function of the spinal cord
    E. There is no way to determine what side of the body will be affected based on what side of the brain is damaged

# Short Answer Questions

*Answer each of the following questions with a brief but complete written answer based on information from your text.*

1.  There seems to be a rather diverse nomenclature (vocabulary) used to describe the structures of the brain. Regions may have names of Latin, Greek, or English origin. Some are described with numbers, others with letters. Briefly explain why such diversity is seen in the nomenclature.

2.  Cerebral spinal fluid is a clear fluid that surrounds the brain and flows through the ventricular system and into the spinal cord. Name at least three possible functions of this fluid.

3.  The term *pons* literally means "bridge." Where is this structure located and why is it referred to as a bridge?

4. Although the hypothalamus comprises less than 1 percent of the brain's weight, it is intimately involved in many aspects of behavior. List at least four behaviors that are influenced by the hypothalamus.

5. The text refers to the cortex as "the ultimate meddler." This is an apt description considering the function of the cortex. Briefly describe what is meant by the term *ultimate meddler* when describing the function of the cortex. Utilize the idea of *top-down processing* in your description.

6. In some sense, the phrase "running around like a chicken with its head cut off" is a reference to features of the spinal nervous system. Briefly explain this statement.

7. Briefly describe the Law of Bell and Magendie.

8. Although many behaviors are controlled by both hemispheres, several functions are lateralized; that is, they are controlled by a single hemisphere in the brain. Language is a good example, being controlled primarily by the left hemisphere. Explain briefly why language might be better controlled by one hemisphere rather than two.

9. Damage to neurons providing excitatory input to a region that produces a behavior will result in a reduction or loss of that behavior. Briefly explain the effect of damage to neurons providing inhibitory input to that same structure. Use a specific behavior as an example.

10. It is sometimes difficult to conceptualize functions as "localized" to a certain region of the brain, especially when they are complex functions such as language. Describe briefly why it might be difficult for a neuroscientist to determine the location of a "language center" in the human brain.

# Matching Questions

*Complete each of the following matching questions based on information from your text.*

1. Match the following neuroanatomy terms with their more common counterparts.

   |  |  |
   |---|---|
   |  | __ Anterior |
   | A. Toward the front | __ Posterior |
   | B. Toward the back | __ Ventral |
   | C. Toward the middle | __ Medial |
   | D. Toward the side | __ Superior |
   | E. Toward the top | __ Inferior |
   | F. Toward the bottom | __ Caudal |
   |  | __ Rostral |

2. Match the following nervous system to the best descriptor.

   | | |
   |---|---|
   | A. Brain and spinal cord | __ Peripheral nervous system (PNS) |
   | B. Everything outside of the CNS | __ Spinal nervous system |
   | C. Primary connections to and from the muscles | __ Central nervous system (CNS) |
   | D. Also called the "autonomic nervous system" | __ Internal nervous system |

3. Match the following structure to the best descriptor.

   | | |
   |---|---|
   | A. Fibers connecting the two hemispheres | __ Hypothalamus |
   | B. Produces and transports CSF | __ Ventricles |
   | C. Used for complex coordinated movements | __ Neocortex |
   | D. It mediates pituitary gland function | __ Cerebellum |
   | E. It can be divided into 6 layers of gray matter | __ Corpus Callosum |

4. List the following regions of the brain from most dorsal (1) to most ventral (4).

    ___ Cortex
    ___ Midbrain
    ___ Diencephalon
    ___ Hindbrain

5. Match the following types of brain damage with the regions they are most likely to affect.

    A. Rabies                    ___ Basal ganglia
    B. Bell's Palsy              ___ May affect many regions of the brain
    C. Parkinson's disease       ___ Pia mater and Arachnoid layer
    D. Meningitis                ___ Limbic system
    E. Stroke                    ___ Facial nerves

# Diagrams

1. Imagine the diagram below represents a frontal section of the hypothalamus. You have been told that damage to the ventromedial hypothalamus will affect eating behavior in rats. Indicate (in general) where the ventromedial hypothalamus is located.

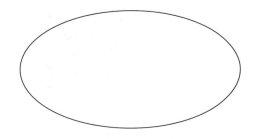

2. Identify the four lobes of the cerebral cortex in the diagram of a human brain below.

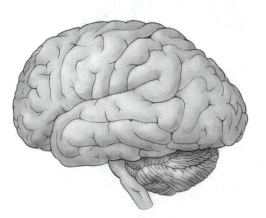

3. Appropriately label the following structures of the hindbrain and midbrain on the diagrams below: pons, medulla, cerebellum, superior colliculus, inferior collicus.

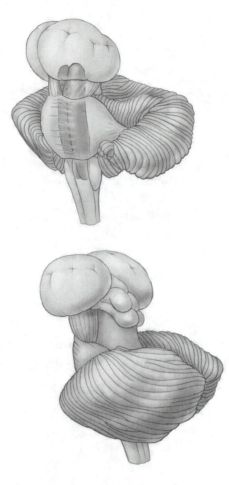

4. Appropriately label the following structures of the forebrain on the diagram below: cerebral cortex, basal ganglia, hippocampus, amygdala.

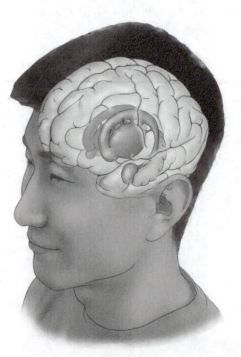

5.  Below is a cross section of the spinal cord. Identify the following: ventral root, dorsal root, gray matter, white matter.

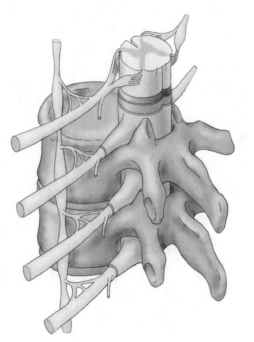

6.  Draw a simple diagram of a spinal cord below. Identify the approximate areas associated with the following five segments: cervical, thoracic, lumbar, sacral, and coccygenual.

7. On the diagram below, draw lines to indicate each of the following: sensory input from the right hand to the appropriate hemisphere, motor output from the right hemisphere to the appropriate hand, sensory input from the left visual field to the appropriate hemisphere.

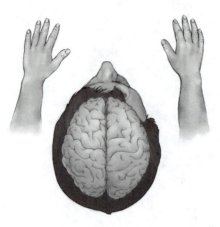

# CD-ROM Exercises

1. Visit module CNS2 of your CD to better visualize the medial, lateral, dorsal, ventral, anterior and posterior planes of the brain. Rotate the brain to conceptualize these planes from different perspectives. Also view the brain sectioned through these different planes.

2. Visit module CNS1 of your CD to examine more closely the surface features of the brain. Pay particular attention to the convolutions that make up the gyri, sulci, and fissures of the cortical surface.

3. Visit module CNS1 of your CD to identify some of the major internal structures of the brain. In particular view information on the ventricular system and corpus callosum (white matter).

4. Visit module CNS3 of your CD to examine the brainstem structures listed in your text. Rotate the brainstem to better visualize the connections of these structures.

5. Visit module CNS1 of your CD to better understand the relationship between the thalamus and hypothalamus. Also note the relationship of the hypothalamus to the pituitary gland and the mammillary bodies.

6. Visit module CNS2 of your CD to visualize the location and relationship between the four major lobes of the cortex. Rotate the brain to better conceptualize the relative size and location of each of the lobes.

7. Visit module CNS1 of your CD to see how the caudate and putamen are integrated to form the basal ganglia. View the olfactory bulb and its connections on the ventral surface of the brain in this same module.

8.   Visit module CNS1 of your CD to review the structures and functions of the spinal cord. Observe the gross anatomy of the entire cord, then examine the afferent and efferent that comprise the dorsal and ventral roots of the cord.

9.   Visit module NC5 of your CD for a wonderful visual demonstration of neural integration. Note particularly the concept of summation as it is described and shown in the video.

10.  Visit module VS2 of your CD for a visual example of how the visual fields are lateralized in the human brain. Note the pathway taken for information from a single visual field. Contrast that with the pathway taken for information from a single eye.


## The Web

*Consider using the following Web sites for additional information on some of the topics from this chapter:*

1.   Virtual Hospital: www.vh.org/Providers/Textbooks/BrainAnatomy/BrainAnatomy.html

2.   Neuroanatomy structures: www.neuropat.dote.hu/anastru/anastru.htm

3.   The human brain with point and click structures: uta.marymt.edu/~psychol/brain.html

4.   Coronal sections and structure labels: www.indiana.edu/~m555/coron/coron.html

5.   Sagittal sections and structure labels: www.indiana.edu/~m555/sagit/sagit.html

The easiest way to get to these sites is to link to them through the student Web site at www.worthpublishers.com/kolb. This site also has further study aids and practice quizzes.

## CROSSWORD PUZZLE

**Across**

2. The "new" outer layer of the brain
6. Structure controlling emotions in 1 down
8. Mediates movement; _____ pallidus
11. Name for small bumps on 2 across
12. 23 across connects them
14. Mediates movement; _____ putamen
19. Temporal or occipital
21. Term meaning "below" 23 down
22. A collection of nuclei controlling movement with 4 down
23. Band of white fibers in the middle of the brain; _____ callosum
25. Liquid in 20 down; abbr.
27. Region below the midbrain
28. 23 across is made up mostly of these
29. Term for "the other side" of the brain
31. Mediates movement; _____ nigra
32. Opposite of ventral

**Down**

1. System containing hippocampus and 6 across
3. Vision to the superior, auditory to the inferior
4. See 22 across
5. Brainstem "bridge"
7. Contains hypothalamus and thalamus
9. A front-to-back cut through the brain
10. The first 2 words of 25 across; abbr.
13. Meninges layer; _____ mater
15. Dorsal or ventral of the spine
16. Term for shallow fissures in 2 across
17. Above the midbrain
18. 12 across singular
20. You have 2 laterals, a 3rd and a 4th
23. Common term for 2 across
24. Common term for disrupted blood flow to brain
25. Brain and spinal cord; abbr.
26. The most anterior 19 across
30. All neurons outside of 25 down; abbr.

CHAPTER

# 3

# What Are the Units of Brain Function?

## CHAPTER SUMMARY

Throughout history researchers have used metaphors to describe the neural basis for behavior. Most recently, the brain has been likened to a computer in its structure and function. Such a comparison serves to enhance the concept that to understand the influence of the brain on behavior, it is essential to understand the components that comprise the brain and the interaction of these components. However, even with our understanding of the many components that comprise sophisticated computers, it is at times still difficult to imagine the complexity of even a single brain cell. For example, single neurons are responsible not only for relatively simple tasks of acquiring and passing on information, but also for tasks as complex as encoding memories. Making the job of determining how neurons accomplish such tasks even more difficult is the fact that neurons exhibit a great deal of plasticity over time. In other words, neurons are constantly changing in structure and, consequently, in function throughout life.

The basic description of a neuron is that it is a specialized cell capable of receiving, integrating, assessing, and ultimately sending information. Some neurons are specialized to receive and pass information from the environment to our brain (*sensory neurons*). Other neurons are specialized to receive and pass information from our brain to our muscles (*motor neurons*). The majority of neurons, however, are cells responsible for processing information within the brain. These cells are generally categorized as *interneurons* and comprise the major difference in brain mass between those animals with small brains and those with large brains.

Although some neurons utilize electrical signals for communication at their *synapses*, the vast majority of neurons communicate using *chemical messengers*. In addition to communicating with other cells, neurons may also receive *feedback* from their own signals in determining if the signal has been adequately sent, or if continued chemical release is required. The initiation of neural signaling is ultimately determined by "weighing" excitatory and inhibitory input. A cell may only initiate firing when excitatory signals outweigh inhibitory signals. The versatility inherent in weighing excitatory and inhibitory signals from multiple interneuron inputs results in enormous possibilities for behavior.

41

*Glial cells* are often described as "support cells" within the nervous system. Unlike neurons, glial cells have not yet been found to establish functional connections for cellular communication. They do, however, engage in numerous activities essential for neural communication and proper brain function. Among these tasks, *ependymal glial cells* produce and secrete cerebral spinal fluid used to mobilize nutrients, eliminate waste products, cushion and possibly cool the brain. *Astroglia* provide a structural framework for neurons and secrete substances needed for maintained health of neurons and healing of injured neurons. Astroglia also comprise the *blood–brain barrier*, binding blood-vessel cells tightly together to inhibit unwanted substances from entering the brain from the bloodstream. These cells also may cause blood vessels to dilate in areas where greater blood flow is needed for increased neural activity. If neurons are injured, astroglia also form a type of scar tissue that is beneficial to the healing process. *Microglia* have a primary function of phagocytosis, engulfing and removing debris left by dead tissue. *Oligodendroglia* provide myelin used to insulate axons and speed neurocommunication in the brain and spinal cord. *Schwann cells* have a similar role in the peripheral nervous system, with the additional benefit of being able to guide regrowth of axons that have degenerated as a result of injury. *Multiple sclerosis* is a disease in which myelin degenerates, resulting in slower and sometimes confused (short-circuited) neural communication.

Electrically charged atoms called *ions* comprise the active *natural elements* found in intracellular and extracellular fluid. These elements may also be found bound together as components of larger *molecules*. For example, the element sodium ($Na^+$) may bind to the element chloride ($Cl^-$) to form a salt (NaCl) molecule. Understanding the role of ions, elements, and molecules required for neural function is one very basic step toward understanding neural control of behavior.

The parts of the cell required for proper function are sometimes likened to work centers in a factory. The *cell membrane*, a *lipid bilayer* designed to keep substances out of the cell, is like an exterior factory wall. A similar membrane surrounding the *nucleus* (*nuclear membrane*), like an interior factory wall, keeps elements of the *intracellular fluid* (*cytosol*) from freely entering the nucleus. *Endoplasmic reticulum* is where *protein products* are assembled in the cell. *Golgi bodies* are where these protein products are packaged and readied for transport. *Microtubules* transport packaged products to different regions within the cell. *Mitochondria* power the cell and all of its functions. *Lysosomes* act as a cleaning and maintenance crew, arranging incoming supplies and disposing of waste products. The nucleus is where the blueprints are kept for all products produced by the cell. These blueprints are *genes* coded in the chemical structure of nuclear *chromosomes*. Copies of these *DNA* blueprints are transported from within the nucleus to intracellular *organelles* in the form of *mRNA*. It is from this mRNA that the organelles of our cell know what type of peptide chain or protein is to be assembled. In particular, the endoplasmic reticulum, which contains a high concentration of *ribosomes*, translates the mRNA and begins the production process. The number of possible combinations of peptide chains that can be manufactured from our 20 different available amino acids is nearly countless. Many of the proteins and polypeptide chains manufactured in the *soma* are transported by motor molecules to sites where they may be imbedded into the cell membrane or excreted from the cell through the process of *exocytosis*. Substances imbedded in the membrane can take the form of *receptors*, *gates*, *channels*, or *pumps*. Receptors respond to neurotransmitters. Gates open and close to allow ion diffusion through membrane channels. Pumps actively transport substances in and out of the cell.

Genes comprise chromosomes and supply the blueprints used to produce the proteins essential for all aspects of neural function. As such, genes ultimately contribute heavily to behavior. With tens of thousands of genes contributing to brain development, it is difficult to speculate on individual contributions. However, it is known that some genetic abnormalities can have severe consequences on behavior. Studying such genetic disorders can provide insight into contributions of some genes. Every normally developed individual has 23 pairs of chromosomes. One pair (*sex chromosomes*) determines primary development of sex characteristics. As chromosomes are paired, genes that make up those chromosomes are also paired into matching *alleles*. When like alleles are matched, the pair is termed *homozygous*. When alleles containing different instructions are matched, the pair is termed *heterozygous*. In the case of a heterozygous pair, the genetic instructions from one allele are generally expressed to a greater extent. This is termed a *dominant* allele, which usually results in greater influence over the *phenotype* (outward appearance) of the organism. *Recessive* phenotypes are generally expressed only when two recessive alleles comprise a homozygous pair. For example, *Tay-Sachs disease* results only when two recessive alleles are present in the individual. On the other hand, *Huntington's disease* (which results from an abnormal dominant allele) is expressed in individuals with only one affected allele. Recessive and dominant features of these genetic abnormalities directly affect the mathematical probability that a person may inherit the disorder from parents who are carriers or affected individuals. *Down's syndrome* is an example of a disorder that results from the addition of an entire chromosome to the genetic makeup of an individual. This disorder is also termed trisomy 21, referring to three 21st chromosomes where only two should exist. Each of these genetic diseases has a significant impact on development and behavior. As such, researchers have learned a great deal about the contributions of individual chromosomes, and even individual genes, to behavior. Technology has recently been developed whereby scientists can manipulate the genetic structure of rodents. With this ability, researchers have been able to develop more accurate models of genetic disorders. Perhaps more important, they are able to assess the general behavioral changes associated with genetic manipulation in an effort to more fully understand the functional role of these most basic contributors to human behavior.

# KEY TERMS

*The following is a list of important terms introduced in Chapter 3. Give the definition of each term in the space provided.*

### Neural Structure and Function

Soma

Axon

Axon hillock

Axon collaterals

Teleodendria

End foot/terminal button

Synapse

Dendrite

Dendritic spines

### Types of Neurons

Bipolar neuron

Interneuron

Somatosensory neuron

Motor neuron

Stellate cell

Pyramidal cell

Purkinje cell

### The Synapse

Electrical signal


Chemical signal


Neurotransmitter


Hormone


Excitatory input


Inhibitory input


### Glial Cells

Ependymal cells


Cerebrospinal fluid


Hydrocephalus


Astroglia


Blood–brain barrier


Microglia


Phagocytosis

Oligodendroglia

Myelin

Schwann cell

Multiple sclerosis

Retrograde degeneration

## Internal Structure of the Cell

Organelles

Element

Trace element

Atom

Neutron

Proton

Electron

Ion

Molecule

Polar molecule

Hydrogen bond

Hydrophilic

Hydrophobic

*Cell Anatomy*

Membrane

Phospholipid

Nucleus

Nuclear membrane

Endoplasmic reticulum (ER)

Golgi body

Microtubule

Mitochondria

Lysosome

Extracellular fluid

Intracellular fluid (cytostol)

**The Nucleus**

Eukaryotic cell

Chromosome

Gene

Deoxyribonucleic acid (DNA)

Nucleotide base

Adenine

Thymine

Guanine

Cytosine

Transcription

Messenger RNA (mRNA)

*Protein Synthesis, Packaging, and Shipment*

Ribosome

Translation

Codon

Transfer RNA (tRNA)

Amino group

Carboxyl group

Peptide bond

Polypeptide chain

Motor molecule

Exocytosis

*Anatomy of the Cell Membrane*

Protein

Receptor

Channel

Gate

Pump

**Chromosomes and Genes**

Sex chromosome

Autosome

Allele

Homozygous

Heterozygous

Wild-type allele

Mutation

Trait

Genotype

Phenotype

Dominant allele

Recessive allele

Complete dominance

Incomplete dominance

Co-dominance

Pleiotropy

## Genetic Disorders and Genetic Engineering

Tay-Sachs disease

Huntington's chorea

Down's syndrome

Cloning

Chimeric animal

Transgenic animal

Knockout technology

## KEY NAMES

*The following is a list of important names introduced in Chapter 3. Explain the importance of each person in the space provided.*

Camillo Golgi

Santiago Ramón y Cajal

Barbara Webb

Fernando Nottebohm

Gregor Mendel

## PRACTICE TEST

## Multiple-Choice Questions

*Answer each of the following multiple-choice questions with the best possible answer based on information from your text.*

1. By our best estimates, the human nervous system contains around . . .
   A. one hundred thousand neurons
   B. one million neurons
   C. one hundred million neurons
   D. one billion neurons
   E. one hundred billion neurons

2.  Neurons show a surprising ability to change form and structure throughout life. This is particularly apparent in which of the following?
    A.  Ability of neurons to multiply
    B.  Neurons constantly sprouting new axons
    C.  Neurons losing old, and producing new, dendrite branches
    D.  All of the above are characteristics of neurons
    E.  None of the above are correct; neurons do not change form and structure throughout life

3.  Which of the following best describes the location of terminal buttons?
    A.  Touching the terminal buttons of other neurons
    B.  Close to, but not quite touching, the terminal buttons of other neurons
    C.  Touching the dendritic spines of other neurons
    D.  Close to, but not quite touching, the dendrite spines of other neurons
    E.  The location of terminal buttons is highly variable and cannot be described in specific terms

4.  Which of the following would *not* be considered a type of neuron?
    A.  Ependymal cell
    B.  Pyramidal cell
    C.  Purkinje cell
    D.  Interneuron
    E.  Bipolar neuron

5.  Neurons generally send messages . . .
    A.  constantly unless they receive inhibitory input
    B.  constantly unless they receive excitatory input
    C.  only when they receive inhibitory input
    D.  only when they receive excitatory input
    E.  generally when excitatory input is greater than inhibitory input

6.  Which of the following is *not* a likely function of cerebral spinal fluid secreted by ependymal cells?
    A.  Cushion the brain when the head is jarred
    B.  Eliminate waste products
    C.  Provide nutrients to the brain
    D.  Mediate electrical signals between neurons.
    E.  Cool the brain

7.  The blood–brain barrier is more of a concept than an actual structure. However, if pressed to describe the makeup of the blood–brain barrier, you could say it is composed primarily of . . .
    A.  astroglia and proteins
    B.  astroglia and blood vessels
    C.  microglia and proteins
    D.  microglia and blood vessels
    E.  The blood–brain barrier contains all of the above

8. The process by which oligodendroglia and Schwann cells form myelin sheathes around axons could best be described as which of the following?
   A. Continuous growth of myelin originating from the soma to the terminal button
   B. Continuous growth of myelin originating from the terminal button to the soma
   C. Continuous growth of myelin originating from both the terminal button and the soma
   D. Intermittent segments of axon are wrapped by outgrowths from adjacent glial cells
   E. All of the above are potential processes for myelin formation

9. In addition to forming an insulating myelin sheath, Schwann cells also provide which function for peripheral neurons following damage?
   A. Act as scavengers to clean debris left by dead axons
   B. Form scar tissue to seal the area around dead axons
   C. Guide regrowth of axons after damage
   D. Repel regrowth of axons by releasing an antigrowth agent
   E. All of the above are correct
   F. None of the above are correct

10. An atom that becomes positively or negatively charged by gaining or losing an electron is called . . .
    A. an element
    B. a trace element
    C. a neutron
    D. a proton
    E. an ion

11. The neuronal membrane can be described as a lipid bilayer formed by phospholipid molecules composed of a "head" and "tail." More specifically, the molecules form the membrane with . . .
    A. hydrophobic heads facing intracellular fluid and hydrophilic tails facing extracellular fluid
    B. hydrophilic heads facing intracellular fluid and hydrophobic tails facing extracellular fluid
    C. hydrophobic heads facing intra- and extracellular fluid, and hydrophilic tails facing each other
    D. hydrophilic heads facing intra- and extracellular fluid, and hydrophobic tails facing each other.

12. The chromosomes within a cell nucleus contain which of the following?
    A. Genes
    B. DNA
    C. Nucleotide bases
    D. Coded instruction for development of all proteins in the cell
    E. All of the above
    F. None of the above

13. The primary function of mRNA is to . . .
    A. synthesize proteins
    B. produce the code for protein sythesis
    C. transport genetic code out of the nucleus
    D. generate DNA
    E. provide energy for the nucleus

14. Regarding the relationship between a protein and a polypeptide chain, it could be said that . . .
    A.  they are two terms to describe the same components
    B.  a protein is formed by a particular configuration of a polypeptide chain
    C.  a polypeptide chain is formed by a particular configuration of a protein
    D.  a polypeptide chain consists of many proteins
    E.  there is no general relationship between these two components

15. Excretion of proteins through a cell membrane is generally accomplished through which of the following?
    A.  Via passive diffusion
    B.  Via mRNA
    C.  Via microtubules
    D.  Via motor molecules
    E.  Via exocytosis

16. One goal of the Human Genome Project is to catalog all of the human genes. How many genes are humans estimated to possess?
    A.  ten thousand
    B.  one hundred thousand
    C.  one million
    D.  ten million
    E.  Researchers have not yet been able to estimate the number

17. Genetic literature often uses the term *wild type* to describe an allele being studied. In this case, "wild type" refers to which of the following?
    A.  An allele that produces abnormal behavior
    B.  An allele that produces exaggerated behavior
    C.  An allele that does not occur in domesticated organisms
    D.  A mutated form of a common allele
    E.  A common allele from which mutations may occur

18. Which of the following could *not* be considered a possible description of a genetic mutation?
    A.  A change in a single nucleotide base
    B.  A change that produces a beneficial change in development of the organism
    C.  A change that produces a disruptive change in development of the organism
    D.  No more than one may occur in any single gene
    E.  Responsible for human hereditary disorders

19. Considering Mendelian genetics and human genetic disorders, which child is most likely to be affected by (express the phenotype of) an inherited disease?
    A.  A child with one parent who is heterozygous for Tay-Sachs disease
    B.  A child with one parent who is heterozygous for Huntington's chorea
    C.  A child with two parents who are heterozygous for Tay-Sachs disease
    D.  A child with two parents who are heterozygous for Huntington's chorea
    E.  A child with one parent who is homozygous for Tay-Sachs disease

20. Which of the following is least likely to be characteristic of a transgenic mouse developed to study Huntington's chorea?
    A. It would have an experimentally induced alteration to its normal genetic makeup
    B. It could potentially to be used for testing therapeutic treatments for Huntington's chorea
    C. It would exhibit abnormal movements
    D. It would have abnormally low production of the protein huntingtin
    E. It would have unusually extensive cell death in some brain regions

## Short Answer Questions

*Answer each of the following questions with a brief but complete written answer based on information from your text.*

1. The particular structure of a neuron is generally a good indicator of the primary function of that neuron. With this in mind, describe the structure of a bipolar cell and how that particular structure serves the function of this cell type. Contrast this description with that of a somatosensory neuron. Explain how the somatosensory neuron structure serves the function of this type of cell.

2. In some cases neurons send axon collaterals back to neurons from which they receive neurochemical signals. What is the reason for having such collaterals?

3.  Describe the condition of hydrocephalus. What are the possible consequences? What is one viable treatment?

4.  One important function of astroglia is the ability to convey signals from neurons to blood vessels. What is this important signal that neurons send to blood vessels via astroglia, and when would you expect this message to be sent?

5.  Define phagocytosis and identify which type of cell is most likely to engage in this activity.

6. Describe the symptoms of multiple sclerosis. Explain in terms of neuronal function the cause of these symptoms.

7. What is a molecule? Give an example of a molecule that is intimately involved in neural function.

8. Each strand of DNA possesses a variable sequence of four nucleotides. These four nucleotides always occur in two predictable pairings. Name the four nucleotides and identify how they are paired in strands of DNA.

9. Describe the general function of each of the following membrane proteins:

Receptor:

Channel:

Gate:

Pump:

10. Describe both the genotype and the phenotype of a Down's syndrome individual

Genotype:

Phenotype:

# Matching Questions

*Complete each of the following matching questions based on information from your text.*

1. Match the following characteristics to the MOST appropriate structure:

A. Vesicles          __ Soma
B. Receptor sites    __ Terminal
C. Nucleus           __ Axon
D. Myelin            __ Dendrite

2. Match the following cell types to their general description:

A. Motor          __ Single short axon and single short dendrite
B. Pyramidal      __ Dendrite connected directly to axon
C. Purkinje       __ Many dendrites extend directly from soma
D. Stellate       __ Long axon with two sets of dendrites extend from
E. Somatosensory     soma
F. Bipolar        __ Many dendritic branches form a fan shape
                  __ Extensive dendrites, large soma, long axon to muscle

3. Identify the following glial cells:

astoglia, microglia, oligodendroglia, Schwann cell, ependymal

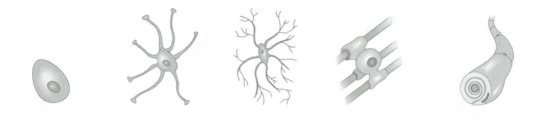

_____     _____     _____     _____     _____

4. Match the following characteristics to the MOST appropriate cell part or organelle

   A.  Phospholipid bilayer        __ Cell membrane
   B.  Contains DNA                __ Endoplasmic reticulum
   C.  Assembles proteins          __ Nucleus
   D.  Packages proteins           __ Microtubules
   E.  Transports proteins         __ Golgi bodies
   F.  Provides cell energy        __ Lysosomes
   G.   Moves and stores waste     __ Mitochondria

5. Match the following disorders to the best descriptor regarding genetic contribution:

   A.  Huntington's chorea        __ Caused by recessive allele
   B.  Tay-Sachs disease          __ Caused by dominant allele
   C.  Down's syndrome            __ No known genetic contribution
   D.  Multiple sclerosis         __ Caused by additional chromosome

# Diagrams

1. Assume messenger output from the sensory neuron below is excitatory. Draw axons
   and axon collaterals from sensory neuron to interneurons, and from interneurons to
   motor neurons so that motor neuron A. is actively inhibited, motor neuron B. is unaffected, and motor neuron C. is actively excited. Use a + to indicate excitation and a – to
   indicate inhibition. Be sure all motor neurons receive interneuron input.

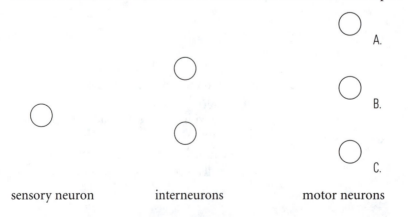

sensory neuron          interneurons          motor neurons

2.  Indicate the location of the following structures on the neuron below:

cell body (soma), axon, dendrites, dendritic spines, axon hillock, axon collateral, teleodendria, end foot, terminal button, nucleus

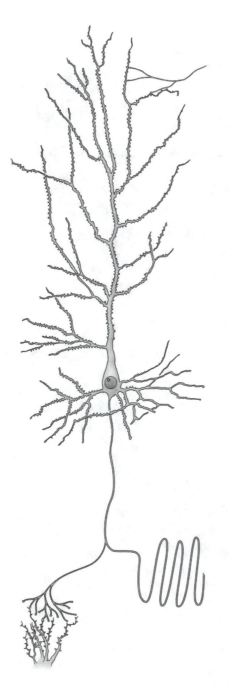

3.  Identify the following cells and cell structures in the diagram below:

    astrocyte, myelinated axon, blood-vessel cells, neuron

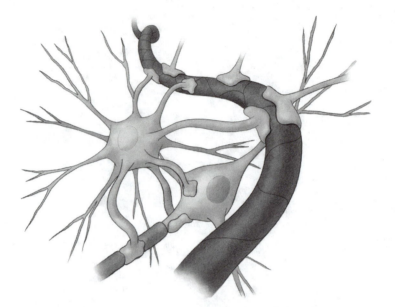

4.  Identify the following organelles in the figure below:

    nucleus, endoplasmic reticulum, mitochondrion, microtubules, Golgi apparatus

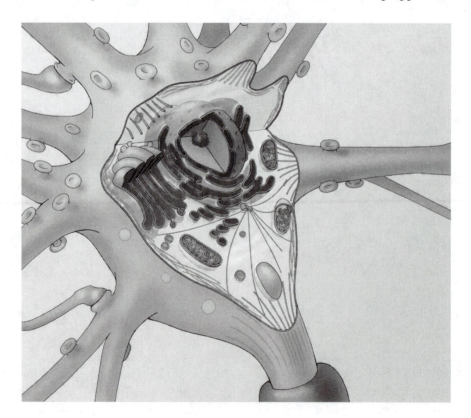

5. Assuming N indicates a chromosome with a normal gene, H indicates a chromosome with a Huntington's chorea gene, and T indicates a chromosome with a Tay-Sachs disease gene, determine the probability that offspring from the following pairs will express the phenotype of the disease.

HN + NN      HN + HN      HH + NN      TN + NN      TN + TN      TT + NN

# CD-ROM Exercises

1. Visit module RM5 of your CD to learn more about staining techniques. Note the variety of techniques for visualizing not only neurons, but also glial cells, cell activity and so on.

2. Visit module NC1 of your CD to view neural structures and learn more about the function of each of these external components. Note the relationship between these structures and how each works as an integral part of the overall function of cell communication.

3. Visit module NC5 of your CD to visualize the "flow" of information as it enters and is then transmitted along a neuron. Use the animated video to show integration of information in the decision-making process of cell communication.

4. Visit module NC3 of your CD to view an animated video showing the function of myelin. Note the difference in conduction speed between a myelinated and unmyelinated axon. Imagine the effects of multiple sclerosis in this regard.

5. Visit module NC1 of your CD to learn more about the structure and function of intracellular organelles. Note how each works as an integral part of overall cell metabolism, structure, and function.

6. Visit module NC2 of your CD to gain a better understanding of differences between intracellular and extracellular fluids. View the animated video to visualize the cell membrane as a functional and active barrier between these fluids.

7. Visit module NC2 of your CD for an animated video showing pumps and channels. Note the function of these proteins in maintaining proper concentration gradients in the resting cell.

# The Web

*Consider using the following Web sites for additional information on some of the topics from this chapter:*

1. National Tay-Sachs & Allied Diseases Association: www.ntsad.org

2. Internet Resources for Huntington's Disease:
   www.lib.uchicago.edu/~rd13/hd/outside.html

3. National Multiple Sclerosis Society: www.nmss.org/

4. National Association for Down Syndrome (NADS): www.nads.org

5. Hereditary Disease Foundation: www.hdfoundation.org/

The easiest way to get to these sites is to link to them through the student Web site at www.worthpublishers.com/kolb. This site also has further study aids and practice quizzes.

# CROSSWORD PUZZLE

**Across**

1. Myelin degeneration; _____ sclerosis
3. Action potential; abbr.
8. Blood-borne chemical transmitter substance
9. Neuron or glial, e.g.
10. Ribonucleic acid; abbr.
11. X and Y determine this
13. Neurons and these cells make up your brain
14. Movement disorder; _____ chorea
16. "It's a boy!"... genetically speaking
18. Neuron lipid bilayer
21. Another name for axon terminal; ____ foot
24. 3rd "b" word in BBB; Blood ____ ____
25. Creator of the robotic cricket
27. Opposite of anterograde
29. Name for local messenger molecule
31. Term for genetic control animal; "____ type"
32. See 23 down
33. Charged particle
34. Cell with axons and dendrites
36. One function of membrane embedded protein; ion _____

**Down**

1. Smallest unit of any substance
2. One function of membrane embedded protein; sodium/potassium _____
4. Appearance of a genotype
5. Genetic blueprint; abbr.
6. Type of CNS glial cell
7. 2nd "b" word in BBB; Blood ____ ____
12. Organelle used for intracellular transport
15. Many of these make up a chromosome
17. Not a motor or sensory neuron
18. Special form of 10 across; abbr.
19. Researching monk
20. "Body" as in a neuron
22. This gene, not recessive, determines 4 down
23. With neutrons and electrons they make up 32 across
26. Found on 35 down, they build proteins
28. A third 21st chromosome results in this syndrome
29. Unmyelinated segment, with Ranvier
30. May be myelinated or unmyelinated
35. Endoplasmic reticulum; abbr.

# 4 How Do Neurons Convey Information?

## CHAPTER SUMMARY

It has been known for some time that electricity is intimately involved in the process of neural communication. Among the earliest findings supporting this notion was that electrical stimulation of a motor neuron resulted in contraction of the muscle that it *innervated*. Prompted by this finding, researchers began utilizing *electrodes* coupled with electrical stimulators to assess the role of electricity in nerve neural communication. Similarly, some experiments have utilized *recording electrodes* to measure changes in electrical activity associated with neural activity. Perhaps the simplest example of a recording-electrode method is an *EEG*, which is used to measure gross changes in electrical brain waves. Early in the history of these studies, researchers realized that although the brain generates electricity (as seen with an EEG) and that electricity may stimulate neural activity, the speed of neural activity was far too slow to be explained as a purely electrical process. Thus, it was reasoned that electricity is a necessary component of neural communication, but not necessarily the means by which all neurons communicate.

Much of what we know about the electrical component of neural communication has been discovered through research using the *giant axon* of the North Atlantic squid. *Hodgkin and Huxley* were pioneers in this field, utilizing stimulating and recording *microelectrodes* in combination with an *oscilloscope* to study electrical changes across the neural membrane. Such electrical changes are a product of positively and negatively charged *ions* flowing into and out of the cell. It has been established that *diffusion, concentration*, and *charge* all influence the movement of ions (and thus the electrical charge of a cell). Diffusion is the process of molecules moving passively and randomly until dynamic equilibrium is reached. Concentration is the orderly movement of molecules from an area of high concentration to an area of low concentration. Charge (or voltage gradient) is the movement of ions toward ions with an opposing charge. These three factors are all mediated by particular features of the neural membrane. For example, *protein channels* may act as pores, allowing passive free movement of molecules. Other proteins may act as *gated channels*, allowing ions to enter and exit the cell at certain times. Still other proteins actively expel some ions, while recruiting others into the cell.

When a neuron is at its *resting potential* there is an electrical imbalance between the intracellular environment and the extracellular environment that is actively maintained.

This *transmembrane voltage* is usually a difference of around *70 mV*, with the intracellular environment more negatively charged. The negative intracellular environment results from *negatively charged proteins* that are too large to pass through any membrane pores. These negatively charged proteins in turn attract a large number of positively charged *potassium ions* into the cell. However, when the concentration gradient inside the cell prevents the entry of additional potassium ions, the cell still maintains a relatively strong negative charge (-70 mV). Positively charged *sodium ions* in high concentration outside of the cell are attracted to the intracellular environment by both electrical and concentration gradients. However, sodium channels are actively gated shut during the resting potential, preventing the entry of these ions. Finally, the cell's *sodium/potassium pump* (another membrane protein) actively works to maintain sodium and potassium imbalances by moving sodium ions from inside the cell to outside, and potassium from outside to in. Negatively charged *chloride ions* contribute very little to this process. The higher extracellular concentration drives these ions toward the intracellular environment, but this force is balanced by the negative charge inside the cell repelling the influx.

*Graded potentials* are seen when the cell potential becomes more positive (*depolarization*) or more negative (*hyperpolarization*) in a graded fashion through small voltage fluctuations. Such a change may be evoked with a small current from a stimulating electrode. Graded potentials are a *local phenomenon*, seen only in the membrane vicinity near the stimulation, and they decay in magnitude as they move from the point of stimulation. Depolarization generally results from sodium ions flowing into a neuron, while hyperpolarization results from potassium ions flowing out of a neuron. *Action potentials* (nerve impulses) are evoked when a neuron is depolarized to a *threshold potential*. Threshold is around -50 mV (compared to resting potential of -70 mV). At threshold the graded nature of the depolarization changes dramatically. The cell membrane rapidly moves in a positive direction, past *equilibrium* (0 mV) to a positive charge of approximately +30 mV, and then quickly returns to its *polarized* state of -70 mV. This brief fluctuation can be explained physiologically by an opening of *voltage-sensitive* sodium and potassium channels at threshold. Sodium gates, which open first, allow a large influx of positively charged ions moving with the force of both concentration and electrical gradients into the cell. Potassium channels open just slightly slower (as the action potential approaches its peak of +30 mV), allowing potassium to flow out of the cell with the force of these same two gradients. A final interesting feature of the action potential is the concept of the *refractory period*. The *absolute refractory* period occurs during an action potential, when sodium and potassium gates are open. During this time it is impossible to stimulate a second action potential. The *relative refractory* period occurs during a brief time after the action potential when the cell is slightly hyperpolarized. During this period, a second action potential may be evoked, but the membrane charge required to reach threshold is greater than that needed during the resting potential.

A nerve impulse is simply the movement (or propagation) of an action potential along the axon of a neuron. The initiation of an action potential anywhere on a cell necessarily changes the membrane potential around that region. With sufficient depolarization, surrounding voltage-sensitive channels will open, initiating a propagation of the signal. The refractory period (mentioned above) prevents an action potential from moving backward over a region that has already been depolarized. This results in propagation in a single direction, usually thought of as along the axon from the cell body to the terminal. With this in mind, an action potential (a nerve impulse) initiated at the juncture of the cell body and the axon (called the axon hillock) will move slowly along the length of the axon until reaching the terminal. This process occurs in *unmyelinated axons*, but is a relatively slow method of propagation. The vast majority of our cells incorporate the use of a *myelin sheath* that acts as an insulator around axons, speeding propagation.

Specifically, propagation is speeded by large numbers of sodium channels clustering in unmyelinated portions of the axon (called *nodes of Ranvier*) and forcing the electrically charged particles to "jump" under myelinated sections of the axon that lack channels. This jumping is called *saltatory conduction*, a process that vastly speeds the neural communication process. The CD provided with your text allows you to visualize how this process works. (It is highly recommended that you review that portion of the CD.)

When a neuron receives synaptic input from innervating terminals, this input may be excitatory (*EPSP*), causing membrane depolarization, or inhibitory (*IPSP*) causing membrane hyperpolarization. Most cells receive many inputs that are combinations of EPSPs and IPSPs. In this regard the neuron must weigh, or *integrate*, these inputs. Integration can be thought of in terms of summation of signals. Signals may be summated from numerous sites in close spatial proximity (*spatial summation*) or they may be summated in time from numerous inputs from the same site in close temporal proximity (*temporal summation*). If summation of excitatory input is sufficient to bring the cell membrane to threshold, an action potential is stimulated. Action potentials are most frequently initiated at the axon hillock where voltage-dependent sodium channels are numerous and sometimes more sensitive to membrane changes than other regions on the neural membrane.

The process of producing neural signals from environmental stimuli (sight, sound, touch, etc.) requires specialized neural receptors capable of transducing environmental energy into neural energy. Likewise, the process of producing a behavior from a neural signal requires stimulation of muscle fibers with neurotransmitters. One example of this is the movement of striated muscles, which is produced by releasing the neurotransmitter *acetylcholine* onto the muscle *end plate*, which in turn contains *transmitter-activated channels*. When these channels are opened in sufficient number, they produce muscle contraction necessary for movement.

Single-cell recording studies have begun to reveal a startling specificity of some cells for certain behaviors. For example, *James Ranck* showed that in rats some neurons are active in response to the head being pointed in a particular direction. These head-direction cells suggest that some cells may actually function to give animals a sense of direction. This study also exemplifies the usefulness of the single-cell recording technique in trying to decipher the function of particular brain regions, structures, and cells. EEG recordings provide information about neural activity on a much grosser level, indicating when large regions of the brain show changes in electrical activity. But studies using the EEG have been equally useful in yielding information about how the brain works as an entire structure. This is particularly useful when studying general behaviors, such as sleep, or brain dysfunction caused by aberrations in electrical function, such as epilepsy. Most recently EEG techniques have been used to study *event-related potentials* (*ERPs*). ERPs allow researchers to study the effects of relatively discrete sensory stimuli using this noninvasive recording technique. Such recordings can also be generated from several regions simultaneously, offering one more potential method for unraveling the functional anatomy of the human brain as it relates to behavior.

# KEY TERMS

*The following is a list of important terms introduced in Chapter 4. Give the definition of each term in the space provided.*

### Electricity and the Nerve Cell

Negative pole

Positive pole

Volts

Electrical potential

Potential

Current

Insulator

Electrical stimulator

Stimulating electrode

Voltmeter

Recording electrode

Electroencephalogram, or EEG

### Modern Tools

Giant axon


Oscilloscope


Milliseconds


Millivolts


Microelectrodes


Patch clamp


### Movement of Ions

Diffusion


Concentration gradient


Voltage gradient, or charge


### Electrical Activity of a Membrane

Transmembrane voltage


Resting potential


Sodium/potassium pump

Graded potentials

Hyperpolarization

Depolarization

Tetraethylammonium (TEA)

Tetrodotoxin

### Action Potential

Threshold potential

Voltage-sensitive channels

Absolute refractory

Relative refractory

### Nerve Impulse

All-or-none law

Glial cells

Schwann cells

Oligodendroglia

Nodes of Ranvier

Saltatory conduction

**_Integrating Information_**

Excitatory postsynaptic potential, or EPSP

Inhibitory postsynaptic potential, or IPSP

Axon hillock

Temporal summation

Spatial summation

Stretch-sensitive channels

Transducing

End plate

Acetylcholine

Transmitter-activated channels

*Studying Brain Function*

Head-direction cell

Alpha rhythms

Event-related potential (ERP)

## KEY NAMES

*The following is a list of important names introduced in Chapter 4. Explain the importance of each person in the space provided.*

Luigi Galvani

Wilder Penfield

Hermann von Helmholtz

Andrew Hodgkin and Alan Huxley

## PRACTICE TEST

## Multiple-Choice Questions

*Answer each of the following multiple-choice questions with the best possible answer based on information from your text.*

1. Early studies of the effects of electricity on brain function were sometimes conducted in awake humans with exposed brain tissue. For example, R. Bartholow stimulated the cortex of a patient and reported which of the following?
   A. He was able to control her speech by stimulating specific parts of the brain
   B. He was able to evoke memories by stimulating specific parts of the brain
   C. He was able to evoke hand movements by stimulating specific parts of the brain
   D. He was able to evoke fear and anxiety by stimulating specific parts of the brain
   E. All of the above are true

2. When recording electrical potentials from the brain, one wire from a voltmeter is attached to a recording electrode. Which of the following is also connected to the voltmeter?
   A. A battery
   B. A stimulating electrode
   C. A ground electrode
   D. A brain cell
   E. The skull

3. Although it was initially believed that electricity progressed as a continuous electrical signal along the nerve pathways, it was later determined that the speed of neural transmission is slower than the speed of electricity. In 1886 Julius Bernstein suggested the slowing of electrical transmission was caused by which of the following?
   A. Myelin
   B. A chemical basis for the electrical charge
   C. Iron in the blood
   D. Density of nerve cells
   E. Gravitational forces

4. The giant axon of the squid has become a popular tool for studying neural transmission and electrical potentials for which of the following reasons?
   A. It is very large, and therefore easily manipulated for study
   B. It is a very slow firing axon, making it easy to study
   C. It is approximately 12 feet long, making it useful for studying transmission patterns
   D. It can be kept functional in a liquid bath of any fluid
   E. All of the above are true

5. An oscilloscope is . . .
   A. similar in design to a television
   B. capable of being used as a sensitive voltmeter
   C. a useful tool for studying electrical potential in neurons
   D. capable of indicating direction, duration, and magnitude of electrical changes
   E. All of the above are true

6. What is the reason that negatively charged proteins inside the cell do *not* move to the extracellular fluid when the cell is at rest?
   A. They are kept in the cell by the concentration gradient
   B. They are kept in the cell by the voltage gradient
   C. They are kept in the cell by both the voltage and the concentration gradient
   D. Channels for these proteins only open during the initiation of an action potential
   E. None of the above are true

7. Movement down a concentration gradient describes which of the following?
   A. Movement of ions from an area of high concentration to an area of low concentration
   B. Movement of ions from an area of low concentration to an area of high concentration
   C. Movement of positively charged ions toward an area with a net negative charge
   D. Movement of positively charged ions toward an area with a net positive charge
   E. All of the above are correct

8.  Which of the following best describes the resting potential of a typical neural membrane?
    A.  The inside charge is approximately equal to the outside charge
    B.  The inside charge is approximately 70 volts less than the outside charge
    C.  The inside charge is approximately 70 volts greater than the outside charge
    D.  The inside charge is approximately 70 millivolts less than the outside charge
    E.  The inside charge is approximately 70 millivolts greater than the outside charge

9.  The number of potassium ions that can accumulate in a resting neuron is restricted by the concentration gradient. What is the primary force preventing sodium ions from accumulating in a resting neuron?
    A.  Concentration gradient
    B.  Voltage gradient
    C.  Both concentration and voltage gradients
    D.  The sodium/potassium pump
    E.  Their entry is restricted by gated channels at rest

10. Which of the following most accurately describes the sodium/potassium pump?
    A.  It is a protein molecule imbedded in the cell membrane
    B.  It is inactive during the resting state of the neuron
    C.  It moves sodium ions into the cell during rest
    D.  It moves potassium ions out of the cell at rest
    E.  All of the above are true

11. Which of the following best describes graded potentials?
    A.  They are all-or-none phenomena
    B.  They appear as a movement of the membrane potential from positive to negative
    C.  They appear as a movement of the membrane potential from negative to positive
    D.  They are produced by the action of the sodium/potassium pump

12. Which of the following phenomena occur when a membrane reaches threshold?
    A.  Voltage-sensitive potassium channels close
    B.  Voltage-sensitive sodium channels close
    C.  Voltage-sensitive sodium channels open
    D.  Voltage-sensitive chloride channels open
    E.  Voltage-sensitive chloride channels close

13. While an action potential is occurring a neuron is said to be in an absolute refractory period, during which time it is incapable of initiating another action potential. For a brief period immediately following the action potential the neuron enters a relative refractory period. Which of the following statements best describes the relative refractory period?
    A.  The cell is slightly depolarized compared to normal resting potential
    B.  Initiation of an action potential requires slightly greater stimulus intensity at this time
    C.  Initiation of an action potential requires slightly less stimulus intensity at this time
    D.  The cell is incapable of initiating another action potential at this time
    E.  None of the above are true

14. The term *saltatory conduction* is derived in part from Latin to describe which of the following?
    A. The movement of a signal in a single direction
    B. The rapid conduction of a signal along an axon
    C. The jumping action of a signal along an axon
    D. The opening of voltage-sensitive channels required for an action potential
    E. The closing of voltage-sensitive channels following an action potential

15. Which of the following is *not* a feature of nodes of Ranvier?
    A. They are an unmyelinated portion of the dendrite
    B. They contain a high density of sodium channels
    C. They are necessary for signal propagation via saltatory conduction
    D. They are necessary for rapid propagation of a neural signal
    E. All of the above are features of nodes of Ranvier

16. Which of the following would be most likely to evoke an IPSP?
    A. An influx of sodium ions
    B. An influx of potassium ions
    C. An influx of both potassium and sodium ions
    D. An influx of chloride ions
    E. An efflux of chloride ions

17. If an IPSP were to occur in close proximity on a neural membrane to an EPSP, what would be the net result?
    A. They would summate to produce a greater depolarization than either one separately
    B. They would summate to produce a greater hyperpolarization than either one separately
    C. They would produce approximately the same depolarization that either would individually
    D. They would produce approximately the same hyperpolarization that either would individually
    E. They would act as opposing forces, each canceling the membrane effect of the other

18. Which of the following describes the axon hillock?
    A. It is found at the junction where the axon meets the terminal button
    B. It is generally affected more by EPSPs and IPSPs initiated at the dendrites than on the cell body
    C. It contains a high concentration of voltage-sensitive chloride channels
    D. It is where most action potentials are initiated
    E. All of the above describe the axon hillock

19. Which of the following neurotransmitters stimulates transmitter-activated channels at muscle fibers?
    A. Dopamine
    B. Serotonin
    C. Acetylcholine
    D. Norepinephrine
    E. Epinephrine

20. Which of the following *cannot* be assessed using EEG?
    A. Amplitude of electrical signals from the brain
    B. Frequency of electrical signals from the brain
    C. Single-cell activity during behaviors
    D. Epilepsy
    E. Levels of sleep

## Short Answer Questions

*Answer each of the following questions with a brief but complete written answer based on information from your text.*

1. Among the early theories of neural communication was the idea that neurons propagated and transmitted electrical signals. Hermann von Helmholtz refuted this theory with a relatively simple experiment. Briefly describe the techniques he used and the results he generated in this experiment.

2. The oscilloscope has become one of the most useful tools for assessing neural activity. This relatively simple device generates a "line" from which neural activity can be interpreted. In general terms, what does a vertical deflection of this line indicate? What is the difference between a small deflection and a large deflection of this line? What is indicated when the vertical deflection is then maintained as a horizontal line?

3. Briefly explain why negatively charged intracellular proteins do not diffuse out of the cell. Also explain why sodium and potassium ions are attracted to these intracellular proteins.

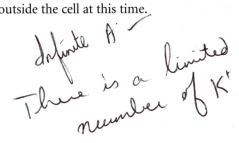

$(\times 12)$  $(\times 10)$
$Cl^-$   $Na^+$

$(\times 20)$
$K^+$  $A^-$

Because the negatively charged intracellular proteins are infinite it is not possible for them to diffuse.
$Na^+K$ are attracted to intracellular proteins because of the sodium/potassium pump. channel.

4. Briefly explain why chloride ions show so little movement into and out of a neuron when it is at its resting potential.

~~Because of the unlimited amount of A⁻ any movement of Cl⁻ will cause loss of resting pot.~~

$Cl^-$ is attracted to $Na^+$ ions. If $Na^+$ cannot get through the hole $Cl^-$ will not be equeally distribtts because it wants to be with $Na^+$

5. Briefly explain why a neuron maintains a negative intracellular charge, even though there is approximately 20 times as many positively charged potassium ions inside the cell relative to outside the cell at this time.

infinite $A^-$
There is a limited number of $K^+$

6. As previously described, when chloride channels are opened in the membrane of a resting neuron, there is very little movement of this ion either into or out of the cell. Briefly explain the role of this seemingly inactive ion in mediating cell activity and neural impulses.

*the Cl⁻ gradient is usually the membrane's resting potential*

7. Novocaine functions in a manner similar to that of tetrodotoxin (the puffer fish toxin). Briefly describe how tetrodotoxin has its effects, and then speculate on how injection of novocaine may work as a local anesthetic.

8. When an action potential is initiated by membrane depolarization it is propagated by opening adjacent voltage-sensitive membrane channels. Why then does a signal move in only one direction along a membrane, and not reverse direction by opening voltage-sensitive channels from which it came?

*Because the gates are briefly inactivated as the action potential is completed*

9. Explain saltatory conduction, including nodes of Ranvier and the myelin sheath in your description.

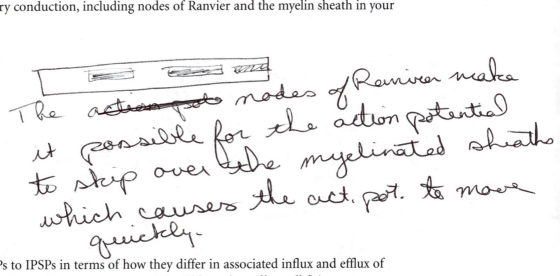

The ~~action pots~~ nodes of Ranvier make it possible for the action potential to skip over ~~the~~ the myelinated sheaths which causes the act. pot. to move quickly.

10. Compare EPSPs to IPSPs in terms of how they differ in associated influx and efflux of ions, how they affect cell membrane potential, and how they affect cell firing rate.

# Matching Questions

*Complete each of the following matching questions based on information from your text.*

1. Match the following ions to their respective charge.

   Positive (+)
   Negative (−)

   + Potassium
   + Sodium
   + Calcium
   − Chloride
   − Intracellular proteins

2. Identify each of the following as being either intracellular (I) or extracellular (E) when a neuron is in a resting state.

_I_ Large negatively charged protein molecules
_I_ Higher concentration of potassium ions
_E_ Higher concentration of sodium ions
_I_ Negative charge
_E_ Higher concentration of chloride ions

3. Identify each of the following events as occurring with an influx of sodium (IS) or with an efflux of potassium (EP).

IS _EP_ Initiation of the action potential
EP _IS_ Hyperpolarization
IS _EP_ Depolarization
EP _IS_ Refractory period

4. Match the following disorder with the appropriate symptom or characteristic.

A. Lou Gehrig's
B. Multiple Sclerosis
C. Epilepsy

_B_ Insensitivity to the chemical messages
_B_ Autoimmune disorder
_C_ Produces abnormal EEG
_A_ Causes degeneration of motor neurons
_C_ Neurons fire synchronously

5. Match the following recording technique to the appropriate feature or characteristic.

A. Single-cell recording
B. EEG
C. ERP

___ First recording technique developed
___ Activity heard as a beep or pop
___ Records alpha rhythms in relaxed subject
___ Records brain response, discrete stimulus
___ Reports N and P waves

# Diagrams

1. On the graph below draw an approximate oscilloscope recording from a neuron. Begin by drawing a resting state. At point A illustrate a subthreshold depolarization. At point B illustrate a hyperpolarization. At point C illustrate a threshold depolarization and action potential.

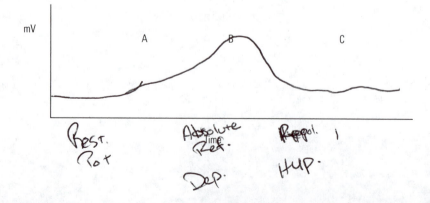

2. On the graph below draw an approximate oscilloscope recording from a neuron. Begin by drawing a resting state. At point A illustrate the response that would be seen with an efflux of potassium ions. At point B illustrate the response that would be seen with an efflux of sodium ions. At point C illustrate the response that would be seen with an influx of calcium ions.

mV

A                    B                    C

Time

3. A diagram of an axon follows. Add to this diagram a typical pattern of myelin. Indicate nodes of Ranvier. Also indicate where you would expect sodium channels to be concentrated.

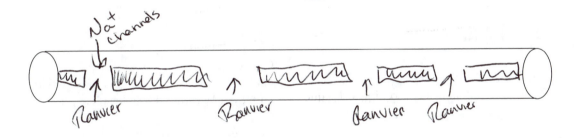

4. Assuming all other variables are held constant, which of the two neurons is more likely to be activated based on the inputs indicated?

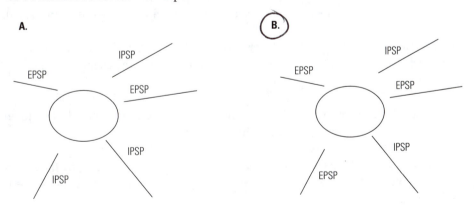

5. Draw approximate EEG patterns that you would expect to see on a subject under the following conditions: Alert, Relaxed, Deep Sleep.

Alert

Relaxed

Deep Sleep

# CD-ROM Exercises

1. Visit module RM2 of your CD to better understand how electrical stimulation studies are currently used. Note that the basic methods employed by earlier researchers (e.g., electrical stimulating electrodes) have changed little over time.

2. Visit module RM4 of your CD to view current techniques used in recording electrode studies. Note the use of these techniques in awake animals and the integration of computers for assessing output from the brain.

3. Visit module NC2 of your CD to view the output from an oscilloscope used for neural recording. Note oscilloscope changes in electrical potential when the cell is stimulated.

4. Visit module NC2 of your CD to better understand how electrical and concentration gradients mediate ionic movement through the membrane. Note the changes on the oscilloscope as ions flow into and out of the cell.

5. Visit module NC2 of your CD to visualize the membrane resting potential. Note the role of active protein pumps in maintaining this potential.

6. Visit module NC2, paying particular attention to the submodule describing the action potential. Note ionic changes associated with this phenomenon and the oscilloscope readout for the action potential.

7. Visit module NC3 for a nice animated video depicting the role of the myelin sheath in conducting an action potential. Note particularly the role of the nodes of Ranvier in this process.

8. Visit module NC4 for an animated depiction of excitatory and inhibitory actions of neurotransmitters at the synapse. Compare and contrast the differences in these activities with regards to postsynaptic function.

9. Visit module NC5 for a nice animated video depicting the process of spatial and temporal summation. Note the additive effect of excitatory input in both cases ultimately producing an action potential and propagating the signal to the next neuron.

10. Visit module RM1 to learn more about modern EEG recording techniques. Note also the description given in the module of ERPs and their role in this technique.

## The Web

*Consider using the following Web sites for additional information on some of the topics from this chapter:*

1. Center for Neural Communication Technology: www.engin.umich.edu/facility/cnct/

2. Epilepsy Foundation of America: www.efa.org/

3. World Federation of Neurology Amyotrophic Lateral Sclerosis: www.wfnals.org/

4. Myasthenia Gravis Foundation of America: www.myasthenia.org/

5. American Board of EEG and Neurophysiology: fhdno2.tch.harvard.edu/www/aben/

The easiest way to get to these sites is to link to them through the student Web site at www.worthpublishers.com/kolb. This site also has further study aids and practice quizzes.

# CROSSWORD PUZZLE

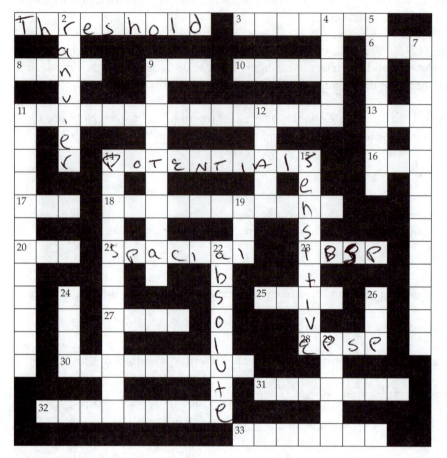

## Across

1. Point where action potential is initiated
3. Peripheral myelin cells
6. Acetylcholine released here on muscle surface; _____ plate
8. Action potential is an (19 down) or _____ phenomenon
9. Used to record brain activity from scalp
10. Membrane recording technique, with 29 down
11. CNS cells that insulate axons
13. # of ions actively pumped at rest
14. Graded and action, e.g.
16. Sodium is pumped out _____ active transport
17. Phenomenon in 8 across is actually termed a _____
18. Neurons are studied by recording and _____
20. Minimum number of cells needed for 10 across technique
21. Signal summation may be temporal or _____
23. Inhibitory signal; abbr.
25. 3 across and 7 across; e.g.
27. What 3 across and 7 across insulate
28. Excitatory signal below 1 across
30. It flows out at the action potential peak
31. Potential between 23 across and 28 across
32. Device used for 18 across
33. 4 down _____ are recorded using 9 across

## Down

2. Proper name for unmyelinated region is node of _____
4. Greek letter
5. Hyperpolarization is this direction
7. 28 across is an example of this
9. Movement of ions creates this type of activity
11. Used as a sensitive voltmeter to measure neural activity
12. Describes squid axons used for research
14. Term for neuron receiving a signal from another neuron
15. Most channels are voltage-_____, some are stretch- _____
19. See 8 across; hope you get this many correct on your next exam
22. Refractory period that is not relative
24. Protein that moves sodium and potassium
26. Event-related potential; abbr.
29. Membrane recording technique with 10 across

**CHAPTER**

# How Do Neurons Communicate?

## CHAPTER SUMMARY

It has been known for nearly a century that neurons communicate with target structures by releasing chemical *neurotransmitters* at their synapses. Beginning in the 1950s, use of the electron microscope provided images of the structural basis for chemical communication. These images show that chemicals are packaged in vesicles, and that vesicles may be contained within *storage granules* in the presynaptic terminal. Electron microscope images also show a variety of protein molecules in both the *presynaptic* and *postsynaptic membranes*. These proteins act as receptors, channels, and pumps, all utilized in neural communication. Although the vast majority of mammalian synaptic connections use chemicals for signal transmission, in some rare cases *electrical synapses* can be found. Chemical communication allows greater flexibility than electrical signals in transmitting a signal at the synapse, however this flexibility comes at the cost of speed. Chemical transmission is slower than electrical in part because of the functional stages required, which include 1) synthesis and storage of chemical molecules; 2) transportation from the cell body to the terminal and from the terminal to the presynaptic membrane at the time of release; 3) interaction of chemicals with postsynaptic membrane receptor sites; and 4) deactivation of transmitter after use. Some neurotransmitters are synthesized from food, while others are simply made from instructions inherent in DNA coding. From the storage vesicles, neurotransmitter is released when an influx of calcium at the terminal binds with *calmodulin* and the resulting calcium/calmodulin complex moves vesicles to the presynaptic membrane. The strength of a neural signal depends on how much calcium enters a terminal and subsequently how many vesicles of neurotransmitter are released into the *synaptic cleft*. The contents of a single vesicle are called a *quantum*. A quantum constitutes the smallest amount of transmitter that can be released, and all neural signals constitute some multiple of this quantum.

Once released into the synaptic cleft, neurotransmitters bind to *transmitter-activated receptors* in the postsynaptic membrane, where they may hyperpolarize or depolarize that cell. In some cases, binding to receptor sites may initiate a chain of chemical reactions in the postsynaptic cell. Deactivation of transmitter once released may result from passive diffusion away from receptors, degradation by enzymes in the cleft, reuptake into the presynaptic terminal, or uptake by neighboring glial cells. Enzymatic degradation

85

may also take place inside the terminal when a neuron produces more neurotransmitter than is needed.

Synaptic connections are generally thought of as occurring between axon terminals and dendrites. Although such *axodendritic* synapses are probably the most common, there are also *axoaxonic*, *axosynaptic*, *axomuscular* (terminating on muscle fibers), *axoextracellular* (terminating in extracelluar space), and *axosecretory* (teminating on blood capillaries). In some cases dendrites synapse on other dendrites (*dendrodendritic*). Regardless of location, all synapses are categorized as either *Type I* (excitatory) or *Type II* (inhibitory) based on the effect they ultimately have on the postsynaptic neuron. Although Type I synapses may intuitively seem "important" in mediating behavior, it should be realized that Type II synapses are equally important in regulating normal function. For example, in neural disorders where Type II synapses are dysfunctional, loss of inhibitory input may result in uncontrolled movements such as *tremors* or *dyskinesia*.

The earliest studies to suggest chemical communication within the nervous system assumed the existence of an excitatory and an inhibitory neurotransmitter combining to mediate behavior. This assumption was correct but oversimplified. Currently, about 50 different substances have been identified that act as neurotransmitters. It is also likely that many such substances are still unidentified. In general terms, for a substance to be considered a neurotransmitter, it should meet four criteria: 1) It must be synthesized in, or present in, a neuron; 2) When the neuron is active it releases the substance which in turn evokes a response; 3) When the substance is experimentally administered at the target, the same response is evoked; and 4) There must be a mechanism for deactivation of the substance in the synaptic cleft. However, even these criteria are considered too strict by some researchers, since a very wide range of substances appear to have some role in mediating neural function.

Currently, neurotransmitters are classified as *small-molecule neurotransmitters*, *peptide neurotransmitters*, and *gases*. Small-molecule neurotransmitters (or their main components) are derived from the food we eat. They are synthesized and packaged in the terminal. They act relatively quickly at target sites and are replaced quickly after use. Many psychoactive drugs are designed to reach the brain in a manner similar to small-molecule neurotransmitters. Examples of small-molecule neurotransmitters include *acetylcholine* (*ACh*, made from *choline* and *acetate*), *dopamine* (made from tyrosine), *norepinephrine* (made from dopamine), and *epinephrine* (made from norepinephrine). *Gammaaminobutyric acid* (*GABA*) and *glutamate* are the primary inhibitory and excitatory brain neurotransmitters respectively (although *glycine* is also a major inhibitory neurotransmitter at many structures). Unlike small-molecule neurotransmitters, peptide neurotransmitters are assembled and packaged in the soma and then transported to the axon terminal. This process makes replacement after use relatively slow. In addition, peptide neurotransmitters do not act directly at ion channels, but rather, produce effects through indirect influence of cell structure and function. *Enkephalins* are one example of peptide neurotransmitters. These substances are known to regulate pain, an effect that can be seen in the response to opium and morphine, both of which mimic the actions of *Metenkephalin*, *Leu-enkephalin*, and *beta-endorphin*. *Nitric oxide* (*NO*) and *carbon monoxide* (*CO*) are gases that act as neurotransmitters. Neither stored in nor released from vesicles, these substances appear to be synthesized in many regions of the cell and then diffuse freely across the membrane as needed.

There are two general classes of receptor sites to which neurotransmitters bind. *Ionotropic* receptors are functionally linked to ion channels, and when activated produce rapid changes in ionic flow and membrane potential of the target cell. *Metabotropic* receptors are associated with one of a family of proteins called *guanyl nucleotide-binding proteins* (*G-proteins*). When these sites are activated they trigger a series of changes within the target cell utilizing a second messenger system. The *second messenger* in turn may alter ion flow through membrane channels. It may also result in production of new channels or the production of other new proteins via a message to the cell's nuclear DNA. Target cells may contain exclusively ionotropic or metabotropic receptor sites, or a combination of the two. Furthermore, these receptors may exert any combination of excitatory or inhibitory influence on the target cell. It is this potential combination of inputs that generates the flexibility of an infinite number of possible responses to individual stimuli.

It was originally believed any given neuron contained only one neurotransmitter substance. This hypothesis has since been disproved with the finding that many combinations of transmitters may coexist within a given neuron or even within a given axon terminal. This coexistence of transmitter substances, in combination with the large number of identified transmitters, and the potential for excitatory or inhibitory postsynaptic effects results in a staggering number of possible combinations for activity within the nervous system.

The skeletal motor system utilizes *cholinergic* neurons releasing ACh at the neuromuscular junction. When stimulated, *nicotinic ACh receptors (nACh)* permit simultaneous efflux of potassium ions and influx of sodium ions, producing an excitatory response. When released with ACh, *calcitonin-gene-related peptide (CGRP)* acts through a second messenger to increase the target cell response. The *autonomic nervous system* contains both *cholinergic* and *adrenergic* neurons. Adrenergic neurons release epinephrine (also called adrenaline) to stimulate the body into a "fight or flight" response. The release of acetylcholine produces the opposite response, sometimes termed the "rest and digest" response. The *central nervous system* utilizes a wide array of transmitter substances, each with a specific function. As mentioned, GABA and glutamate have inhibitory and excitatory effects respectively throughout this system. In addition, four other neurotransmitter systems exert major influence in what are referred to as the *ascending activating systems*. These systems are the ascending cholinergic, dopaminergic, noradrenergic, and serotonergic systems. In very general terms, the cholinergic system is associated with normal alert behaviors including learning and memory. The dopaminergic system controls movement and has been implicated in drug addiction and schizophrenia. The noradrenergic system is associated with mania when overactive, and depression when underactive. The serotonergic system is also associated with depression and some forms of schizophrenia.

It is now known that changes in synaptic function, including release and response to neurotransmitters, are associated with learning. Pioneering studies by *Kandel* and colleagues using Aplysia have shown, for example, that *habituation* results from a reduction in neurotransmitter release associated with repeated stimulation. This reduced transmitter release appears to result from reduced calcium influx at the terminal. However, it is still unknown why calcium channels exhibit this change in the habituation process. *Sensitization*, the learned behavioral response opposite that of habituation, appears to result from serotonin released by interneurons in Aplysia. Acting as a second messenger, serotonin increases the response of the target neuron, evoking an exaggerated postsynaptic response. *Donald Hebb* proposed a synaptic basis for learning more than 50 years ago. The theory that learning requires some conformational change at the synapse is sometimes termed the *Hebb synapse*. The development and application of technology since Hebb originally proposed his theory has supported his original contention. In particular, research on hippocampal cells has shown that *long-term enhancement (LTE)* can occur when glutamate receptors are stimulated as the cell membrane is depolarize. This state of high excitation results in calcium influx that is thought to act as a second messenger producing conformational changes in both the presynaptic and the postsynaptic membrane. One of these changes is production of retrograde plasticity factor that is thought to ultimately stimulate further release of glutamate. This self-perpetuating process eventually leads to relatively permanent changes, as suggested by Hebb. *Associative* learning is thought to occur when two stimuli are paired in time to create a neurotransmitter response vigorous enough to evoke LTE synaptic changes. Finally, recent research has shown dendritic processes to be very plastic. That is, they have the potential to increase or decrease surface area and spiny projections. The ability to undergo such physical changes further increases the potential for synaptic conformations to underlie the process of learning.

## KEY TERMS

*The following is a list of important terms introduced in Chapter 5. Give the definition of each term in the space provided.*

### Chemical Message

Epinephrine (EP)

Chemical neurotransmitters

Presynaptic membrane

Postsynaptic membrane

Synaptic cleft

Storage granules

Electrical synapses

Calmodulin

Transmitter-activated receptors

Miniature postsynaptic potentials

Quantum

Transporter

Axodendritic

Axomuscular

Axosomatic

Axoaxonic

Axosynaptic

Dendrodendritic

Axoextracellular

Axosecretory

Type I synapses

Type II synapses

Tremor

Dyskinesia

### *Kinds of Neurotransmitters*

Small-molecule transmitters

Choline

Acetate

Dopamine

Norepinephrine

Rate limiting

Glutamate

Gamma-aminobutyric acid (GABA)

Met-enkephalin

Leu-enkephalin

Beta-endorphin

Nitric oxide (NO)

Carbon monoxide (CO)

*Types of Receptors*

Ionotropic

Metabotropic

Guanyl nucleotide-binding (G-proteins)

Second messenger

*Neurotransmitter Systems*

Cholinergic

Nicotinic ACh receptor (nACh)

Calcitonin-gene-related peptide (CGRP)

Adrenergic

Ascending activating systems

*Synapses and Learning*

Habituation

Sensitization

Hebb synapse

Field potentials

Ammon's horn

Perforant pathway

Dentate granule cells

Mossy fiber

CA1 and CA3

Schaeffer collateral

Trisynaptic pathway

Long-term enhancement (LTE)

Doubly gated channels

Retrograde plasticity factor

Associative learning

Confocal microscope

## KEY NAMES

*The following is a list of important names introduced in Chapter 5. Explain the importance of each person in the space provided.*

Otto Loewi

Eric Kandel

Donald O. Hebb

## PRACTICE TEST

## Multiple-Choice Questions

*Answer each of the following multiple-choice questions with the best possible answer based on information from your text.*

1. Neurotransmitter mediation of heart rate is one example of chemical communication regulating behavior. When the puffin dives beneath the surface of the water it undergoes a behavior called diving bradycardia. What is the functional purpose of this neurotransmitter-mediated response?
   A. To increase oxygen consumption when not breathing
   B. To conserve oxygen while under water
   C. To increase heart rate
   D. To increase metabolism and raise body temperature
   E. The reason for this response is unknown

2. Early researchers, including Loewi, determined that _____ increased heart rate, whereas _____ decreased heart rate.
   A. acetylcholine, epinephrine
   B. epinephrine, acetylcholine
   C. electricity, acetylcholine
   D. electricity, epinephrine
   E. electricity, lack of electricity

3. Neurotransmitter is known to be stored in synaptic vesicles. However synaptic vesicles may also be stored in larger vesicles. What is the name given to these large storage vesicles?
   A. Golgi apparatuses
   B. Terminal vesicles
   C. Giant vesicles
   D. Storage granules
   E. Terminal storage units

4. Which of the following ions plays an important role in transporting vesicles to the membrane and in the release of neurotransmitters into the synaptic cleft?
   A. Sodium
   B. Potassium
   C. Chloride
   D. Magnesium
   E. Calcium

5. The process of presynaptic neurotransmitter reuptake requires a transporter membrane protein that most closely resembles which of the following in its function?
   A. Sodium channel
   B. Ionotropic receptor
   C. Metabotropic receptor
   D. Sodium-potassium pump
   E. Potassium channel

6. It could be said that glutamate is generally found at . . .
   A. Type I synapses
   B. Type II synapses
   C. gamma-aminobutyric acid synapses
   D. axoaxonic synapses
   E. all synapses in approximately equal frequency and amount

7. Type I synapses are typically located on the _____ , whereas Type II synapses are usually found on the _____.
   A. dendrites, axon terminals
   B. dendrites, cell body
   C. axon terminals, dendrites
   D. cell body, dendrites
   E. cell body, axon terminals

8. Regarding the kinds of neurotransmitter substances that exist, currently approximately how many have been identified through experimental research?
   A. 5
   B. 25
   C. 50
   D. 100
   E. 1000

9. The Renshaw loop describes which of the following?
   A. A device designed to loop around axons and isolate terminals for experimental studies
   B. The process of synthesizing and then breaking down neurotransmitter substances
   C. A feedback loop by which a neuron inhibits itself from continued transmitter release
   D. The sequence of motor neuron, interneuron, sensory neuron, back to interneuron.
   E. The process of excitation followed by inhibition found at most synapses

10. Neurotransmitters that are synthesized and packaged for use in the axon terminal also have what feature?
    A. They are generally synthesized from substances in the food we eat
    B. They are usually proteins
    C. They are relatively slow to act at target sites
    D. They are relatively slow to be replaced after use
    E. None of the above are true of these substances

11. Regarding the neurotransmitter acetylcholine, which of the following is *not* considered a substance used in the synthesis of this chemical?
    A. Choline
    B. Acetate
    C. Acetylcholinesterase (AChE)
    D. A compound that is found in vinegar
    E. A compound that is found in egg yolk

12. Glycine is considered the primary inhibitory neurotransmitter in the brain stem and spinal cord. Which of the following is considered the primary inhibitory neurotransmitter in regions such as the forebrain and cerebellum?
    A. Glutamate
    B. Gamma-aminobutyric acid (GABA)
    C. Acetylcholine (ACh)
    D. Epinephrine (Ep)
    E. Glycine

13. Opium and morphine are drugs that mimic the effects of several peptide neurotransmitters. Which of the following is *not* mimicked by these drugs?
    A. Met-enkephalin
    B. Leu-enkephalin
    C. Beta-endorphin
    D. Alpha-endorphin
    E. These drugs mimic the effects of all of the above

14. Which of the following is *not* true of ionotropic receptor sites?
    A. They mediate rapid change
    B. They are functionally linked to a membrane channel
    C. They are structurally similar to voltage-sensitive channels
    D. When activated they allow ions to flow across the membrane
    E. When activated they generally alter cell metabolism through a series of steps

15. The nicotinic ACh receptor is located at all neuromuscular junctions on skeletal muscles. Which of the following is true of this receptor?
    A. Stimulation permits an influx of sodium ions
    B. Stimulation permits an efflux of potassium ions
    C. This receptor can be stimulated by nicotine
    D. Effects of ACh at the receptors can be altered by calcitonin gene-related peptide (CGRP)
    E. All of the above are true of this receptor

16. As an example of how loss of neurotransmitter function may affect behavior, it is known that humans with Alzheimer's disease show extensive loss of _____ neurons.
    A. Dopaminergic
    B. Serotonergic
    C. Cholinergic
    D. Opiate
    E. All of the above

17. Which of the following is true of the neural basis of learning the habituation response as shown in experiments with Aplysia?
    A. Ability to produce action potentials is reduced in sensory neurons
    B. Ability to produce action potentials is reduced in motor neurons
    C. Calcium influx in response to stimuli is increased
    D. The amount of neurotransmitter released in response to stimuli is reduced
    E. All of the above are true of synaptic changes associated with habituation

18. The neurophysiological process of sensitization is a prolonging of the action potential brought about by which of the following?
    A. Slowing of sodium channels opening, resulting in reduced calcium inflow
    B. Slowing of potassium channels opening, resulting in reduced calcium inflow
    C. Slowing of sodium channels opening resulting in increased calcium inflow
    D. Slowing of potassium channels opening, resulting in increased calcium inflow
    E. Increase in threshold potential required for cell firing

19. Why was Donald Hebb unable to directly support his hypothesis that learning is mediated by structural changes at the synapse?
    A. At the time he developed this hypothesis technology was not available to test it directly
    B. Other researchers of the time opposed his experiments
    C. His proposal is theoretical and could not be demonstrated through experiments
    D. Hebb was not interested in directly testing his hypothesis
    E. The hypothesis was incorrect and thus could not be supported through testing

20. Which of the following neurotransmitter/receptor site combinations has been implicated as contributing to synaptic changes associated with learning and memory?
    A. Dopamine/dopamine
    B. Acetylcholine/nicotinic
    C. Acetylcholine/cholinergic
    D. Glutamate/NMDA
    E. GABA/GABA

# Short Answer Questions

*Answer each of the following questions with a brief but complete written answer based on information from your text.*

1. Though rare, humans utilize some electrical synapses. Other animals, such as the crayfish, rely much more heavily on such synapses. Briefly describe the primary advantage of electrical synaptic transmission and the primary advantage of chemical neurotransmission.

2. The concept of a quantum of neurotransmitter is important in understanding the magnitude or potential magnitude of a postsynaptic response. Briefly explain what a quantum of neurotransmitter is, and how it relates to postsynaptic neuron response.

3. Briefly describe the four means by which neurotransmitter can be removed from postsynaptic receptor sites to terminate the response.

4. There are four general criteria for identifying a substance as a neurotransmitter. List those four criteria in general terms.

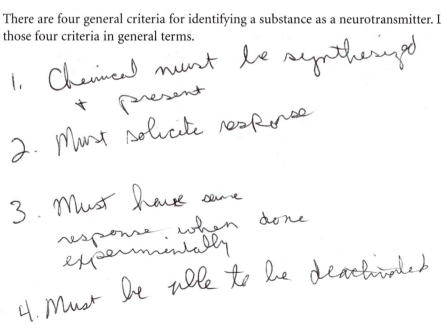

1. Chemical must be synthesized + present

2. Must solicite response

3. Must have some response when done experimentally

4. Must be able to be deactivated

5. One of the most unusual neurotransmitters to be identified is nitric oxide (NO). This neurotransmitter substance is unusual in part because it is a soluble gas (rather than a chemical compound). Briefly describe at least two other ways in which NO is different from chemical neurotransmitters.

6. Briefly describe similarities and differences between ionotropic and metabotropic receptors.

7. Dale's law, put forth when researchers first began studying neurotransmitters, states that one neuron may contain only one neurotransmitter. Considering recent research findings in the area of neurotransmitters, briefly describe the validity of Dale's law.

8. The autonomic nervous system uses neurotransmitters to regulate body states during times of arousal and times of relaxation. Briefly explain the primary neurotransmitters that are used by the autonomic nervous system, and how these transmitter substances affect body functions.

9. Eric Kandel and others have done extensive work assessing synaptic changes associated with simple learning in the Aplysia. Two types of learning that they have assessed are habituation and sensitization. Briefly describe what is meant by these terms in the sense of learned behaviors.

10. Describe in general terms what is proposed by the Hebb synapse.

# Matching Questions

*Complete each of the following matching questions based on information from your text.*

1. Match each of the following neurotransmitter substances to the best descriptive feature.

   A. Acetylcholine          ___ Main excitatory transmitter
   B. Glutamate             ___ Found at neuromuscular junction
   C. GABA                 ___ Main inhibitory transmitter
   D. Opioid peptides        ___ Synthesized as a gas
   E. Nitric oxide            ___ Used for pain reduction

2. Match the following neurotransmitter systems with the disorder in which they are implicated (note in some cases dysfunction of more than one substance has been implicated; those disorders have two spaces for matching).

                                ___, ___ Depression
   A. Dopamine            ___, ___ Schizophrenia
   B. Serotonin             ___ Drug abuse
   C. Acetylcholine       ___ Parkinson's disease
   D. Norepinephrine     ___ Alzheimer's disease
                                ___ Manic behavior

3. Match the following types of substantia-nigra-damaged individuals with features of their disorder.

                                ___ Identified in California in the 1980s
   A. Parkinson's disease patient       ___ Result of severe influenza
   B. Post-encephalitic Parkinson patient   ___ Idiopathic
   C. Frozen addict                     ___ Result of MPTP
                                ___ Disease of aging

4. Identify each of the following as features of either Ionotropic (I) or metabotropic (M) receptors.

   ___ Binding site attached directly to membrane pore
   ___ Changes cell activity through a series of steps
   ___ Associated with G-proteins
   ___ Mediates rapid changes in membrane voltage
   ___ Structurally similar to voltage-sensitive channel
   ___ Often utilizes second messenger systems

5. Mark each of the following as being associated with sympathetic (S) or parasympathetic (P) nervous system arousal.

   ___ Rest and digest
   ___ Heart rate increase
   ___ Cholinergic neurons
   ___ Adrenergic neurons
   ___ Fight or flight

# Diagrams

1. On the diagram of a synaptic connection depicted below, identify the following: mitochondria, synaptic vesicle, storage granule, synaptic cleft, presynaptic membrane, postsynaptic membrane.

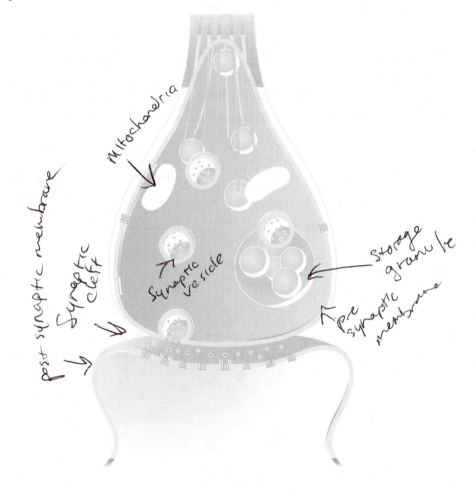

2. Draw a simple diagram to represent each of the following synaptic connections:
   axodendritic, axosomatic, axoaxonic, axosynaptic, dendrodendritic, axoextracellular,
   axosecretory.

3. The diagram below depicts the synthesis pathway for the neurotransmitter epinephrine. Fill in the empty boxes.

4. Below is a diagram depicting normal innervation between a sensory and motor neuron. Draw a simple diagram to depict changes in these connections that would be expected with sensitization. Draw a second diagram to depict changes in these connections that would be expected with habituation.

5. Numerous synaptic changes are thought to be associated with learning and memory. Identify at least 4 possible changes that may occur and draw arrows indicating where such changes would be found in the synapse.

# CD-ROM Exercises

1. Visit module NC4 of your CD to better visualize the structure and function of the axon terminal. Note the internal components and how they work as a unit to release neurotransmitter substances into the synapse.

2. Visit module NC4 of your CD to improve your understanding of synaptic transmission. In particular, visit the submodules describing both excitatory and inhibitory synapses.

3. Visit module NC2 to review ionic flow across the cell membrane. Try to imagine this flow being associated with ionotropic receptor stimulation to induce action potentials and neural signals.

4. Visit module RM6 of your CD to improve your understanding of the confocal microscope. Note the advantages of this particular microscope in certain aspects of neural tissue inspection.

# The Web

*Consider using the following Web sites for additional information on some of the topics from this chapter:*

1. Neurotransmission/Neurotransmitters: web.indstate.edu/thcme/mwking/nerves.html

2. Center for the Neural Basis of Cognition: www.cnbc.cmu.edu/

3. Cambridge Neuroscience (neuropharmaceuticals): www.cambneuro.com/

4. Parkinson's Disease Foundation, Inc.: www.pdf.org/

5. World Parkinson's Disease Association: www.wpda.org/

The easiest way to get to these sites is to link to them through the student Web site at www.worthpublishers.com/kolb. This site also has further study aids and practice quizzes.

# CROSSWORD PUZZLE

## Across

3. One of two enkephalin prefixes
5. Soluble gas messenger; _____ monoxide
8. Receptor stimulation may evoke this type of messenger system
10. Endoplasmic reticulum; abbr.
11. Very common excitatory transmitter
13. Abbreviated term for "endogenous morphine"
14. Term for the synaptic space
15. Very common inhibitory transmitter; abbr.
17. Involuntary movement sometimes seen with L-dopa treatment
19. Enzymes convert 2 down into this neurotransmitter
21. One of two enkephalin prefixes
22. Growing used to a stimulus, also considered a simple form of learning
24. Term for pump that actively takes neurotransmitters back into terminal
27. First word in 15 across; abbr.
28. Researcher devoted to synaptic changes
29. Enzymes convert 19 across into this neurotransmitter

## Down

1. Prefix with 13 across
2. This neurotransmitter is depleted in Parkinson's disease
3. Long-term enhancement; abbr.
4. 13 across singular
5. Prefix for region 1 or 3 in the hippocampus
6. 19 across, 29 across, and 2 down
7. Term for movement from terminal to soma
8. Opposite form of learning from 22 across
9. In simple terms, a neurotransmitter is a _____
12. Involuntary movements seen in Parkinson's disease
13. Epinephrine; abbr.
14. 5 across; abbr.
16. nicotinic acetylcholine receptor; abbr.
18. Acetylcholine is made up of choline and _____
19. Soluble gas messenger; abbr.
20. Large vesicles are called _____ granules
23. Second word in 19 down; abbr.
24. Number of classifications of synapses
25. 1st neurotransmitter to be identified; abbr.
26. Place in England to enjoy a drink and stimulate 15 across receptors

# 6 How Do Drugs and Hormones Influence Behavior?

---

## CHAPTER SUMMARY

*Psychoactive drugs* are chemical compounds that act to alter mood, thought processes, or behavior. Such drugs may be used to manage neuropsychological illness or may conversely become *abused substances*. Psychoactive drugs may be administered via numerous routes, including oral ingestion, inhalation, absorption through the skin, or injection into the blood, muscle, or brain. Although oral ingestion is usually the most convenient route, injection and inhalation are generally more effective, bypassing digestive breakdown and other potential barriers.

The effectiveness of a drug is based in part on the route by which it is administered. In general, an effective oral dose is about ten times greater than that required to be effective if inhaled or injected intravenously. In turn, the effective inhaled or injected dose is about ten times greater than that required to be effective if injected into cerebral spinal fluid. There are also individual differences in determining the effective dose of a drug. For example, large people are less sensitive than small people, men are less sensitive than women, and middle-aged people are less sensitive than the elderly.

Alcohol is an example of a drug that can be effectively administered through oral ingestion. Being a weak acid, alcohol is absorbed directly through the stomach wall. Other drugs that are weak bases do not pass readily through the stomach wall and must therefore traverse more of the digestive system, generally resulting in degradation of the psychoactive effects. All drugs (unless injected directly into the brain) must pass through the *blood–brain barrier*, a term for the small capillary and glial network that form *tight junctions* restricting most substances in the bloodstream from entering the brain. For drugs to pass the blood–brain barrier, they must be non-ionized fat-soluble small molecules, or they must have a chemical structure resembling substances that are moved through the barrier by an *active transport system* (such as glucose). There are some regions where the blood–brain barrier is quite permissive in allowing substances to pass into the brain. The *median eminence* allows passage of hormones to mediate pituitary function. Toxic substances may pass through *area postrema* of the lower brainstem to stimulate a defensive vomiting response.

Drugs have their effect by acting as *agonists* (increasing effectiveness) or *antagonists* (decreasing effectiveness) of neurotransmission at receptor sites. As an example, *black widow spider venom* acts as an acetylcholine agonist by promoting release of this transmitter. The effect is excess activity at the neuromuscular junction that can result in paralysis. *Botulinum toxin* is an antagonist at these same sites. The result of too little stimulation at these receptors is also paralysis. Understanding how a drug affects a synapse is the first step in effective use of the compound. For example, low concentrations of botulinum toxin have potential for use in treating uncontrolled muscle twitches. South American Indians have also used the acetylcholine antagonist *curare* on their arrow tips to induce paralysis in animals they hunt. *Organophosphates* are a potent class of acetylcholine antagonists that bind irreversibly to receptors and have been used as insecticides and in chemical warfare.

Psychoactive drugs may be classified in a number of ways. Most frequently they are classified based on their most pronounced psychoactive effect. In this regard psychoactive drugs fall into the five broad categories of *sedative-hypnotic antianxiety agents*, *antipsychotic agents*, *antidepressants*, *narcotic analgesics*, and *stimulants* (which include *psychedelic drugs*).

Sedative-hypnotic and antianxiety agents include *alcohol*, *benzodiazepines* (also known as *minor tranquilizers* or antianxiety agents) and *barbiturates*. These drugs all work as agonists at the $GABA_A$ receptor site to reduce neural activity. *Tolerance* is the phenomenon whereby with continued use, increasingly greater doses of these drugs are required to evoke a desired effect. *Cross-tolerance* refers to the fact that chronic use of one drug from this class may result in tolerance to another drug from the same class.

Antipsychotic agents are sometimes called *neuroleptics* or *major tranquilizers*. These drugs are used to reduce the symptoms of schizophrenia. However, since they are dopamine antagonists (particularly at the *D2 receptor* subtype) they have a side effect of producing symptoms similar to Parkinson's disease, including *dyskinesia*. The effectiveness of these drugs in treating schizophrenia was a basis for the development of the *dopamine hypothesis of schizophrenia*, which states that symptoms of this disease result from overactivation of the dopamine system.

Antidepressants include *monoamine oxidase (MAO) inhibitors* and the *tricyclic antidepressants*. MAO inhibitors prevent the breakdown of serotonin and dopamine in the synaptic cleft, acting as an agonist for these neurotransmitters. Similarly, tricyclic antidepressants act as agonists by blocking the reuptake transporter for these neurotransmitters. *Second-generation antidepressants* include *selective serotonin reuptake inhibitors* (*SSRIs*), including fluoxetine (marketed under the name Prozac). Although these drugs are quite successful in reducing symptoms in many patients, about 20 percent of patients do not respond to drug therapy or cannot tolerate the side effects of these treatments.

Narcotic analgesics include *opium*, *morphine*, and *codeine*, all of which are derived from seeds of the opium poppy. All of these drugs are endorphin agonists and act as potent painkillers. *Heroin* is a semi-synthetic form of morphine that is more fat-soluble and thus more readily penetrates the blood–brain barrier. *Naloxone* and *nalorphine* are endorphin antagonists and have therapeutic value in treating individuals who have overdosed on endorphin agonists.

Stimulants include *cocaine* and *amphetamine* and act as potent dopamine agonists. Cocaine, derived from the coca shrub, acts by blocking reuptake of dopamine into the presynaptic terminal. Amphetamine is a synthetic compound that shares the reuptake blocking effect of cocaine, but also has the effect of increasing dopamine release, making it a more potent agonist. Caffeine is a relatively mild stimulant that indirectly increases *cyclic adenosine monophosphate* (*cyclic AMP*, or *cAMP*), subsequently increasing glucose utilization. *Psychedelic drugs* include *mescaline*, *tetrahydrocannabinol* (*THC*), *lysergic acid diethylamide* (*LSD*), and *psilocybin*. These drugs share a general agonist effect, although the specific neurotransmitter systems they affect may vary.

Tolerance to drugs may develop in several ways. *Metabolic tolerance* usually results when, after continued exposure, the system begins to produce more enzymes needed to break down a drug. *Cellular tolerance* refers to compensatory changes in cell structure and activity after repeated exposure to a drug. *Learned tolerance* refers to the ability of an individual to exhibit increasingly normal behavior with repeated use of a drug. Conversely, *sensitization* is when an individual shows an increase in responsiveness to successive drug use. Sensitization appears to occur when drugs are used occasionally (rather than continuously, which produces tolerance), and is thought to result from increased neurotransmitter release with each successive use. Also unlike tolerance, sensitization appears to be more selective in the behaviors affected and the environment in which it occurs.

*Substance abuse* is excessive reliance on and chronic use of a drug. This condition can advance to *drug addiction* and is usually accompanied by physical dependence on the drug. *Withdrawal* is the unpleasant physical condition that accompanies drug disuse. Withdrawal symptoms range from sweating, anxiety, and nausea to convulsions and death, depending on the drug and the extent of dependence. Although a wide range of psychoactive agents are abused, all seem to share the quality of producing *psychomotor activation*, likely through activation of dopamine neurons. It is not clear why humans abuse and become addicted to drugs. The dependence hypothesis suggests that individuals become addicted to drugs in an attempt to avoid unpleasant withdrawal symptoms. However, this does not explain why people return to drug use long after withdrawal symptoms have subsided, or why some drugs that produce few if any unpleasant withdrawal effects are potentially addictive. A more recent hypothesis is that addiction begins through *associative learning* when the *pleasure* of drug intoxication is *classically conditioned* to drug use. Terry Robinson and Kent Berridge have proposed the *wanting-and-liking theory* whereby drug use is initiated by liking the pleasurable effects. As tolerance develops, greater doses are required to increase the liking response. Eventually, very little liking is experienced and the behavior is continued predominantly through wanting because of conditioning to cues associated with drug use. Robinson and Berridge suggest that opiod neurons may be responsible for the liking aspect of drug use, while *mesolimbic dopamine neurons* control wanting behavior.

Uncontrolled alcohol consumption is the most common form of abnormal drug use and offers a useful model for assessing behavioral changes during drug intoxication. Abnormal behavior patterns under alcohol intoxication have been explained using the *disinhibition theory*, which states that cortical function that normally mediates reasoning and higher level cognitive function is depressed by alcohol. The term *alcohol myopia* has also been used to describe how, when under the influence of alcohol, individuals tend to respond much more strongly to cues in their immediate environment, while giving less consideration to distant cues. In both cases, alcohol is thought to reduce normal functioning of brain regions associated with reasoning. Research suggests that genetics may predispose some individuals to addiction. However, at this time the evidence is based in large part on correlation research, and a genetic abnormality has not been identified that causes addictive behavior.

Some drugs of abuse are known to directly produce neurodegeneration in animal models. For example, administration of MDMA (ecstasy) in doses used by humans results in degeneration of fine serotonergic fibers in rats and monkeys. In other cases, drug addiction may indirectly result in neurodegneration. For example, chronic alcohol consumption is often accompanied by poor diet and vitamin deficiency that can cause damage to specific brain structures. Other drugs that produce profound psychoactive effects, such as LSD, have not been shown to produce cell loss in animals when administered in doses used by humans.

Hormones are a class of endogenous chemicals that circulate through the bloodstream to target organs. Once reaching their targets, they act in a manner similar to neurotransmitters altering cell function and ultimately behavior of the organism. Hormones are used to maintain *homeostasis* (such as eating), to regulate *reproductive function* and in response to *stress*. The hypothalamus utilizes *releasing factors* to stimulate the pituitary gland into releasing hormones that then control release of hormones throughout the system. For example, the hypothalamus regulates insulin release from the pancreas, which controls glucose storage and utilization, ultimately mediating eating behavior. They hypothalamus also regulates hormones of the menstrual cycle. Interestingly, changes in ovarian hormones such as estrogen and progesterone during the menstrual cycle in turn appear to affect performance on some motor and cognitive tasks. Stress hormones include *epinephrine*, responsible for rapid effects associated with the adrenaline surge, and *cortisol*, which is utilized for preparing the body for extended periods of stress by decreasing digestion, immune responses and reproductive functioning. Stress responses activated by these hormones occur during "good stress" as well as "bad stress." Although the response is generally considered adaptive, Sapolsky and his colleagues have recently shown that prolonged and/or extreme stress can result in neurodegeneration, particularly to hippocampal cells.

# KEY TERMS

*The following is a list of important terms introduced in Chapter 6. Give the definition of each term in the space provided.*

### Principles of Drug Action

Drug

Psychoactive drugs

Abused substances

Blood–brain barrier

Endothelial cells

Tight junctions

Active transport systems

Median eminence

Area postrema

Agonists

Antagonists

Lecithin

Black widow spider venom

Botulinum toxin

Curare

Organophosphates

### *Classification of Psychoactive Drugs*

Sedative-hypnotics

Antianxiety agents

Alcohol, barbiturates

Benzodiazepines

Minor tranquilizers

Tolerance

Cross-tolerance

GABA$_A$

Antipsychotic agents

Major tranquilizers

Neuroleptics

Dyskinesia

D2 receptor

Dopamine hypothesis of schizophrenia

Antidepressants

Monoamine oxidase inhibitors

Tricyclic antidepressants

Second-generation antidepressants

Selective serotonin reuptake inhibitors

Narcotic analgesics

Opium

Codeine

Morphine

Heroin

Nalorphine

Naloxone

Endorphins

Stimulants

Cocaine

Amphetamine

Cyclic AMP

Psychedelic drugs

Mescaline

Lysergic acid diethylamide

Psilocybin

### Drugs, Experience, Context, and Genes

Tolerance

Metabolic tolerance

Cellular tolerance

Learned tolerance

Sensitization

Substance abuse

Substance dependence

Addiction

Physical dependence

Withdrawal

Psychomotor activation

Dependence hypothesis

Pleasure

Associative learning

Classical conditioning

Incentive salience

Incentive sensitization

Mesolimbic dopamine system

Disinhibition theory

Time out

Alcohol myopia

Analogue

Kainate

MGluR4

MDMA

***Hormones***

Testosterone

Endocrine glands

Homeostasis

Reproductive functions

Stress hormones

Releasing factors

Homeostatic hormones

Reproductive hormones

Stress hormones

Stress

Stressor

Stress response


Epinephrine


## KEY NAMES

*The following is a list of important names introduced in Chapter 6. Explain the importance of each person in the space provided.*

Candice Pert


Solomon Snyder


Sigmund Freud


Terry Robinson


Jill Becker


Kent Berridge


Ian Whishaw


Tara MacDonald


Robert Sapolsky

# PRACTICE TEST

# Multiple-Choice Questions

*Answer each of the following multiple-choice questions with the best possible answer based on information from your text.*

1. Which of the following is true of psychoactive drugs?
   A. They may alter mood
   B. They may alter behavior
   C. In high doses some may act as toxins in the brain
   D. They have the potential to become abused substances
   E. All of the above

2. Which of the following is a feature associated with orally administered drugs that have a rapid effect?
   A. They are weak acids
   B. They are hydrophobic
   C. They are large molecules
   D. They are easily metabolized by the liver
   E. All of the above

3. Which of the following is the most accurate statement regarding the blood–brain barrier?
   A. It does not allow any substances into the brain from the bloodstream
   B. It is composed of tight junctions formed by endothelial cells
   C. It is especially effective in keeping lipid-soluble drugs from entering the brain
   D. It utilizes no active transport of substances, only passive diffusion
   E. It effectively prevents L-dopa in the bloodstream from entering the brain

4. Which of the following is *not* generally considered an individual difference that is likely to alter the effectiveness of a drug?
   A. Individual differences in sensitivity to drug effects
   B. Age
   C. Ethnic origin
   D. Size
   E. Gender

5. The venom from the bite of a black widow spider would likely do which of the following?
   A. Kill a human
   B. Affect dopamine
   C. Act as an agonist
   D. Cause muscle twitches in an area around the bite
   E. Block release of a neurotransmitter

6. Organophosphates bind irreversibly to acetylcholinesterase. As such they are highly potent agonists at acetylcholine receptor sites. What is a potential use for these compounds?
   A. Treating myesthenia gravis
   B. Treating Parkinson's disease
   C. Reducing muscle twitches
   D. A toxin for chemical warfare
   E. None of the above

7. Which of the following is *not* considered a member of the drug classification sedative-hypnotics?
   A. Barbiturates
   B. Alcohol
   C. Prozac
   D. Benzodiazepines
   E. Minor tranquilizers

8. Many drugs that reduce anxiety or have minor tranquilizing qualities act as agonists at the $GABA_A$ receptor subtype. What is the ionic change associated with activation of this receptor?
   A. An influx of sodium ions
   B. An influx of potassium ions
   C. An influx of calcium ions
   D. An influx of chloride ions
   E. An efflux of all the ions listed above

9. Antipsychotic agents are effective in reducing the symptoms of what disorder?
   A. Depression
   B. Mania
   C. Parkinson's disease
   D. Chronic pain
   E. None of the above

10. Antidepressants are thought to act by improving chemical transmission of serotonin, noradrenaline, histamine, acetylcholine, and dopamine. However, agonists for one of these neurotransmitters have been particularly successful in alleviating symptoms of depression. Select that transmitter from the list below.
    A. Serotonin
    B. Noradrenaline
    C. Histamine
    D. Acetylcholine
    E. Dopamine

11. Opium is derived from seeds of the opium poppy. Which of the following is synthesized directly from opium?
    A. Heroin
    B. Morphine
    C. Endorphins
    D. Naloxone
    E. Nalorphine

12. Cocaine and amphetamine share the feature of blocking dopamine reuptake, making them effective dopamine agonists. What additional feature does amphetamine have at the synapse that makes it an even more potent agonist than cocaine?
    A. It enhances dopamine release from the terminal
    B. It blocks enzymatic breakdown of dopamine
    C. It directly stimulates postsynaptic dopamine receptor sites
    D. It blocks reuptake of serotonin
    E. All of the above

13. Which of the following is *not* classified as a psychedelic drug?
    A. Mescaline
    B. Tetrahydrocannabinol (THC)
    C. MDMA (ecstasy)
    D. Lysergic acid diethylamide (LSD)
    E. Psilocybin

14. The liver produces enzymes that are used to degrade alcohol. With regular alcohol consumption a liver will begin to produce more of this enzyme than it did prior to alcohol exposure. This phenomenon is termed . . .
    A. cellular tolerance
    B. metabolic tolerance
    C. behavioral tolerance
    D. sensitization
    E. intoxication

15. Tolerance appears to develop with frequent repeated drug use. Sensitization is thought to develop with which of the following?
    A. Frequent repeated drug use
    B. Frequent repeated drug use followed by long periods of abstinence
    C. Initial exposure to the drug
    D. Following an episode of drug overdose
    E. Occasional use

16. Which of the following is *not* a feature of addiction as defined in your text?
    A. It develops as an advanced state of substance abuse
    B. It usually is based on use of drugs that inhibit psychomotor activation
    C. It usually includes physical dependence
    D. It usually includes development of tolerance
    E. Withdrawal symptoms are usually experienced if drug use is discontinued

17. Which of the following is true of how addicts report drug use experience?
    A. Initial drug experience is unpleasant, but pleasure is derived with repeated use
    B. Initial drug experience is pleasant, but pleasure decreases with repeated use
    C. Initial drug experience is pleasant, and pleasure is maintained with repeated use
    D. Initial drug experience is pleasant, and pleasure increases with repeated use
    E. All of the above are reported with approximately equal frequency

18. MacDonald and coworkers have proposed that some undesirable behaviors associated with alcohol intoxication result from an inability to attend to distant cues combined with a strong influence of salient cues in the immediate environment. What is the term used by MacDonald to describe this phenomenon?
    A.  Cue inattention
    B.  Selective intoxication syndrome
    C.  Alcohol-induced blindness
    D.  Alcohol myopia
    E.  Beer goggles

19. The hypothalamus produces releasing factors to stimulate which gland into releasing hormones?
    A.  Pineal
    B.  Pituitary
    C.  Gonads
    D.  Adrenal
    E.  Pancreas

20. Sapolsky contends that the type of stress that stimulates a hormone response is which of the following?
    A.  Stress associated with fear
    B.  Stress associated with aggression
    C.  Stress associated with sadness
    D.  Stress associated with happy events
    E.  Stress associated with any of the above

## Short Answer Questions

*Answer each of the following questions with a brief but complete written answer based on information from your text.*

1.  The blood–brain barrier (bbb) may be viewed as both a blessing and a curse. Briefly describe the make-up of the bbb. As a blessing, describe a useful function of the bbb. As a curse, explain how the bbb may hinder pharmacological therapy for some brain disorders.

2. The effectiveness of neuroleptics at reducing symptoms of schizophrenia led to development of the dopamine hypothesis of schizophrenia. Briefly describe this hypothesis and how it was formulated from results of neuroleptic treatments.

3. Briefly explain the effect of MAO inhibitors on neural transmission. Also identify the disorder for which these drugs are most frequently prescribed.

4. Early in its history, amphetamine had several potential benefits for which it was used. List at least three reasons amphetamine was used for reasons other than recreation. Also include a statement as to why it is now seldom used therapeutically.

5. Briefly describe tolerance and sensitization. Give a general explanation of synaptic changes in neural transmission that are thought to underlie these phenomena.

6. Briefly describe the difference between substance abuse and addiction. Include in your explanation how the two are related.

7. Briefly describe the dependency hypothesis of drug addiction. Include in your explanation at least two weaknesses in this theory.

8. Briefly explain the disinhibition theory of how alcohol produces behavioral effects. Include in your explanation the primary region proposed to be affected in this model.

9. There is a body of evidence suggesting that alcoholism, and possibly drug addiction in general, may have a genetic basis. Give at least two examples of research to support this contention. Also explain a weakness in interpreting results from this research.

10. Hormones are generally thought of as mediating sexual behavior. However, a separate class of hormones is utilized in response to stress. Give an example of at least two stress hormones, and explain how these hormones affect behavior.

# Matching Questions

*Complete each of the following matching questions based on information from your text.*

1. Number from 1 to 5 (1 being the fastest, 5 being the slowest) the relative speed with which a drug would have its action when delivered via the following routes of administration.

   _4_ Oral (eaten)
   _5_ Topical (applied to the surface of the skin or mucus)
   _2_ Intravenous (injected into a vein)
   _1_ Intracranial (injection into the brain)
   _3_ Inhalation (smoked)

2. Label each of the following actions as agonists or antagonists.

   _Ant_ ~~agonist~~ block presynaptic reuptake of neurotransmitter from synapse
   _Ant_ block enzyme that breaks down neurotransmitter
   _Ag_ _Ant_ block postsynaptic receptor site
   _Ag_ _Ant_ block release of neurotransmitter from presynaptic terminal
   _Ag_ _Ag_ increase effectiveness of neurotransmission
   _Ant_ _Ant_ decrease effectiveness of neurotransmission

3. Match the following drugs to the appropriate feature or characteristic.

   A. Alcohol            _B_ Block dopamine receptor sites
   B. Neuroleptics       _A_ Affects GABA_A_ receptor
   C. MAO Inhibitors     _E_ Increases cyclic AMP
   D. Opium              _D_ Among the most potent analgesics
   E. Caffeine           _C_ Contributed to development of Prozac

4. Match the following drug class to the appropriate source.

   A. Norepinephrine psychedelics    _E_ Fermented and distilled
   B. Tetrahydrocannabinol           _C_ Coca plant
   C. Psychomotor stimulant          _B_ Hemp plant
   D. Narcotic analgesics            _D_ Poppy seeds
   E. Sedative-hypnotics antianxiety _A_ Peyote cactus sugars

5. Match the following disorders to the appropriate symptoms or characteristics.

   _C_ More common in women than in men
   A. Fetal alcohol syndrome   _A_ Poor nutrition may increase symptoms
   B. Drug-induced psychosis   _A_ Associated with underdeveloped brain
   C. Depression               _C_ Sometimes treated with electroconvulsive therapy
                        C B   ___ May be co-diagnosed with schizophrenia

# Diagrams

1. In several regions, the blood–brain barrier is very permissive (or even lacking), allowing chemicals from the blood to pass easily into the brain. Use the sagittal brain diagram below to identify three regions where chemicals pass readily from the bloodstream into the brain.

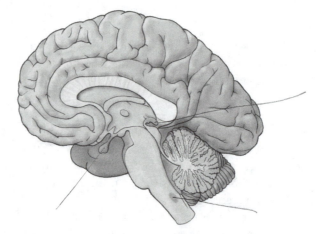

2. Below are three dopamine synapses. The first synapse shows normal function. Depict on the other two synapses the effects of 1) Cocaine, 2) A neuroleptic drug.

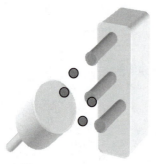

**Normal**

**Cocaine**

**Neuroleptic**

● Dopamine

▬ Receptor

3. Continuous drug use may result in both behavioral tolerance and a physiological tolerance. For example, as individuals consume alcohol over time tolerance develops for signs of intoxication (behavioral) and for blood alcohol level (physiological). Below is a graph depicting an individual's drinking behavior over a three-week period. Graphically illustrate what would be expected with regards to level of intoxication and blood alcohol level on the other two graphs.

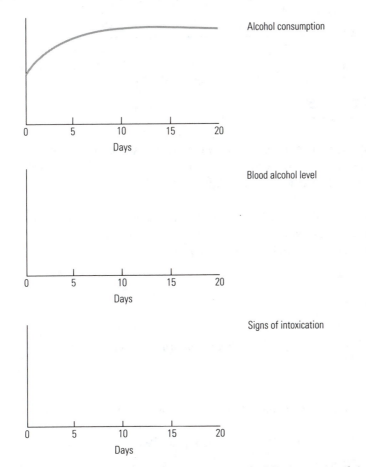

4. Robinson and Berridge have described the process of addiction as involving separate brain mechanisms responsible for both wanting and liking drug use. They further hypothesize that the relative influence of these two mechanisms changes over time with continued drug use. On the graph below, depict with lines the change in relative influence of wanting and liking mechanisms with continued drug use. Assume both mechanisms start at approximately the same level.

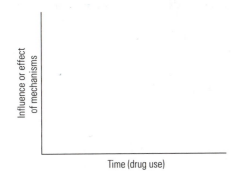

5. Sapolsky and colleagues have suggested a self-perpetuating cycle whereby stress can produce significant brain damage. Complete the diagram below indicating 1) cells affected, 2) change in cortisol secretion, 3) effect of changes in 1) & 2).

Stress → 1) *hippocampal cells* → 2) *Release of cortisone* → 3) *Damage to hippocampal*

## CD-ROM Exercises

1. Visit module NC4 of your CD to review the processes of excitatory synaptic function. Consider this module with particular consideration given to drugs that act as agonists, such as acetylcholine at striated muscles.

2. Visit module NC4 of your CD to review the processes of inhibitory synaptic function. Consider this module with particular consideration given to drugs that act as antagonists, such as GABA in the central nervous system.

## The Web

*Consider using the following Web sites for additional information on some of the topics from this chapter:*

1. National Organization on Fetal Alcohol Syndrome: www.nofas.org/

2. National Institute on Alcohol Abuse and Alcoholism: etoh.niaaa.nih.gov/

3. Narcotics anonymous personal experiences: members.aol.com/GlennS1956/index.html

4. Partnership for a Drug-Free America: www.drugfreeamerica.org/

5. APA division of Psychopharmacology: www.apa.org/divisions/div28/index.html

The easiest way to get to these sites is to link to them through the student Web site at www.worthpublishers.com/kolb. This site also has further study aids and practice quizzes.

# CROSSWORD PUZZLE

## Across

1. Term for physiological balance
5. Keeps unwanted substances out of the brain; abbr.
6. Drug commonly called "ecstasy"; abbr.
8. Potent serotonin hallucinogen; abbr.
9. Source of venom that causes ACh release
10. Similar effects, but more potent than cocaine
13. Codeine and morphine mimic these natural chemicals
17. Prozac, e.g.
18. One who uses drugs inappropriately or excessively
19. Benzodiazepine is an example of this class
22. Addicts experience when drug is not taken
24. The "O" in MAO
25. 6 across is one of these, at serotonin neurons
27. Class of drugs for opium; _____ analgesics
28. Gland that releases hormones

## Down

2. Near the hypothalamus, where hormones enter the CNS; with 12 down
3. Alcohol and barbiturates
4. System affected by 3 down; abbr.
5. Word for the second letter in 5 across
7. Substance synthesized from morphine
11. Area _____, weak spot in 5 across
12. Second word in 2 down structure
14. Dopamine system implicated in drug abuse
15. Effect shown by Robinson and Becker after a single injection of amphetamine
16. Extracted from berries, it blocks ACh receptors
17. Type of learning thought to link drug use to pleasure
19. It occurs in a number of stages after repeated drug use
20. System that moves glucose into the brain; with 23 down
21. Potent opiate antagonist
23. First word in system from 20 down
26. Street name for lysergic acid diethylamide

CHAPTER

# 7 How Does the Brain Develop?

## CHAPTER SUMMARY

To understand the influence of brain development on emergence of behaviors, several strategies may be used. One method is to analyze structural development and correlate these changes to the emergence of behaviors. A second method is to first assess behavioral changes, and then draw conclusions about neural development based on these observations. Finally, factors that affect both brain and behavior may be assessed. Such factors include the influence of hormones, toxins, and injury during development.

The study of brain development has roots in philosophical discussions nearly 2000 years old. Early philosophers subscribed to the concept of *preformation*, or the idea that fetal development constituted a time when the organism was miniaturized, and that development was merely an enlargement process. Preformation was the dominant theory until the mid-nineteenth century, when detailed analysis of embryos began to reveal too many anatomical differences during gestation to support this theory. Today we know that brain development begins in a curled sheet of cells called the *neural tube. Neural stem cells* proliferate in this tube, which later forms the ventricular system for the brain. Stem cells give rise to *progenitor cells* that may further divide and produce nonproliferating *neuroblasts* and *glioblasts*. During development, neural tissue does not take on the appearance of a brain until about 100 days, and the human cortex surface features of gyri and sulci do not become apparent until nearly seven months.

It is believed that cell development into specific types of cells is mediated in large part by genetic codes contained in the DNA. However, chemical *neurotrophic factors* may also be involved. Two examples of such chemicals are *epidermal growth factor* (EGF), which stimulates stem cells to produce progenitor cells, and *basic fibroblast growth factor* (bFGF), which stimulates progenitor cells to produce neuroblasts.

*Neurogenesis* (the process of forming neurons) is complete at around 4.5 months of gestation. Cell migration from the neural tube to appropriate destinations begins shortly after cell production begins, and continues for about six weeks after neurogenesis ceases. Migration of most neurons is guided by *radial glial cells*, while a small number of cells appear to be guided by chemical signals. Migration guides cells first to deep brain structures, with layers of cells added on until the outermost cortical layers are formed at the end of development. Once in place, cells begin to mature or differentiate. This process

129

includes relatively rapid axon development, with a slower though more extensive process of growth and *arborization* of dendrites. Axonal development is lead by a *growth cone*, which then divides into several *filopodia* (or finger-like projections), which eventually form terminals. Growth cones are attracted to or repelled from sites by *tropic molecules*. Only one group of such molecules, called *netrins*, has been identified, but researchers are quite certain more exist. *Cell-adhesion molecules (CAM)* are a class of molecules that allow growth cones to adhere to a surface to guide growth or to form a connection.

The nervous system has a propensity to vastly overproduce both cells and neural connections during development, after which time nonfunctional connections are pruned and nonessential neurons degenerate. This process is sometimes referred to as neural Darwinism. The most inactive neurons are most susceptible to cell death, and it is believed that lack of cell activity results in reduced neurotrophic factor and ultimately a genetically programmed death termed *apoptosis*. Cells likely to survive are those that are highly active, especially clusters of cells that fire simultaneously forming neural circuits for sensory and motor systems.

Once neurons are established, glial development finalizes myelin sheath production around established axons. In fact, myelin formation has been correlated to development of behavioral processes after birth. One example of this is motor coordination that develops in synchrony with myelination of axons in the motor cortex, located in the frontal lobe. Language development also closely correlates to neural development of cortical neurons near Broca's area, located in this same general region. Complex cognitive development has been described in detail beginning with observations of *Jean Piaget*. Piaget and others have described a series of four major cognitive development stages seen in all normally developing children. These stages occur at roughly the same time that *growth spurts* appear in brain development, suggesting that expansion of neural tissue underlies the development of increasingly complex cognitive strategies. Animal models have shown that similar growth spurts appear in monkeys and are accompanied by increasing ability in task-solving strategies.

*Brain plasticity* refers to the ability of the brain to change throughout life in response to experiences. Such experiences include external stimuli as well as internal stimuli, such as hormones, toxins, and genetic aberrations. Donald Hebb was among the first to show that developing animals exposed to a stimulus-enriched environment developed greater brain mass and neural complexity than animals raised in an environment deprived of such stimuli. From this work it was proposed that increasing neural stimulation during development can reduce synaptic pruning. It has further been proposed that early exposure to language, music, and other culturally influenced stimuli results in long-lasting familiarity with those stimuli. Such plasticity allows an infinite number of possible neural connections modified by experiences during development, generated from a single genetic blueprint.

Particular *critical periods* of development have been identified during which time establishment of neural connections can lead to lasting behaviors. The demonstration by Konrad Lorenz of *imprinting* in baby goslings serves as a prototypical example. Imprinting occurs during a critical period, after which it cannot be established. In cases where imprinting does not occur, or occurs with an inappropriate model, birds exhibit abnormal sexual and social behaviors in adulthood suggesting a permanent change in neural structure and function. Other abnormal experiences encountered during critical periods of neural development (such as deprivation of social contact) have been shown to have long-lasting and sometimes devastating effects in both animals and humans. Internal experiences such as hormones also have their effect during a critical period. For example, the presence of testosterone during development masculinizes neural development, leading to male-pattern behavior later in life. Similarly, females exposed to testosterone during their critical period exhibit some male-pattern behaviors later in life.

Regarding brain injury during development, it appears the second half of the gestational period is a particularly vulnerable time. During this period, after neurogenesis is complete and migration is occurring, damage can produce severe cognitive and motor deficits. *Spina bifida* is a condition in which the back portion of the neural tube does not completely close, resulting in incomplete formation of the spinal cord and severe motor disturbance. *Anencephaly* occurs when the front portion of the neural tube does not completely close. In this case, brain development is severely affected and survival of the infant is generally limited to only a few days. In cases of mental retardation, it appears that dendritic arborization is impaired, resulting in abnormal neural connections. Similar malformation in neural connections may underlie a host of neurological disorders that become apparent later in life, including seizures, dyslexia, schizophrenia, and other mood disorders. Although abnormalities in neural plasticity appear to result in numerous disorders, this same feature of the nervous system serves a very adaptive function of allowing "normal" development in the face of a wide range of internal and external factors.

# KEY TERMS

*The following is a list of important terms introduced in Chapter 7. Give the definition of each term in the space provided.*

### Brain Development

Preformation

Neural tube

Sexual dimorphism

Neural stem cells

Ventricular zone

Progenitor cells

Neuroblasts

Glioblasts

Neurotrophic factors

Epidermal growth factor

Basic fibroblast growth factor

Neurogenesis

Migration

Differentiation

Radial glial cells

Dendritic arborization

Growth cones

Filopodia

Cell-adhesion molecules

Tropic molecules

Netrins

Synaptic pruning

Neural Darwinism

Apoptosis

### Behavior and Development

Object permanence

Conservation of volume

Growth spurts

Nonmatching-to-sample

### Environment and Development

Brain plasticity

Chemoaffinity hypothesis

Amblyopia

Critical period

Imprinting

Masculinization

Spina bifida

Anencephaly

Phenylketonuria (PKU)

Down's syndrome

Fetal alcohol syndrome

Rubella

Cerebral palsy

Kwashiorkor

Schizophrenia

## KEY NAMES

*The following is a list of important names introduced in Chapter 7. Explain the importance of each person in the space provided.*

Jean Piaget

Donald Hebb

Harry Harlow

# PRACTICE TEST

## Multiple-Choice Questions

*Answer each of the following multiple-choice questions with the best possible answer based on information from your text.*

1.  In assessing the relationship between brain and behavior by examining how structural development correlates to behavior, we would anticipate that growth of brain structure associated with language would . . .
    A.   precede development of any language skills
    B.   occur after development of basic language skills
    C.   occur after development of sophisticated language skills
    D.   parallel some aspects of language skills
    E.   not be related in any way to development of language skills

2.  Some factors may abnormally alter neural development and as a result alter behavioral development, offering insight into the parallels between brain development and behavior. Which of the following may abnormally alter neural development in this way?
    A.   Exposure to very high or very low levels of hormones
    B.   Genetic aberrations
    C.   Exposure to toxins
    D.   Injury to the developing brain
    E.   All of the above are capable of altering neural development

3.  The neural tube is sometimes thought of as the nursery in which neural cells proliferate. What happens to this neural tube as the brain develops into adult form?
    A.   It is absorbed into brain tissue
    B.   It becomes the basal ganglia
    C.   It becomes the cerebral cortex
    D.   It becomes the vertebra surrounding the spinal cord
    E.   None of the above

4   Which of the following is the term used for cells lining the neural tube?
    A.   Neurons
    B.   Neural stem cells
    C.   Progenitor cells
    D.   Neuroblasts
    E.   Glioblasts

5.  Which of the following is the primary function of neurotrophic factors?
    A.   Guide axon growth
    B.   Prune nonfunctional axons
    C.   Stimulate cell production
    D.   Speed neural signals
    E.   Block the action of hormones

6. Neurogenesis is . . .
   A. the pruning of little-used axonal connections
   B. the final stage of brain development
   C. the myelination of axons
   D. the process of forming neurons
   E. another term for apoptosis

7. Which of the following is true of the process cells undergo when migrating to their appropriate regions of the brain?
   A. Most follow chemical signals, a small number utilize radial glial cells
   B. Most follow radial glial cells, a small number utilize chemical signals
   C. Approximately equal numbers utilize radial glial cells and chemical signals
   D. Most migrate randomly, a small number use both radial glial cells and chemical signals
   E. Most use both radial glial cells and chemical signals, a small number migrate randomly

8. The process of neural development forming the brain appears to follow which of the following sequences?
   A. Posterior forms first, then anterior
   B. Anterior forms first, then posterior
   C. Outer structures form first, then inner structures
   D. Inner structures form first, then outer structures
   E. Development varies considerably between individuals

9. Which of the following is true of dendritic arborization?
   A. It is a relatively slow process of pruning dendrites
   B. It is a relatively slow process of forming dendritic branches
   C. It is a relatively fast process of pruning dendrites
   D. It is a relatively fast process of forming dendritic branches
   E. It is a process that is thought to be unaffected in Down's syndrome

10. During development, growth cones may send out finger-like projections known as . . .
    A. radial glial
    B. netrins
    C. tropic molecules
    D. dendritic branches
    E. filopodia

11. Which of the following is true of myelination?
    A. It is not well correlated to maturation of cerebral structures
    B. Cells cannot function until they are myelinated
    C. All myelination is generally completed about the time of birth
    D. Areas that control the highest level of functioning are thought to be myelinated last
    E. All of the above are true

12. Which of the following is *not* true of language development?
    A. It is mediated solely by development of controlled movements of the mouth
    B. It is controlled in large part by structures in the cerebral cortex
    C. Areas controlling language increase dendritic density dramatically between 15 and 24 months
    D. About 1 percent of all children with normal intelligence show marked delays in speech development
    E. Language acquisition is largely complete by age 12

13. Piaget noted distinct stages of cognitive development in children that correlate with growth spurts seen in neural development. How many stages of development did Piaget propose?
    A. Four
    B. Eight
    C. Twelve
    D. Sixteen
    E. Twenty

14. Which of the below is true of animals raised in a stimulus-enriched environment compared to animals raised in an impoverished environment?
    A. Enriched-environment rats perform better in maze-learning tasks
    B. Enriched-environment rats have larger neurons
    C. Enriched-environment rats have a greater number of synaptic connections
    D. Enriched-environment rats have more and larger astrocytes
    E. All of the above are true

15. When Martha Constantine-Patton implanted a third eye into the head of a frog embryo, her results were as hypothesized in that this third eye . . .
    A. did not form functional connections
    B. formed functional connections with random brain regions
    C. formed functional connections with tectum regions for both eyes
    D. formed functional connections with the tectum region for a single eye
    E. formed functional connections with the visual cortex

16. Abnormal experiences during early critical periods of brain development may have long-lasting effects on behavior. An example of this was demonstrated by researchers who raised Scottish terriers in isolation and darkness. When removed from this environment, these animals showed which of the following behaviors?
    A. They showed virtually no reaction to people
    B. They showed virtually no reaction to other dogs
    C. They exhibited a marked reduction in sensitivity to pain
    D. They performed very poorly on a dog intelligence test
    E. All of the above are true

17. Which of the following is the most accurate statement regarding the influence of hormones on neural plasticity?
    A. Hormones do not influence neural plasticity
    B. Hormones influence plasticity only during fetal development
    C. Hormones influence plasticity through childhood
    D. Hormones influence plasticity through adolescence
    E. Hormones influence plasticity throughout an entire lifetime

18. Which of the following is the most accurate statement regarding the influence of hormones on neural development?
    A. Hormones do not influence neural development
    B. Hormones act alone to influence neural development
    C. Hormones act to reverse the effects of environmental influences on neural development
    D. Hormones may mediate the effects of environmental influences on neural development
    E. Hormones affect neural development only in males

19. Which of the following is *not* a similarity between spina bifida and anencephaly?
    A. Both result in death soon after the infant is born
    A. Both have a genetic basis
    A. Both result from malformation of the neural tube
    A. Both are disorders of fetal neural development
    A. Both are considered nontreatable conditions

20. Which of the following is a common feature of many types of mental retardation?
    A. Elongated axons
    A. Abnormal dendritic growth
    A. Shortened axons
    A. Small cell bodies
    A. Abnormally low number of neurons

## Short Answer Questions

*Answer each of the following questions with a brief but complete written answer based on information from your text.*

1. For more than a thousand years the theory of *preformation* dominated research in fetal development and consequently neural and behavioral development. Briefly define preformation, and explain why this theory was eventually abandoned.

2. Neurogenesis is completed within the first half of a full-term pregnancy. During the second half of the pregnancy neurons undergo the process of pruning and forming functional connections. During which time period is the fetus particularly vulnerable to injury or trauma? Briefly explain your answer.

3. Both trophic molecules and tropic molecules are discussed in this chapter. The terms are so similar they are easy to confuse. Briefly describe the function of each of these molecules that are essential for normal neural development.

4. The term *neural Darwinism* is used when describing brain cell development. Briefly describe what is meant by this term.

5. Growth spurts seen in neural development of young children correlate nicely with changes seen in capacity for cognitive function. Growth spurts, however, are not simply periods of cell proliferation. In fact, few if any new neural cells are added to the brain after the first 4.5 months of gestation. What then accounts for neural growth spurts in children?

6. In one of the more interesting methodological approaches to assessing brain plasticity, Donald Hebb allowed a group of young laboratory rats to grow up in the kitchen of his home. What was his rationale for this and what were his findings?

7. Roger Sperry proposed a theory that formed the basis for the *chemoaffinity hypothesis* used to explain neural connections during development. Briefly explain the chemoaffinity hypothesis.

8. Explain the concept of a critical period of neural development. Use the example of birds imprinting in your explanation.

9.  Briefly describe spina bifida as it relates to neural development. Compare this disorder to anencephaly.

10. Plasticity is often used to describe a response to brain injury.  However, plasticity is a part of normal development and normal brain function. Give an example of how plasticity can be thought of in terms of normal brain development and function.

# Matching Questions

*Complete each of the following matching questions based on information from your text.*

1.  Indicate from first (1) to last (5) the order of development of the following structures and neurons.

    ___ Progenitor cells
    ___ Neural groove
    ___ Neural stem cells
    ___ Neuroblasts and glioblasts
    ___ Neural tube

2. Match the following substances involved in development with their appropriate feature or description.

   A. Epidermal growth factor (EGF)      ____ Stimulates production of progenitor cells
   B. Basic fibroblast growth factor (bFGF)      ____ Guide growth cones to the cell
   C. Radial glial cells      ____ Guide cell migration from neural tube
   D. Netrins      ____ Stimulates production of neuroblasts
   E. Cell-adhesion molecules      ____ Provide adhesive surface for guiding cells

3. Match the following terms with the most appropriate definition or description.

   A. Neurogenesis      ____ Axonal projections
   B. Arborization      ____ Dendritic branching
   C. Filopodia      ____ Programmed cell death
   D. Apoptosis      ____ Cell proliferation
   E. Neural Darwinism      ____ Process of eliminating neurons

4. Number from earliest (1) to latest (4) Piaget's stages of behavioral development. Then draw an arrow from each stage to the appropriate characteristic(s) of that stage.

   A. Conservation, mathematical transformations      ____ Formal operational
   B. Pretend play, language development      ____ Sensorimotor
   C. Object permanence, stranger anxiety      ____ Concrete operational
   D. Abstract logic      ____ Preoperational

5. Match the following disorders of neural development with the appropriate feature or description.

   A. Amblyopia      ____ Lazy eye syndrome
   B. Impoverished environment      ____ Serious motor problems
   C. Spina bifida      ____ Abnormal intellect and social behaviors
   D. Anencephaly      ____ Mental retardation
   E. Down's syndrome      ____ Fatal soon after birth

# Diagrams

1. On the figure below, identify the approximate location of the following regions: fore-brain, midbrain, hindbrain, spinal cord, neural tube.

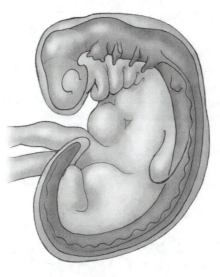

2. Draw below three cortical neurons. Assume Neuron A comes from a rat raised in a dark isolated cage, Neuron B comes from a rat raised with one other rat in a normal caged environment, and Neuron C comes from a rat raised with 10 siblings in a garbage dump.

   <u>Neuron A</u>                        <u>Neuron B</u>                        <u>Neuron C</u>

3. Below is a diagram roughly illustrating neural projections from each eye to the optic tectum in a frog. Draw a third eye representing an eye implanted during embryonic development, as was done by Martha Constantine-Patton. Show how projections from that third eye would develop.

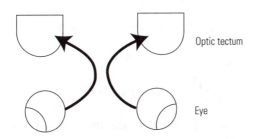

4. Below are two neurons, one representative of a normal individual, the other representative of a mentally retarded individual. Draw appropriate dendritic arbors on the two neurons.

5. Which of the groups of hippocampal neurons below is most characteristic of those seen in schizophrenic patients?

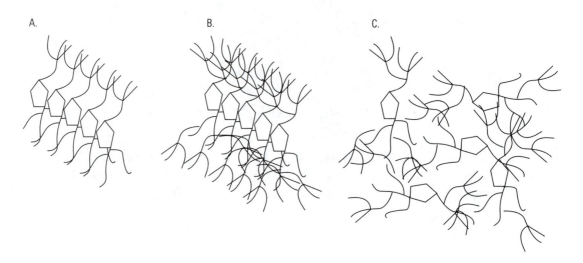

# CD-ROM Exercises

1. Visit module NC1 of your CD to review the structure of dendrites. Visualize the process of arborization during development of dendrites.

2. Visit module NC3 of your CD to review myelination of axons and how this process affects neural transmission. View this process in terms of development, imagining neural signals for movement in infants being transported along unmyelinated axons compared to those same signals being transported as the axon becomes myelinated.

# The Web

*Consider using the following Web sites for additional information on some of the topics from this chapter:*

1. Abnormal Fetal Anatomy: www.cpdx.com/cpdx/abfetana.htm

2. Rebuilding a Nervous System: www.medinfo.ufl.edu/other/profmed/slides/pm011399/

3.  Virtual Hospital:
    www.vh.org/Providers/Textbooks/FetalYoungCNS/FetalYoungCNS.html

4.  National Association for Down Syndrome: www.nads.org

5.  Spina Bifida and Hydrocephalus Association of Canada: www.sbhac.ca/

The easiest way to get to these sites is to link to them through the student Web site at www.worthpublishers.com/kolb. This site also has further study aids and practice quizzes.

# CROSSWORD PUZZLE

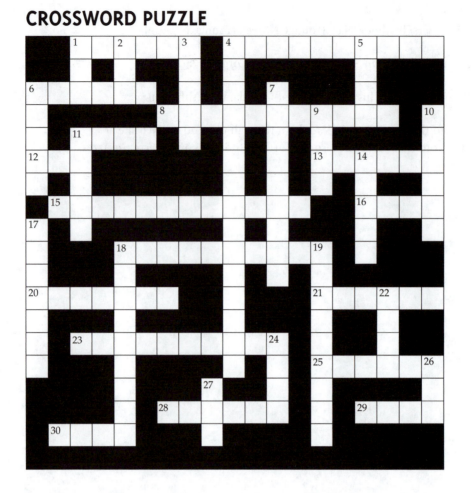

## Across

1. Time when brain development is most sensitive; critical _____
4. Reference to the brain's ability to change throughout life
6. Growth _____ in the brain coincide nicely with stages of cognitive development
8. When the front of the neural tube fails to close during development
11. Cell-adhesion molecules; abbr.
12. Prefix with natal
13. With 6 down, when back of neural tube fails to close during development
15. The birth of neurons, literally
16. Form taken after groove
18. An axon "foot" extended out during development
20. German measles, may cause birth defects
21. Guides axon growth; with 11 down
23. Lorenz showed this phenomenon with ducks
25. Signal molecules are also called _____ molecules
28. He showed monkeys raised in social isolation developed abnormally
29. Progenitor cells are derived from this type of cell
30. They guide most axon growth, then form the myelin sheath

## Down

1. 4 down; abbr.
2. Common animal for studying development
3. Chromosome abnormality causes this syndrome
4. Genetic abnormality of metabolism
5. Neuron or glial
6. See 13 across
7. Type of branching that is abnormal in mental retardation
9. He let lab rats live in his kitchen
10. Study childhood development through human observation
11. Second word in 21 across
14. Development before birth
17. A class of tropic molecules, meaning "to guide"
18. Like 18 across, except "feet"
19. What cells do during development, and birds do in the spring and fall
22. Glia do this around axons to form a sheath
24. Cells do this as they mature, grass and flowers do it as well
26. 11 across singular; abbr.
27. Divisions of 14 down development; _____ mesters

# 8 How Do We See the World?

## CHAPTER SUMMARY

As we begin discussion of sensory systems it should be noted that our version of the world, or reality as we know it, is a creation of our brain based on sensory information collected from the environment. For example, our experience of sound is simply the brain's interpretation of energy waves moving through the air. In response to the philosophical question "If a tree falls in the woods and there is nobody there to hear it, does it make a sound?" the answer is an unequivocal "no." The falling tree simply produces waves of energy. The experience of "sound" is a phenomenon of the auditory system.

Vision is considered the "primary" sensory system for humans because of our reliance on this system. As such, much of sensory-system research (and this book) has been dedicated to understanding vision. Simply stated, vision is a system designed to capture electromagnetic energy, transform that energy into a neural signal, and then interpret the neural signal. Human visual perception is dependent on undertaking this process within a relatively small range (from approximately 400 to 700 nanometers) of electromagnetic energy waves. Beyond the range of our visual perception are ultraviolet waves (too small for us to interpret) and infrared waves (too large for us to interpret). Our visual perception of the world does not include objects that generate or reflect these wavelengths. However, other animals do see and interpret visual information from these ranges, including honey bees, which perceive ultraviolet wavelengths.

The structure of the eye is designed to capture light energy. Light passes into the eye through a *cornea* (outer covering) and a pupil. The pupil constricts and dilates, based on movement of the *iris*, in response to high or low light conditions, respectively. The *lens* focuses light energy onto the *fovea*, an area of the *retina* at the back of the eye that contains the greatest density of receptor cells designed for acute vision. It is also worth noting that images are inverted in this process. In other words, our eyes see the world upside down, but our brain is capable of reversing this effect so we perceive our environment as it truly is (right-side up). Visual information leaves the eye via a bundle of neurons through the *optic disc*, a region of the retina that contains no receptors. The optic disc is also known as the *blind spot* because, with no receptor cells, there is no interpretation for the portion of our visual field that falls on this region.

Photoreceptors may be categorized as *rods* or *cones*. Rods, which make up the vast majority of photoreceptors, are long slender cells that are sensitive to dim light and are concentrated in areas outside of the fovea. Cones are cone-shaped cells that are densely packed into the fovea and are used for color vision and for acute visual processing. In general terms, humans have three subtypes of cones that are commonly called "blue," "green," and "red," based on their maximum response to wavelengths of light interpreted as these colors. Some women appear to possess two subtypes of the red cone, potentially increasing to some degree the spectrum of color they can interpret from the environment.

After photoreceptors have transformed light energy into a neural signal, that neural signal is then sent via bipolar cells to ganglion cells and then to the brain. Ganglion cells that receive input primarily from rods are called *magnocellular cells* (or M cells), while those that receive input primarily from cones are called *parvocellular cells* (or P cells). In the process of cell transmission from receptors, to bipolars, to ganglion, the signal may also be modified by *horizontal* and *amacrine cells* found in the retina.

Fiber tracts from both eyes merge at the optic chiasm on the ventral surface of the brain. Here half the fibers from each eye cross to the opposite hemisphere. Input from the left side of our visual field (as seen by both eyes) goes to the right hemisphere of the brain, while input from the right visual field goes to the left hemisphere. Beyond the chiasm two distinct pathways are formed. All of the projections from P ganglion cells and a few from M cells form the *geniculostriate system*, which sends information first to the lateral geniculate nucleus (LGN) of the thalamus and then on to the *primary and secondary visual cortex* of the occipital lobe. The remaining M cells form the *tectopulvinar system*, which sends information to the *pulvinar* region of the thalamus.

*Margaret Wong-Riley* and colleagues have identified regions within the visual cortex of the occipital lobe that appear to interpret color (called *blobs*) and regions that interpret motion (*interblobs*). This finding suggests that we have independent systems for different aspects of visual perception that are highly integrated, allowing us to distinguish numerous features of a single object simultaneously. Perception of objects occurs in our *visual field*, which is basically the portion of the environment that we can see. Individual rods and cones have a *receptive field*, the portion of the visual field from which they receive information. As rods and cones converge on a ganglion cell, they form the receptive field for that ganglion. As ganglion cells converge on a visual cortex cell, they similarly form a receptive field that represents the part of the retina to which they are connected. In this way, signals from ganglion cells to cortical regions can produce a *topographical representation* of the entire visual field, allowing us to interpret location of any object we see. It is also worth noting that a particularly large volume of brain tissue is devoted to the interpretation of information coming from the part of our visual field that strikes our fovea.

Intracellular recordings taken from cells in the visual pathways have increased our understanding of how the brain perceives shape. Researchers have found that cells may be either excited or inhibited by light, depending on its location in the receptive field. An *on-center* cell, for example, increases firing when light strikes the center of its receptive field, and decreases firing when light is moved to the periphery of this field. *Off-center cells* show the opposite response to light location. Such cells respond particularly well to edges of light, generating a comparison of light and dark known as *luminance contrast*. By emphasizing the edges of objects, the visual system is capable of perceiving shapes based on light contrast. Information about light contrast interpreted by ganglion cells is sent to *simple*, *complex*, and *hypercomplex cells* of the visual cortex. Simple cells respond vigorously to a stationary bar of light. Complex cells respond best to a moving bar of light. Hypercomplex cells also respond best to a moving bar of light, but have a strong inhibitory area at one end of the receptive field. All of these cells share the feature of responding to luminance contrast along the edge of a stimulus.

Some visual information is processed in area TE of the temporal lobe. This region appears to be responsible for interpreting particularly complex stimuli, including facial recognition and recognition of the same complex object from different orientations (a phenomenon known as *stimulus equivalence*). Cells in this region appear to integrate characteristics such as orientation, size, color, and texture.

Color vision is explained with two separate but integrated theories. The *trichromatic theory* states that color perception is achieved by weighing a ratio of activity from the three separate types of cones, each of which responds greatest to a different wavelength of light. Color perception is achieved by summing the input from each of these types of cells. According to this theory, lacking one of the three types of cones would result in impaired color vision, which is precisely what happens in some types of human color blindness. Furthermore, lacking two types of cones results in an inability to compare ratios and a complete loss of color perception. The *opponent-process theory* is based on the observation that there appear to be four natural colors: red, green, blue, and yellow. Furthermore, red and green, and blue and yellow, appear to oppose each other in the visual system, as demonstrated by the phenomenon of afterimages. This phenomenon is explained at the level of ganglion cells that exhibit on-center and off-center properties in response to opposing wavelengths.

Injury to the visual system beyond the eye results in a variety of blindness disorders. *Homonymous hemianopia* occurs when damage occurs along the visual pathway in one hemisphere and results in loss of perception of an entire visual field. *Scotomas* are blind spots in a visual field produced by small lesions of the occipital lobe. Such blind spots generally go unnoticed (much like our natural blind spot) because involuntary eye movements *(nystagmus)* allow us to process all of the visual field with intact receptors very quickly. *Visual-form agnosia* is an inability to recognize objects, although the ability to manipulate objects remains in tact. Another form of agnosia is an inability to see objects when they are in motion. Both types of agnosias result from damage to the ventral stream of visual information, affecting the ability to determine "what" the object is, but not the ability to interact with the object. *Optic ataxia*, on the other hand, is an ability to recognize stimuli but an inability to incorporate appropriate motor patterns for interacting with objects. This deficit results from damage to the dorsal stream of visual information. Visual-form agnosia and optic ataxia illustrate that our sensory systems may utilize numerous strategies, each with different neural pathways, to interpret information from our environment.

# KEY TERMS

*The following is a list of important terms introduced in Chapter 8. Give the definition of each term in the space provided.*

### The Eye

Cornea

Lens

Iris

Sclera

Retina

Pupil

Photoreceptors

Blind spot

Fovea

Optic disc

Papilloedema

### Photoreceptors

Rods

Cones

Wavelength

*Retinal Neurons*

Bipolar cells


Horizontal


Amacrine cells


Magnocellular


Parvocellular


*Visual Pathways*

Optic chiasm


Geniculostriate system


Striate cortex


Superior colliculus


Pulvinar


Tectopulvinar


Ventral stream


Dorsal stream

Lateral geniculate nuclei (LGN)

Cortical columns

### *The Occipital Cortex*

Primary visual cortex

Extrastriate cortex

Secondary visual cortex

Blobs

Interblobs

### *Coding Location in the Retina*

Visual field

Receptive field

Topographic representation

### *Seeing Shape*

Luminance contrast

Orientation detectors

Simple cells

Complex cells

Hypercomplex cells

Ocular dominance columns

*Seeing Color*

Trichromatic theory

Opponent-process theory

*Injury to the Visual Pathway to the Cortex*

Homonymous hemianopia

Scotomas

Nystagmus

Visual-form agnosia

Optic ataxia

# PRACTICE TEST

## Multiple-Choice Questions

*Answer each of the following multiple-choice questions with the best possible answer based on information from your text.*

1. Regarding individual sensory experience of color in men who are not color blind, which of the following is the most accurate statement?
   A. All have the same basic physiological mechanisms and experience the same colors
   B. All have the same basic physiological mechanisms but experience different colors
   C. Each has a different physiological mechanism and each experiences different colors
   D. Each has a different physiological mechanism but each experiences the same colors
   E. There are two basic physiological systems dividing men into two groups that experience slightly different colors

2. The fact that vision is the primary sensory experience for humans is evidenced by which of the following?
   A. That eyes are located at the top of the body
   B. That eyes are located very close to the brain
   C. That eyes are located in the front of the head
   D. That eyes are very large sensory organs
   E. That more brain tissue is associated with vision than with any other sensory system

3. What is the approximate range of wavelengths of electromagnetic energy that a human can perceive as light?
   A. 1–400 meters
   B. 1–400 nanometers
   C. 400–700 meters
   D. 400–700 nanometers
   E. The human visual system does not perceive electromagnetic energy

4. The blind spot occurs in a region at the back of the eye that . . .
   A. contains no rods
   B. contains no cones
   C. contains nerve fibers leaving the eye
   D. contains blood vessels entering the eye
   E. All of the above

5. The human visual system usually contains three different types of cones used in perception of color. How are these cone types distributed across the retina of the eye to maximize color vision?
   A. Short wavelength on the dorsal surface, long wavelength on the ventral surface
   B. Long wavelength on the dorsal surface, short wavelength on the ventral surface
   C. Short wavelength on the lateral region, long wavelength on the medial region
   D. Long wavelength on the lateral region, short wavelength on the medial region
   E. More or less randomly

6. The primary function of amacrine cells within the retina is to . . .
   A. convert light energy into neural activity
   B. process color vision
   C. perceive shape
   D. transmit information between ganglion and bipolar cells
   E. All of the above

7. Which of the following best describes the representation of visual information from our environment in the brain?
   A. Approximately half of the information from our visual field is represented in the brain
   B. All information from the left eye is represented in the right brain
   C. All information from the left eye is represented in the left brain
   D. Approximately half of the information from the left eye is represented in the left brain
   E. Visual information from our environment enters the left and right brain randomly

8. Which of the following does *not* receive visual input via a primary visual pathway?
   A. Frontal lobe
   B. Occipital lobe
   C. Parietal lobe
   D. Temporal lobe
   E. All of the above receive input via a primary visual pathway

9. Which of the following is *not* found in the occipital lobe of the human brain?
   A. Primary visual cortex
   B. Extrastriate visual cortex
   C. Lateral geniculate nucleus
   D. Blobs
   E. Interblobs

10. At what level of the visual system are shapes perceived?
    A. Rods
    B. Cones
    C. Ganglion cells
    D. Thalamus
    E. Cortex

11. Utilization of luminance contrast by the visual system would be best employed under what condition?
    A. Trying to view a moving object
    B. Trying to establish the location of the edge of an object
    C. Trying to distinguish a difference in the shade of two colors
    D. Trying to determine which of two objects was larger
    E. Trying to establish which of two objects was closer

12. Which of the following characteristics differentiates hypercomplex cells from complex cells?
    A. Hypercomplex cells are sensitive to color
    B. Hypercomplex cells are sensitive to a moving bar of light
    C. Hypercomplex cells are located in the visual cortex
    D. Hypercomplex cells have a strong inhibitory area at one end of their receptive field
    E. Hypercomplex cells are orientation detectors

13. Using the trichromatic theory of color vision, how would you explain the most common type of color blindness experienced by humans?
    A. It is caused by absence of retinal receptors
    B. It is caused by an absence of all cones
    C. It is caused by an absence of one type of cone
    D. It is caused by an absence of blobs
    E. The basis for this color blindness can only be explained using opponent-process theory

14. Which of the following cortical cells or regions are thought to process color vision?
    A. Simple cells
    B. Complex cells
    C. Hypercomplex cells
    D. Blobs
    E. Interblobs

15. Scotomas, or blind spots in the visual field, may be caused by which of the following?
    A. Loss of rods
    B. Loss of cones
    C. Lesions of the occipital lobe
    D. Lesions of the temporal lobe
    E. All of the above

16. Visual-form agnosia may be caused by extensive lesions of the lateral occipital region. Which of the following is the correct definition for the general term *agnosia*?
    A. Not knowing
    B. Not seeing
    C. No color
    D. No form
    E. No eyes

17. Which of the following would you expect to observe in a person who suffers from an optic ataxia?
    A. Inability to recognize objects
    B. Unimpaired ability to handle objects
    C. Damage to the retinal surface
    D. All of the above
    E. None of the above

18. A visual aura has been reported by some individuals to precede which of the following?
    A. Psychotic episodes
    B. Sleep
    C. Migraine headache
    D. Auditory hallucinations
    E. Child birth

19. Approximately 50 percent of the population is affected by myopia. Which of the following is the primary cause of this visual disorder?
    A. Lesions of the optic tract
    B. Lesions of the occipital lobe
    C. Lack of cones
    D. An eyeball that is too long
    E. The cause of myopia is unknown

20. Which of the following is considered to be among the most common permanent neurological symptoms of carbon-monoxide poisoning?
    A. Migraine headache
    B. Visual agnosia
    C. Optic ataxia
    D. Color blindness
    E. Blindness

# Short Answer Questions

*Answer each of the following questions with a brief but complete written answer based on information from your text.*

1. "If a tree falls in the woods and there is no one there to hear it, does it make a sound?" Answer this very old philosophical question using an explanation of neurophysiology of sensory experiences.

2. Beyond our range of color perception are waves of electromagnetic energy that, though invisible to our sensory system, may be perceived by other animals. What are the terms used for wavelengths too short and too long for us to perceive? Also give an example of an animal that can perceive these wavelengths.

3. Most individuals have three distinct types of cones. Briefly explain what feature of these cones differs and why this difference is important for our visual perception.

4. Jerison's principle of proper mass states that the amount of neural tissue responsible for a particular function is directly proportional to the complexity of that function. With this in mind, explain how neural tissue for visual processing is distributed in relation to cells in the retina.

5. You have learned that the corpus callosum is an important structure for transmitting information between the two hemispheres. There are, however, very few corpus callosum connections between the occipital lobes. Why are there so few connections, and what is the most likely explanation for the few connections that are made between these visual regions?

6.  Briefly describe the difference between simple cells, complex cells, and hypercomplex cells of the primary visual cortex.

7.  Briefly describe the physiological function of cones proposed in the trichromatic theory of color vision.

8.  People who are color blind generally do see some color, they simply have difficulty distinguishing between some colors. What is the physiological basis for color blindness?

9. Visual agnosia can result in an inability to recognize objects, but not to interact with them. Optic ataxia, on the other hand, does not impair ability to recognize objects, but can severely impair ability to reach for and manipulate objects. Briefly explain the importance of characterizing these two disorders in terms of understanding visual processing.

10. Briefly explain the disorders of myopia and hyperopia. Explain the characteristics of these disorders, and the underlying causes.

# Matching Questions

*Complete each of the following matching questions based on information from your text.*

1. Match the following structures of the eye with the appropriate feature or function.

   A. Cornea          ___ Contains photoreceptors
   B. Lens            ___ Directs image onto the fovea
   C. Iris            ___ Controls amount of light entering eye
   D. Retina          ___ Contains blood vessels entering eye
   E. Blind spot      ___ Outer covering of eye

2. Indicate whether the following is a characteristic of rods (R) or cones (C).

   ___ used primarily for night vision
   ___ used for color vision
   ___ highest density found in the fovea
   ___ used for acute vision
   ___ long and slender in shape
   ___ most of the receptors in the eye are this type

3. Indicate whether the following is a characteristic of magnocellular cells (M) or parvocellular cells (P).

   ___ receive input primarily from rods
   ___ found in the periphery of the retina
   ___ are sensitive to color
   ___ are the smaller of the two ganglion cells
   ___ are more sensitive to light

4. Match each of the following disorders of vision with the appropriate feature or symptom.

   A.  Scotomas                   ___ Deficit in reaching using visual guidance
   B.  Homonymous hemianopia      ___ Usually compensated for by nystagmus
   C.  Color blindness            ___ Caused by complete lesion of one optic tract
   D.  Visual-form agnosia        ___ More common in males than females
   E.  Optic ataxia               ___ Inability to recognize objects

5. Indicate from first (1) to last (5) the pathway of neural signals through the visual system.

   ___ Optic chiasm
   ___ Occipital lobe
   ___ Lateral geniculate nucleus
   ___ Fovea
   ___ Temporal lobe

# Diagrams

1. In the diagram of an eye below label the following structures: cornea, lens, iris, sclera, retina, fovea, blind spot, pupil, optic nerve.

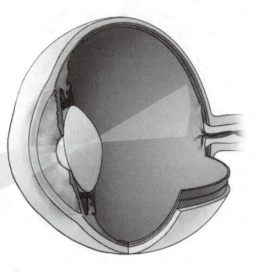

2. In the diagram of a retina below, label the following cells: cones, rods, ganglion cells, horizontal cells, amacrine cells, bipolar cells.

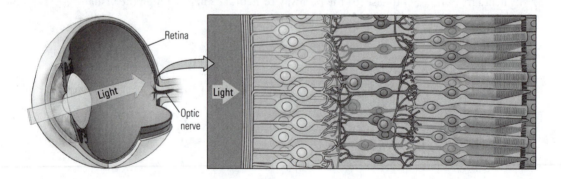

3. Show the pathway for visual information as it moves from the visual field to the brain. Use particular care when showing the pathway's movement through the optic chiasm. (Figure. 8-11)

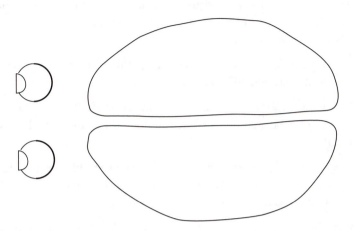

4. Based on the diagram below showing cone responses in the color spectrum, what color would you expect to see at wavelengths indicated by A and B?

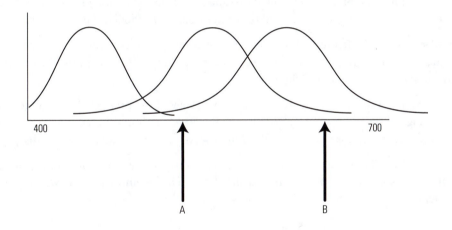

5. Regarding the columnar organization of cells in the primary visual cortex, the diagram below shows a vertical bar of light to which cells in one column respond. Indicate the approximate stimuli required to evoke responding from the adjacent columns.

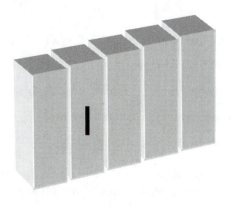

# CD-ROM Exercises

1. Visit module VS1 of your CD to better visualize the anatomy of the eye and the structure of the retina. Take full advantage of noting the three-dimensional detail of the eye in visualizing the retina and the blind spot.

2. Visit module VS3 of your CD to visualize the visual pathways to the LGN. Pay particular attention to how input is layered within this structure.

3. Visit module VS5 of your CD to visualize visual connections to the occipital cortex. Pay particular attention to how the cortex is layered in this region, and how this layering parallels that seen in the LGN.

4. Visit module VS2 of your CD to better understand the concept of visual fields. Note how these fields are perceived within the eye and how information about these fields moves through the optic tracts and nerves to the LGN and cortex.

5. Visit module VS6 of your CD to better conceptualize the location and anatomy of the LGN. Pay particular attention to inputs to this structure as noted in this module.

6. Visit module VS5 of your CD for further explanation of how shape is perceived within the cortex. Pay close attention to information about organization and analysis of cortical neurons.

7. Visit module VS1 for a more detailed explanation of how ganglion cells integrate information. Submodules on off-center and on-center cells are particularly useful in this regard.

8. Visit module VS5 of your CD for a nice explanation of how cortical cells contribute to visual perception. In particular note the differences in function of simple cells compared to complex cells in this module.

9. Visit module VS1 of your CD for an excellent review of the process of color vision. Take advantage of the interactive CD by moving the wavelength to different locations and noting the receptor ratios that are involved in processing these various wavelengths.

10. Visit module VS6 of your CD to view video recordings of patients with damage to visual pathways. Note the variety of agnosias and the patients' seeming lack of awareness of their deficits.

# The Web

*Consider using the following Web sites for additional information on some of the topics from this chapter:*

1. Blindness information site, Mississippi State University: www.blind.msstate.edu/irr/

2. Check to see if you're color blind: www.geocities.com/Heartland/8833/coloreye.html

3. Brain scans of disorders: www.psych.nwu.edu/psych/people/faculty/paller/B10/KAP5a/

4. Color vision information site: www.yorku.ca/eye/color.htm

5. Ataxia Web site: www.studyweb.com/links/4124.html

The easiest way to get to these sites is to link to them through the student Web site at www.worthpublishers.com/kolb. This site also has further study aids and practice quizzes.

# CROSSWORD PUZZLE

**Across**

2. Visual cortex cells that respond best to a moving bar of light
4. The "L" in LGN
8. Striate cortex is sometimes referred to as the ___ visual cortex
9. Prefix with chiasm, nerve, and tract
10. Opponent-process is an example of one of them for color vision
12. Visual system is to see, as auditory system is to ___
13. The "higher" stream for visual information
14. Like 2 across, but with a strong inhibitory area at one end of the field
17. The "G" in LGN
20. Where the visual receptors are located in your eyes
22. Secondary visual cortex is sometimes referred to as _____ cortex
27. Interpreted from wavelengths of light
29. On/off pairing for opponent process; abbr.
30. Dark staining cortex regions thought to process color
31. Blind _____ , where axons leave the eye
32. Light-gathering organs
33. Another term for 31 across, optic ____
34. Term for an inability to visually guide movements

**Down**

1. Holes in the eyes through which light passes
3. M cells are magnocellular, P cells are ____
5. With 10 across, this is the other
6. They are found among 7 down and horizontal cells
7. Cells that receive input from 26 down
9. Number of eyes on a cyclops
10. Sad eye excretion
11. Cortical cell that responds best to a stationary bar of light
15. Clear protective covering over eye
16. It directs light to the fovea
18. Smell with your nose, see with your ____
19. Areas near 30 across that don't stain dark
21. _____ colliculus receives visual input
23. 10 across; singular
24. May be blue, green, or brown . . . not a cone!
25. Means "stripe," used to describe visual cortex sometimes
26. Most abundant visual receptor
27. Outer layer of occipital and temporal lobes that processes vision
28. Visual part of the thalamus; abbr.
30. Without sight

# 9 How Do We Hear, Speak, and Make Music?

## CHAPTER SUMMARY

As with vision, the perception of sound requires a transformation of environmental energy into neural energy. However, unlike the visual system that utilizes electromagnetic energy, the auditory system utilizes pressure waves formed from vibrating air molecules. Sound waves have three properties that we are able to discern: *frequency*, *amplitude*, and *complexity*. Frequency of sound waves is measured in *hertz* (cycles per second). Variations in hertz are perceived as differences in pitch. As with the visual system, the human range of audition is not infinite, and other animals use energy beyond the range humans can perceive. Humans hear from about 20 Hz (low pitch) to about 20,000 Hz (high pitch). Very few sounds are of a pure or single frequency. Rather, sounds are made up of combinations of frequencies called complex tones. Complexity is perceived as quality of tone patterns. Random sounds that are not interpreted as single frequencies or complex tone patterns are perceived as noise. Amplitude of sound waves is measured in *decibels*, and perceived as volume or intensity of sound by humans. Our auditory system is also designed to localize the source of sound production.

Perception of different sounds is a function of interpreting different sequences of neural activity. This interpretation is largely a process through which meaning about our environment is gained. The process of auditory analysis is far more complex than simply detecting the presence of sound. For example, we can understand speech at a rate of nearly 30 segments per second, which is approximately 5 times the rate at which we can interpret random sounds. We are also capable of discerning three perceptual qualities from music, including *timbre*, which allows us to differentiate numerous sources of a musical tone of the same pitch and volume.

Perception of sound begins in the ear where the *pinna* acts to catch and deflect sound waves into the external ear canal. Next the energy waves vibrate the *eardrum*, which in turn vibrates a series of small bones commonly called the *hammer*, *anvil*, and *stirrup* in synchrony with the sound waves. These bones then flex a small membrane called the *round window* on the *cochlea* of the inner ear. Movement of the round window results in movement of the fluid inside the cochlea. In the center of the cochlea, the *basilar membrane* contains approximately 15,000 *hair cells* that are the receptors for transforming physical energy (waves of fluid inside the cochlea) into neural energy.

Over 100 years ago Hermann von Helmholtz proposed that movement of different regions of the basilar membrane (and thus stimulation of different groups of hair cells) was perceived as different frequencies or pitches. In the 1960s George von Bekesy supported this general idea by showing that high-frequency sounds produce greater displacement of hair cells near the base of the basilar membrane while low-frequency sounds produce the greatest displacement near the apex. As a region along the membrane is maximally displaced by waves of fluid, hair cells are displaced to varying degrees. Maximum displacement in one direction results in a maximum influx of calcium (depolarization) and a strong excitatory signal. Hair cell displacement in the opposite direction closes calcium channels, resulting in hyperpolarization. Integration of multiple signals along the membrane ultimately results in a signal perceived as a particular pitch. Loudness of all tones is determined by the intensity of the signal. That is, how much displacement of cells has occurred and how much neurotransmitter is released as a result of calcium influx.

As with the visual system, the auditory system also utilizes bipolar and ganglion cells to propagate the signal from the receptor cells. Projections from ganglion cells enter the medulla at the *cochlear nucleus*. The signal is then sent to the nearby *superior olive* and the *trapezoid body*, and from these structures to the *inferior colliculus* and then the *medial geniculate nucleus*. Ultimately, auditory information is processed in cortical regions. Among these cortical regions is the *planum temporale*, which is physically larger in the left hemisphere than in the right hemisphere of right-handed individuals. The planum temporale includes *Wernicke's area*, a region that is known to be important in comprehension of speech.

Understanding how hair cells are arranged along the basilar membrane to respond maximally to a particular pitch (known as *tonotopic representation*) has allowed researchers to develop cochlear implants. These tiny devices contain a microphone to receive sound and a series of wires that are differentially stimulated based on the pitch of the sound received. Electrically stimulating auditory neurons ultimately produces a signal similar to stimulation encountered in an intact inner ear, making these devises relatively effective in restoring some aspects of auditory perception to many deaf individuals.

The one known exception to tonotopic representation of the basilar membrane is that very low tones (<200 Hz) do not maximally displace a region along the membrane, but rather, move a length of the apex of the membrane in synchrony with the waves. For these low tones, the system appears to simply utilize frequency of movement of the membrane apex to determine differences in pitch.

Location of sounds is determined using two methods. First, the timing of sounds stimulating receptors is determined. Receptors in the ear nearest to the sound source fire slightly ahead of those on the other side of the head. Second, high-frequency sounds are noticeably dampened by the head when entering the ear opposite the source of the sound. In both cases, sounds coming from directly in front, behind, above, or below the head are particularly difficult to localize. When this happens, there is a natural tendency to turn or tilt the head slightly to help localize the sound source.

Regarding interpretation of complex sounds, there appear to be regions in the right and left temporal cortex for assessing music and language, respectively. Damage to these regions can result in specific disruption of ability to interpret these complex stimuli. Also interesting is the finding that damage to what is considered the "language region" in monkeys results in a disruption of ability to recognize vocalizations of that species.

In the 1960s Noam Chomsky proposed that language production and interpretation had features of an inherited trait, suggesting that humans were predisposed to learning language. Since that time additional evidence has supported this contention. For example, elegantly complex languages are learned with very little apparent effort by children of all cultures, and language structure develops with no formal training. Children also show a sensitive period for learning language, after which time learning language is very difficult.

Language appears to be centered in at least two regions within the human cortex (usually in the left hemisphere). *Broca's area*, located at the posterior region of the frontal lobe, is responsible for language production. Damage to this area results in a disruption of normal speech with few obvious effects on language comprehension and is known as *Broca's aphasia*. Wernicke's area, located in the posterior region of the temporal lobe, is responsible for language comprehension. Damage to this area results in disruption of language comprehension. Speech production is fluent, but usually nonsensical. This type of language disruption is known as *Wernicke's aphasia*. In the 1930s Wilder Penfield expanded the understanding of speech centers using electrical stimulation of the human brain in awake subjects. Penfield was able to induce vocalizations in subjects by stimulating regions he termed *supplementary speech areas*. He was also able to induce aphasias and speech arrest by stimulation of four different cortical regions (including Broca's and Wernicke's).

With technological advances, including the refinement of *positron emission tomography (PET)*, researchers are now able to view brain activity during speech in a noninvasive manner. Such studies, comparing brain activity during speech to brain activity in a control state, have shown separate regions for analysis of simple and complex auditory stimulation. While simple stimulation affects primarily A1 regions, complex stimuli (e.g., syllables) produce the greatest activity in secondary auditory regions. Although all auditory stimuli are processed in both hemispheres, the left hemisphere generally shows a greater response. PET scans have also shown that Broca's area becomes active not only when producing speech, but also during speech comprehension.

Analysis of music is generally thought of as a function of the right hemisphere. However, PET studies have shown that some aspects of music comprehension appear to require left hemisphere input. The distinction may be that the left hemisphere is involved with more sophisticated analysis of music (i.e., discerning sequences of pitches).

Auditory communication is prevalent in many species. Birds provide a particularly useful model for study, in part because birdsong parallels human language on several levels. There is a diversity and complexity of song across many species. The final song utilized by a bird is affected by experiences during development, particularly during a sensitive period early in life. Control of birdsong appears to be asymmetrical, controlled primarily by the left hemisphere. Finally, there are separate structures for producing and interpreting song in the bird brain.

Bats also utilize auditory signals, but primarily for the purpose of echolocation rather than for communication. Bats emit a range of high-frequency noises from which echoes can be analyzed to guide flight. Interestingly, the bats' auditory system has developed a "cochlear fovea," or a region that is particularly responsive to the range of sounds used for echolocation. The brain region dedicated to analysis of this range is particularly large, aiding in complex analysis of echoes for location, movement, and even surface texture.

## KEY TERMS

*The following is a list of important terms introduced in Chapter 9. Give the definition of each term in the space provided.*

### *Sound*

Frequency


Hertz


Perfect pitch


Amplitude


Decibels


Noise


Loudness


Quality


Timbre


Pitch


Prosody

### Anatomy of the Auditory System

Pinna

External ear canal

Hammer

Anvil

Stirrup

Eardrum

Oval window

Cochlea

Basilar membrane

Hair cells

Tectorial membrane

### Auditory Receptors

Hair cell

Bipolar cells

Ganglion cells

Cochlear nucleus

Superior olivary complex

Trapezoid body

Inferior colliculus

Medial geniculate nucleus

**Auditory Cortex**

Heschl's gyrus

Planum temporale

Wernicke's area

**Neuronal Activity**

Tonotopic representation

Tuning curve

Cochlear implants

*Anatomy of Language*

Creolization


Broca's area


Broca's aphasia


Wernicke's aphasia


Aphasia


Supplementary speech area


Positron emission tomography (PET)


Echolocation


# KEY NAMES

*The following is a list of important names introduced in Chapter 9. Explain the importance of each person in the space provided.*

Hermann von Helmholtz


George von Békésy


Noam Chomsky


Paul Broca

Karl Wernicke


Wilder Penfield


## PRACTICE TEST

## Multiple-Choice Questions

*Answer each of the following multiple-choice questions with the best possible answer based on information from your text.*


1. What was found in the cave of Neanderthals that changed the way anthropologists and neuroscientists viewed language and music development in this early culture?
   A. Paintings on the cave wall
   B. Pottery with elaborate inscriptions
   C. A primitive flute
   D. A primitive drum
   E. A primitive writing utensil

2. What form of energy do animals perceive as sound?
   A. Waves of air molecules
   B. Waves of electromagnetic energy
   C. Waves of volatile chemicals
   D. Waves of heat energy
   E. All of the above may be perceived as sound

3. The frequency range in which humans can distinguish sound is approximately
   _____ hertz.
   A. 2–200
   B. 20–200
   C. 20–2,000
   D. 20–20,000
   E. 200–20,000

4. A person with perfect pitch is able to do which of the following?
   A. Perceive a larger range of frequencies than normal individuals
   B. Perceive sounds at lower amplitudes than normal individuals
   C. Identify by sound any note on the musical scale
   D. Sing extraordinarily well
   E. Play musical instruments extraordinarily well

5. A sound characterized as 80 decibels and 80 hertz could be described as which of the following?
   A. A high-pitched soft sound
   B. A high-pitched loud sound
   C. A low-pitched soft sound
   D. A low-pitched loud sound
   E. You cannot describe pitch and volume based on these measures

6. Which of the following is *not* true of speech perception?
   A. It is affected by experience
   B. It is mediated in large part by the temporal lobe
   C. It can occur at rates faster than perception of nonspeech sounds
   D. It shares many features of music perception
   E. It is most fully developed in cultures that produce rapid speech

7. Which of the following structures is *not* located inside of the cochlea?
   A. Basilar membrane
   B. Tectoral membrane
   C. Inner hair cells
   D. Outer hair cells
   E. Cochlear nucleus

8. Which of the following best describes the way in which high-pitch sounds are transformed into neural signals along the basilar membrane?
   A. They maximally displace hair cells near the apex of the basilar membrane
   B. They maximally displace hair cells near the base of the basilar membrane
   C. They maximally displace hair cells near the middle of the basilar membrane
   D. They displace hair cells equally along the entire length of the basilar membrane
   E. They do not displace any hair cells along the basilar membrane

9. Displacement of hair cells along the basilar membrane initiates an excitatory neural signal by which of the following?
   A. Causing an influx of calcium
   B. Causing an influx of sodium
   C. Causing an influx of potassium
   D. Causing an efflux of chloride
   E. Causing an efflux of sodium

10. At what region do axons from the auditory ganglion cells enter the brain?
    A. Temporal lobe
    B. Frontal lobe
    C. Parietal lobe
    D. Occipital lobe
    E. Brain stem

11. While Wernicke's area is specialized for language comprehension in one hemisphere, the same area in the other hemisphere is specialized for which of the following functions?
    A. Language comprehension
    B. Music comprehension
    C. Speech production
    D. Producing written language
    E. Reading

12. Tonotopic representation predicts that . . .
    A. humans can identify any rhythmic sound
    B. perfect pitch is innate
    C. each hair cell is maximally responsive to a particular frequency
    D. audition is difficult to achieve without visual representation of the object
    E. All of the above

13. Which of the following mechanisms of neural signaling is used to indicate an increase in the volume of a sound?
    A. An increase in the size of action potentials
    B. A decrease in the size of action potentials
    C. An increase in the frequency of cell firing
    D. A decrease in the frequency of cell firing
    E. Perception of increased volume cannot be accounted for by neural firing

14. What technique could you employ to help localize sounds that are difficult to pinpoint because they arrive at the same time with the same intensity at both of your ears?
    A. Tilting your head
    B. Holding perfectly still
    C. Closing your eyes
    D. Nodding your head up and down
    E. All of the above are equally useful

15. Which of the following is *not* true of language and language development?
    A. Language acquisition is nearly effortless for children
    B. Technically advanced cultures tend to have the most complex languages
    C. If language is not learned in the first 6 years of life, skills will be severely compromised
    D. Children do not learn the structure of language from their parents
    E. All human populations have language

16. Which of the following is true of Broca's area?
    A. It is primarily responsible for language production
    B. It is located in the frontal lobe
    C. It is generally localized to the left hemisphere
    D. PET studies show that it becomes active during language/sound discrimination tasks
    E. All of the above are true

17. Which of the following is true of the electrical brain stimulation studies conducted by Wilder Penfield?
    A. He was able to evoke complex speech patterns from patients
    B. He was able to induce complex auditory signals perceived by patients
    C. He was able to induce both aphasia and complete arrest of speech
    D. He identified approximately 30 cortical areas for language comprehension and production
    E. All of the above are true

18. Which of the following is true of neural analysis of music?
    A. Most analysis of music occurs in the right hemisphere
    B. Most analysis of music occurs in the left hemisphere
    C. Analysis of music occurs approximately equally in the left and right hemispheres
    D. Broca's area is critically involved in analysis of music
    E. Wernicke's area is critically involved in analysis of music

19. Which of the following is *not* a feature of birdsong that parallels a feature of human language development?
    A. There exists a sensitive period for learning
    B. There are structures for both production and comprehension
    C. There are regional dialects for the same song/language
    D. The left hemisphere appears responsible for the majority of neural processing
    E. Neural structures responsible for song/language are sexually dimorphic and larger in males

20. Which of the following features can a bat detect using echolocation?
    A. Location of an object
    B. Velocity of a moving object
    C. Surface texture of an object
    D. Distance of an object
    E. All of the above

# Short Answer Questions

*Answer each of the following questions with a brief but complete written answer based on information from your text.*

1. Both complex tones and noise are made up of combinations of frequencies. Briefly describe the difference between complex tones and noise as they are perceived by humans.

2. Describe in general terms the theory of pitch perception as proposed orginally by Hermann von Helmholtz and later modified by George von Békésy.

3. Cochlear implants have a small microphone that picks up sounds in the environment. Briefly describe how these implants transfer that information to the brain?

4. Briefly describe the two ways in which our auditory system may localize the source of sound.

5.  Noam Chomsky shook up the world of language research with his theory that language may in fact be an inherited trait. Give at least two examples of characteristics of language that support Chomsky's contention.

6.  Early slave traders attempted creolization with a language they created and called "pidgin." Why did pidgin fail as a language, and what does its failure tell us (in general) about the development of language?

7.  Briefly describe deficits you might observe in an individual who has damage to Broca's area.

8. Briefly describe deficits you might observe in an individual who has damage to Wernicke's area.

9. List at least three factors that can affect the development of birdsong in young birds.

10. Describe the concept of a "cochlear fovea" as it relates to the use of echolocation in bats.

# Matching Questions

*Complete each of the following matching questions based on information from your text.*

1. Match the following terms with the appropriate feature or description.

   A. Frequency
   B. Amplitude
   C. Location
   D. Language
   E. Music

   ___ Measured in decibels
   ___ Primarily right hemisphere
   ___ Measured in hertz
   ___ Time difference between ears
   ___ Posterior temporal lobe

2. Indicate from first (1) to last (5) structures that are utilized along the auditory pathway.

   ___ Ganglion cells
   ___ Inferior colliculus
   ___ Bipolar cells
   ___ Cochlear nucleus
   ___ Superior olive

3. Match the following sound descriptions to their appropriate waveforms: A) Low pitch loud, B) Low pitch quiet, C) High pitch loud, D) High pitch quiet

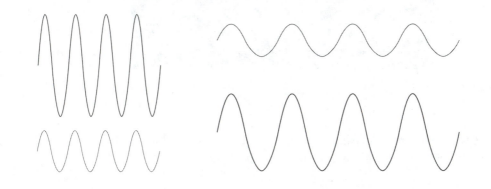

4. Match the following structures associated with hearing with the brain structures in which they are located.

   A. Wernicke's area
   B. Medial geniculate nucleus
   C. Inferior colliculus
   D. Olivary complex
   E. Round window

   ___ Cortex
   ___ Hindbrain
   ___ Cochlea
   ___ Thalamus
   ___ Midbrain

5.  Match the following location from which a sound originates with the appropriate perception strategy.

    A.  Looking straight ahead, quieter in left ear        ___ From straight right
    B.  Looking left, quieter in left ear                        ___ From ahead
    C.  Looking right, arriving first at the right ear     ___ From behind
    D.  Looking behind, arriving first in left ear          ___ From the left

# Diagrams

1.  On the diagram below, identify the following inner ear structures: A) Inner hair cells, B) Outer hair cells, C) Basilar membrane, D) Tectorial membrane

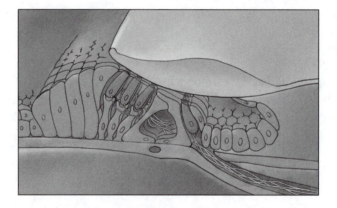

2.  Show where you expect maximum displacement of hair cells along the basilar membrane below for the following instruments: Tuba, Flute, Trumpet

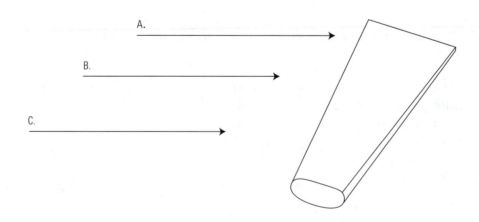

3.  Which of the following sound waves would be the most difficult for this person to localize?

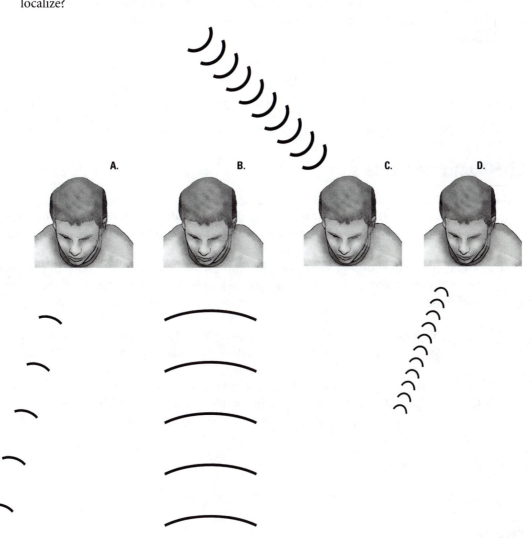

4.  On the figure below, identify the approximate location of the following regions:
    A) Motor area for face, B) Broca's area, C) Wernicke's area, D) Arcuate fasciculus

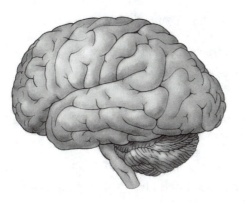

5.  Arrange the following sounds in their approximate location along the dB scale provided below: A) Your professor's voice when lecturing, B) A fire alarm in your building, C) A person whispering at the desk next to you, D) A low-flying helicopter passing over your building

|   |   |   |   |   |   |   |   |   |   |   |
|---|---|---|---|---|---|---|---|---|---|---|
| 0 | 20 | 40 | 60 | 80 | 100 | 120 | 140 | 160 | 180 | 200 |

## CD-ROM Exercises

1.  Visit module CNS1 of your CD for a detailed map of auditory pathways within the brain. Look in the functional neuroanatomy submodule for this audition sensory information.

2.  Visit module CNS1 of your CD to visualize cortical anatomy and the 4 lobes. In particular visualize the location of the planum temporale located in the dorsal region of the left temporal lobe.

3.  Visit module CNS1 of your CD to visualize Broca's and Wernicke's areas. The language submodule is particularly useful when reviewing information on these cortical structures.

4.  Visit module RM9 of your CD to better understand the method of PET scanning. Note the apparatus and imagine how this method could be utilized for analyzing neural functioning in brain regions during speech and language comprehension.

## The Web

*Consider using the following Web sites for additional information on some of the topics from this chapter:*

1.  National Association of the Deaf: nad.policy.net/

2.  American Academy of Audiology: www.audiology.org/

3.  Graphic tour of the inner ear: www.sissa.it/bp/Cochlea/

4.  National Aphasia Association: www.aphasia.org/

5.  Development of cochlear implants: www4.nas.edu/beyond/beyonddiscovery.nsf/web/cochlear

The easiest way to get to these sites is to link to them through the student Web site at www.worthpublishers.com/kolb. This site also has further study aids and practice quizzes.

# CROSSWORD PUZZLE

## Across

1. Measure of loudness
6. Waves used to detect pitch
7. Rhythm of speech
8. Cochlear _____ may help restore hearing
11. Tuning _____ are sometimes used to produce 6 across
12. Region essential for language comprehension
14. Organ designed to capture and direct sound waves
15. Snail-shaped inner ear compartment
17. Another term for volume
21. Basilar and tectoral, e.g.
24. Scan for watching brain activity; abbr.
25. Bats use it to guide flight
26. Type of cell found in the inner ear
27. Canaries use it instead of language
29. Another term for 17 across
31. One of the 3 small ear bones
33. Inferior _____ is essential for processing auditory input
34. Vision and hearing both use these cells right after bipolar cells
35. Without hearing

## Down

2. It doesn't sing, but it does caw
3. Region essential for language production
4. Common name for tympanic membrane is the ear _____
5. He produced 20 down, electrically stimulating brains of conscious patients
7. _____ pitch allows you to hear and then identify any note on the scale
9. That outer fleshy part of 14 across
10. 2 down is an example of one
13. The second word abbreviated in 24 across
16. One of the 3 small ear bones
18. The first word abbreviated in 24 across
19. _____ ear canal leads to 4 down
20. Term for disrupted speech or language comprehension
22. The researcher who identified and named a region essential for speech
23. Vision utilizes the lateral geniculate _____ , hearing utilizes the medial geniculate _____
28. Random strings of 30 down
30. What you perceive from compressed air waves
32. Loss of hearing may come with an increase in this

# 10 How Does the Brain Produce Movement?

## CHAPTER SUMMARY

Movement involves many brain regions arranged in a *hierarchical organization*. This means that movement controlled by higher brain regions are more complex and under greater voluntary control than those controlled by lower regions. John Hughlings-Jackson proposed three levels of hierarchical organization, mediated roughly by the forebrain (highest level), the brainstem, and the spinal cord (lowest level). He further suggested damage to the higher levels could produce dissolution (the opposite of evolution), whereby primary movements would become very simple under the control of lower levels. In the 1950s Karl Lashley suggested that the central nervous system was capable of producing *motor sequences* that could control streams of rapid complex behaviors (such as those required for playing a musical instrument or producing speech) without sensory feedback. It was later determined that the frontal lobe indeed has four primary motor regions, including one for planning complex behaviors (prefrontal cortex) and two for producing appropriate movement sequences (supplementary and premotor cortex). The fourth region, primary motor cortex, is involved in executing the details of movements as planned and arranged by the other three regions.

The brainstem is responsible for species-typical behavior. This is evidenced when regions of brainstem are stimulated with electrodes in awake animals. Depending on the specific region stimulated the animal may respond with aggressive behaviors, fear behaviors, feeding behavior and so on. Damage to the brainstem during fetal development or in early infancy can result in a condition known as *cerebral palsy* in which a person of normal intellect may exhibit profound movement disruption including, in some cases, an inability to speak.

The primary function of the spinal cord in the execution of movement is relaying information from the brain to the appropriate skeletal muscles. Damage to the spinal cord, depending on the location, can result in *paraplegia* or *quadraplegia*. In addition to this function, the spinal cord also contains some simple reflexive motor patterns, including a walking pattern for the legs, and a *scratch reflex*, which can be seen in many animals.

Electrical stimulation studies in animals and humans have led to a mapping of the motor cortex relative to the body regions it controls. The distribution is topographically similar to the body, with control of head adjacent to control of neck, adjacent to control of shoulder, and so on. However, the amount of tissue devoted to movement of body regions is highly disproportionate. Small body regions that are utilized for highly skilled and rapid movements (e.g., lips, hands) are controlled by the greatest amount of neural tissue. A *homunculus* is often used to show the disproportionate distribution of tissue as it relates to specific body regions. In general, damage to a portion of the motor cortex associated with a particular region of the body will result in motor deficits in that region.

The *corticospinal tracts* (or *pyramidal tracts* as they are sometimes called) are the main pathways from the motor cortex to the brainstem and spinal cord. The somas of motor neurons are located in the ventral horn of the spinal cord, with axons that stretch to (and innervate) muscles throughout the body. Motor neurons innervating the arms and legs are controlled by the motor cortex on the opposite side of the brain (contralateral). Motor neurons that innervate the trunk regions are controlled by the same side of the brain (ipsilateral).

*Synergies* are basic patterns of movements that are common to a species. These shared patterns suggest that some motor control is likely encoded in neural connections and therefore innate to some degree. Neural recordings show that motor cortex regions are utilized prior to and during movement patterns. In different species, depending on the type of movements that best ensure survival, motor cortex regions also vary in size. For example, monkeys have large regions associated with hands, whereas rats have large regions associated with face muscles. If cortical regions controlling movement are damaged, there may be some reorganization, with nearby regions assuming control of muscles normally controlled by the damaged area. Furthermore, this reorganization is enhanced if the body region affected by the neural damage is forced into use during the recovery period.

The *basal ganglia* are several nuclei of the forebrain that make connections with the overlying motor cortex and with the midbrain. The *caudate* comprises the largest portion of this region and receives primary input from the cortex and dopaminergic input from the substantia nigra. Damage to the basal ganglia results in a full spectrum of motor disruption. Loss of dopamine input from the substantia nigra results in a *hypokinetic* state, the most common example being the rigidity associated with Parkinson's disease. Direct damage to the caudate results in a *hyperkinetic* state, as seen in the uncontrollable limb movements associated with Huntington's disease or the uncontrollable tics and vocalizations associated with Tourette's syndrome. The "volume theory" of basal ganglia control over behavior suggests that these structures mediate the extent (volume) of movement planned and executed by cortical regions.

The *cerebellum* contains nearly half of the neurons in the central nervous system and is critical for acquiring and maintaining skilled motor patterns. It also controls many aspects of balance and eye movement. The primary function of the cerebellum is timing movements and maintaining movement accuracy. Repetition of movement patterns results in improved motor skills with enhanced cerebellar control of the motor pattern.

The motor system is intimately integrated with the *somatosensory system*. Sensory feedback from muscles sends signals to the primary *sensory neocortex* located directly adjacent to the motor cortex. The vestibular system, located within the middle ear, provides primary information to the cerebellum about balance. Sensory receptors are located in *hairy skin* and *glabrous* (hairless) *skin*. Glabrous skin includes the lips and hands and is more sensitive to stimuli than hairy skin that covers the majority of our bodies. Dendrites of sensory receptor cells may be stimulated by pressure for the sense of *hapsis* (touch), by chemicals for the sense of *nocioception* (pain), or by stretch for the sense of *proprioception* (body location). Cell bodies for sensory receptors are located in the *dorsal root ganglion* of the spinal cord, with long dendrites reaching the target sites of the body.

Proprioceptive and haptic information is conveyed rapidly along large myelinated axons, whereas nocioceptive information moves much slower along thin axons with less myelin. In rare cases individuals have become deafferented (losing all sensory information from the body). When this happens, movement is profoundly affected and many motor patterns (including limb movement) require visual guidance. In this regard, sensory input can be thought of as the "eyes" that guide movement.

The *dorsal spinothalamic tract* is made up of haptic-proprioceptive axons traveling from the brainstem through the *medial lemniscus* to the *ventrolateral thalamus*. From there, information is sent primarily to the somatosensory cortex, but also to the motor cortex. Nocioceptive axons comprise the *ventral spinothalamic tract* that follows a path similar to that of the dorsal tract.

The spinal cord contains some basic motor programs like the knee-jerk response evoked by a monosynaptic reflex. Within the spinal cord, the dorsal and ventral tracts may interact as well. The gate theory of pain suggests that signals from the ventral tract (pain) may be blunted by vigorous stimulation of the dorsal tract. This *pain gate* is noticed when we rub the area of a minor injury to reduce the sensation of pain. Opiates such as morphine are also thought to work by gating pain signals along this tract. In some instances, the sensation of pain in one region of the body is actually evoked by neural signals from a nearby region that does not contain pain receptors. This *referred pain* is obvious in heart attack victims who feel pain in shoulders or arms as a result of strong neural signals originating in the heart where there are no pain receptors.

The *vestibular system* provides sensory information about body position from the *semicircular canals* and the *otolith organs* of the middle ear. *Endolymph*, the fluid within the semicircular canals, flows and splashes in response to body movements. Endolymph movement in turn bends hair cells that send neural signals about the direction and speed of body movement.

Somatosensory information is processed in the somatosensory cortex located just posterior from the central sulcus and the motor cortex in a region called the post-central gyrus. As with the motor cortex, a homunculus can be used to represent the relative areas of cortex assigned to each body region sending somatosensory information. Like the motor homunculus, the sensory homunculus shows disproportionately large regions dedicated to hands, fingers, and lips. Damage to somatosensory cortex impairs movements of associated regions, often resulting in *apraxia*, and is likely due to lack of feedback necessary for guiding movement. Apraxia is a disorder in which the motor pattern needed for a movement is in tact, but the ability to sequentially execute the movement is lost. As with the motor cortex, somatosensory cortex appears capable of reorganization in response to damage or in response to loss of input from sensory neurons.

# KEY TERMS

*The following is a list of important terms introduced in Chapter 10. Give the definition of each term in the space provided.*

### Organization of Movement Control

Hierarchy

Dissolution

Motor sequences

Primary motor cortex

Cerebral palsy

Spinal cord

Paraplegia

Quadraplegia

Scratch reflex

*Organization of the Motor System*

Homunculus

Corticospinal

Pyramids

Pyramidal tracts

Lateral corticospinal tract

Ventral corticospinal tract

Ventral horn

Dorsal horn

Movement Synergies

*Basal Ganglia and Cerebellum*

Basal ganglia

Caudate putamen

Caudate

Autism

Tourette's disease

Hyperkinetic

Hypokinetic

Cerebellum

Flocullus

**Somatosensory system**

Hairy skin

Glabrous

Nocioception

Hapsis

Proprioception

Rapidly adapting receptors

Slowly adapting receptors

Dorsal root ganglion neurons

Deafferented

Dorsal spinothalamic tract

Dorsal column nuclei

Medial lemniscus

Ventrolateral thalamus

Somatosensory cortex

Ventral spinothalamic track

Monosynaptic reflex

Gate theory of pain

Pain gate

Referred pain

Vestibular system

Semicircular canals

Otolith organs

Utricle

Saccule

Endolymph

Otoconia

Apraxia

## KEY NAMES

*The following is a list of important names introduced in Chapter 10. Explain the importance of each person in the space provided.*

Karl Lashley

Wilder Penfield

## PRACTICE TEST

## Multiple-Choice Questions

*Answer each of the following multiple-choice questions with the best possible answer based on information from your text.*

1. Motor regions of the neocortex receive input from which of the following?
   A. Visual regions of the cortex
   B. The basal ganglia
   C. Sensory systems
   D. Cerebellum
   E. All of the above

2. According to the theory of hierarchical organization of the motor system, which of the below structures would likely be considered at the top of the hierarchy?
   A. Spinal cord
   B. Motor cortex
   C. Brainstem
   D. Basal ganglia
   E. Substantia nigra

3. When brain injury occurs, complex control of behaviors may be lost and replaced by simpler behaviors. Which of the following is the correct term for this phenomenon that is considered the opposite of evolution?
   A. Deevolution
   B. Disevolution
   C. Deafferentation
   D. Dissolution
   E. Disillusion

4. In what lobe of the cerebral cortex can you find the primary motor cortex, supplementary motor cortex and premotor cortex?
   A. Occipital
   B. Frontal
   C. Parietal
   D. Temporal
   E. These regions span all four of the lobes

5. Hess's brainstem stimulation studies suggested that this region was important in producing which of the following?
   A. Sleep
   B. Fear responses
   C. Aggressive responses
   D. Grooming behavior
   E. Species-typical behaviors

6. Christopher Reeve suffers from a condition known as . . .
   A. cerebral palsy
   B. paraplegia
   C. quadraplegia
   D. apraxia
   E. homunculitis

7. What structure controls the scratch reflex in a dog?
   A. Spinal cord
   B. Cerebellum
   C. Basal ganglia
   D. Motor cortex
   E. The structure controlling this reflex is currently unknown

8. Which of the following would be represented as disproportionately large in a human motor cortex homunculus?
   A. Hands
   B. Arms
   C. Legs
   D. Trunk
   E. None of the above would be disproportionately represented

9. Recent studies conducted to confirm Penfield's original studies mapping the human homunculus have revealed which of the following?
   A. That no such mapping pattern can be deduced using this technique
   B. That no areas of the body are disproportionately represented in the motor cortex
   C. That two distinct homunculi may be represented in the motor cortex
   D. That as many as ten homunculi may be represented in the motor cortex
   E. That the human homunculi representation is nearly identical to that of the rat

10. The corticospinal tracts from motor cortex to spinal cord give rise to large bumps on each side of the ventral surface of the brainstem. The shape of large bumps is the basis for which common term for the corticospinal tracts?
   A. Pentagonal tracts
   B. Spherical tracts
   C. Pyramidal tracts
   D. Mogul tracts
   E. Rough tracts

11. Basic patterns of many skilled movements are found to be common among members of a species. What is the term used to describe these potentially innate basic patterns of movement?
   A. Synergies
   B. Monosynaptic reflexes
   C. Instincts
   D. Spinal reflexes
   E. Fixed motor patterns

12. Bucy and colleagues reported behaviors of a man who had the corticospinal tract cut on one side. Immediately after surgery the patient was unable to move one side of his body. What was the condition of that patient seven months after the surgery?
   A. He was dead
   B. He was unable to move either side of his body
   C. In addition to loss of movement, he also eventually lost sensory input on one side
   D. He was able to stand alone and walk with assistance
   E. He made a near full recovery with only slight motor impairments

13. Which of the following is the most prominent structure within the basal ganglia?
   A. Cerebellum
   B. Caudate putamen
   C. Amygdala
   D. Substantia nigra
   E. Limbic cortex

14. Which of the following is *not* true of the somatosensory system?
   A. Unlike other sensory systems, it is distributed across the entire body
   B. It utilizes dendrites that respond to chemical stimulation
   C. It utilizes dendrites that respond to mechanical stimulation
   D. Animals adapt relatively easily to loss of all somatosensation
   E. It includes sensory systems utilized for both balance and movement

15. Which of the following describes the speed with which pain signals are sent compared to the speed with which touch and pressure signals are sent?
   A. Pain signals move approximately 10 times faster
   B. Pain signals move approximately twice as fast
   C. Pain signals move slightly faster
   D. Both types of signals utilize the same dendrites and move at the same speed
   E. Pain signals generally move slower

16. When a doctor evokes a knee-jerk response from a patient by tapping the petellar tendon, the doctor is in fact stimulating which of the following?
    A. Nocioceptive receptors
    B. Hapsis receptors
    C. Monosynaptic reflex
    D. Pain gate response
    E. Slowly adapting receptors

17. According to the pain gate theory, which of the following could be used to reduce a pain sensation?
    A. Acupuncture
    B. Electrical stimulation of some brain sites
    C. Rubbing the area near the painful sensation
    D. Giving an endogenous opiate such as morphine
    E. All of the above

18. Which of the following is *not* considered a function of the vestibular senses?
    A. Providing information about body position
    B. Providing information about body temperature
    C. Providing information about direction of body movement
    D. Providing information about speed of body movement
    E. None of the above are functions of the vestibular system

19. Damage to the primary and secondary somatosensory cortex has *not* been shown to result in which of the following?
    A. Reorganization of body regions represented by cortex surrounding the damage
    B. Paralysis of the affected body part
    C. Impaired motor function of the affected body part
    D. Loss of sensation from the region associated with the damaged region
    E. Apraxia

20. Abnormal development of which of the following structures has been associated with autism?
    A. Cerebellum
    B. Primary motor cortex
    C. Primary somatosensory cortex
    D. Basal ganglia
    E. Spinal cord

# Short Answer Questions

*Answer each of the following questions with a brief but complete written answer based on information from your text.*

1. Give a brief explanation of what is meant by hierarchical organization. Use control of movement as an example of this type of organization.

2. If you were to map the motor cortex of an elephant, what would you expect to find with regards to the distribution of neural tissue for body parts. Briefly explain your answer.

3. The basal ganglia has been implicated in both hyperkinetic and hypokinetic disorders. Briefly describe what this tells us about the function of the basal ganglia.

4. Briefly describe the types of symptoms you would expect to observe in an individual who suffers from cerebellar damage.

5. Briefly describe the difference between hairy skin and glabrous skin both in terms of location and in terms of physical features and function.

6. Deafferentation resulting in loss of somatosensation would result in a fairly rapid demise and death of any animal but a human. What happens to humans who experience such deafferentation and how do they compensate for the loss of sensory input?

7. Briefly explain the concept of referred pain. Use for an example the pain felt by a heart attack victim.

8. Briefly explain why the homunculus for the motor cortex looks so similar to the homunculus for the somatosensory cortex.

9. Briefly describe what is meant by the term *apraxia*. Give an example of an apraxia and a possible cause of this dysfunction.

10. Briefly characterize Tourette's disease. Include in your description behavioral features of the disorder and the underlying cause.

# Matching Questions

*Complete each of the following matching questions based on information from your text.*

1. Match the following motor structures with their appropriate feature or description.

   A. Caudate putamen          ___ "Volume control" for movement
   B. Prefrontal cortex        ___ Planning movement
   C. Primary motor cortex     ___ Monosynaptic reflexes
   D. Spinal cord              ___ Executing movement
   E. Cerebellum               ___ Regulating posture

2. Match the following motor disorder with the associated damaged or dysfunctional region.

   A. Cerebral palsy           ___ Somatosensory cortex
   B. Ataxia                   ___ Brainstem
   C. Tourette's               ___ Spinal cord
   D. Autism                   ___ Cerebellum
   E. Paraplegia               ___ Basal ganglia

3. Match the following somatosensory systems with the appropriate feature or description.

                               ___ Utilizes free nerve endings that release chemicals
   A. Hapsis                   ___ Encapsulated nerve endings monitoring tendons
   B. Nocioception             ___ Utilizes small unmyelinated fiber
   C. Proprioception           ___ Responds best to pressure
                               ___ Processes information on body position

4. Number from first (1) to last (5) the structures utilized in the dorsal spinothalamic tract to transmit information about body position.

___ Dorsal column nuclei
___ Ventrolateral thalamus
___ Muscle stretch receptors
___ Medial lemniscus
___ Somatosensory cortex

5. Match the following components of the vestibular system with their appropriate description.

A. Otoliths
B. Semicircular canals
C. Endolymph
D. Otoconia
E. Hair cells

___ May send excitatory or inhibitory signals
___ Senses changes in 3 planes of different orientations
___ Small crystals of calcium carbonate
___ Fluid filling the semicircular canals
___ Consists of the ultricle and saccule

# Diagrams

1. In the diagram below identify the approximate location of the following regions associated with movement and somatosensation: Primary motor cortex, Primary somatosensory cortex, Cerebellum, Caudate putamen, Substantia nigra

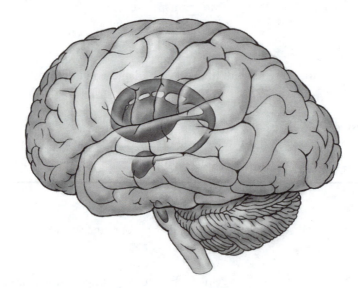

2.  Draw a homunculus that approximately represents the relative volume of neural tissue associated with movement and somatosensation in a human.

3.  Indicate on the diagram below where stroke damage would occur resulting in:
    A) Paralysis of the hand, B) Loss of sensory input from the face.

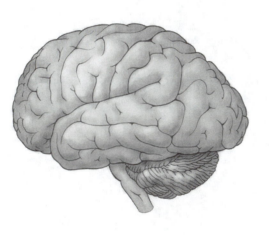

4.  The diagram below is useful for explaining the gate theory of pain. Complete this diagram by indicating where there are question marks (I?) whether the input is excitatory or inhibitory. Also indicate at questions marks (A?) whether axons are large or small and whether they are myelinated or unmyelinated.

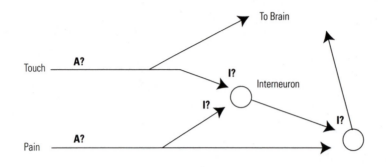

5.  Identify the following regions on the diagram of the vestibular system structures shown below: A) Utricle, B) Saccule, C) Neural fibers, D) Semicircular canals.

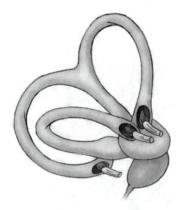

# CD-ROM Exercises

1.  Visit module CM1 of your CD for a simplified explanation of the organization of movement and motor systems. Notice the intricate roles of brain, spinal cord, and muscles in this organization.

2.  Visit module CM5 of your CD for a more detailed analysis of the human homunculus. Notice the exaggerated body parts associated with fine motor control in this representation of the human motor cortex.

3.  Visit module CM4 of your CD for a concise representation of the corticospinal tracts. This visual representation should help simplify this rather detailed area of research.

4. Visit module CM6 of your CD for more detail on the control of movement mediated by the central nervous system. Note not only cortical influences, but also influences of sub-cortical structures including those of the basal ganglia.

5. Visit module CM6 of your CD for more information on the contributions of the cerebellum and basal ganglia to control of movement. Take time to browse through the cerebellum section and the basal ganglia section. Note especially what happens when there is damage to these regions.

6. Visit module CNS1 of your CD for a nice explanation of somatosensory systems. Some of the CNS module information will be familiar from earlier chapters, but it's unlikely you would have understood the details of the somatosensory information the way you do now after reading this chapter.

7. Visit module CM3 for a detailed analysis of the spinal cord. Pay particular attention to the presentation of information regarding spinal reflexes in this module.

# The Web

*Consider using the following Web sites for additional information on some of the topics from this chapter:*

1. Circle of Friends, Spinal Cord Injury Site: www.circleoffriends.org/

2. Spinal Cord Injury Resources: www.kansas.net/~cbaslock/sci.html

3. Tourette's Syndrome Association: tsa.mgh.harvard.edu/

4. National Ataxia Foundation: www.ataxia.org/

5. United Cerebral Palsy: www.ucpa.org/

The easiest way to get to these sites is to link to them through the student Web site at www.worthpublishers.com/kolb. This site also has further study aids and practice quizzes.

# CROSSWORD PUZZLE

**Across**

2. Fluid that fills 21 across
6. Only card that beats a king
8. Somatosensation information enters the spinal cord via the dorsal _____
9. Simple term for nocioception
10. Syndrome that includes tics and vocalizations
12. This and a saccule make up 15 across
13. In the middle, as in _____ lemniscus
15. One of the organs that makes up the vestibular system
16. _____ cortex in the frontal lobe mediates movement
17. To the bottom on the side, as in _____ thalamus
20. The opposite of evolution, seen after brain damage
21. 5 down; singular
22. Lumpy cells on the ventral surface of the brainstem involved in movement
25. Type of skin on your arm
26. Type of reflex seen in knee-jerk response
28. Ventral _____ of the spinal cord contain motor neurons and interneurons
31. Hypo_____ means less movement
32. Fancy word for a basic movement pattern
33. Wilder to his friends, did brain stimulation studies

**Down**

1. Vestibular, motor, or somatosensory
3. _____ root ganglion, where sensory information enters the spinal cord
4. Like 31 across, but meaning more movement
5. They're semicircular in the vestibular system
7. Meaning from the cortex to the spinal cord
11. Small crystals of calcium carbonate in the vestibular system
14. A collection of cells, as in basal _____
17. Sensory system that helps you keep your balance
18. Motor disorder, cerebral _____
19. Fancy term for sense of pressure or touch
23. Karl to friends, he suggested the concept of motor sequences
24. Some reflexes are found in the spinal _____
25. 28 across, singular; or a trumpet
27. One less than ten
29. May be hairy or glabrous
30. To discover; let's hope we do this for effective medical treatments

# 11

# What Causes Behavior?

## CHAPTER SUMMARY

The focus of this chapter is analysis of *motivated* (purposeful) *behavior*. In attempting to identify a cause of behaviors, early researchers found that both animals and humans appeared to engage in some behaviors with no obvious function but simply to stimulate the brain. Later researchers developed a "drive" theory concluding that behaviors were driven by some form of internal energy, and that the vigor and duration of engaging in a behavior reflected the amount of energy stored for that specific action. Most recently researchers have begun to establish a neurochemical basis for many aspects of behavior. Sexual behavior, for example, correlates strongly with levels of circulating hormones. Electrical brain stimulation of areas releasing, or affected by, these mediating neurochemicals can evoke specific behaviors. A neural basis for behaviors may be an important evolutionary adaptation to enhance species-specific behaviors that increase chances for survival. These neural circuits are closely linked to a neural "reward" system, increasing the likelihood that behavior will be undertaken. The idea that a rewarding neural circuitry underlies the generation of behaviors suggests that modifying some behaviors may be difficult. The term *innate releasing mechanism (IRM)* is used to describe neural control of adaptive behaviors that appear without the influence of learning.

Not all behaviors are controlled by IRMs, nor are IRM behaviors incapable of modification. *B. F. Skinner* was among the first researchers to show *reinforcers* and punishment could modify many adaptive behaviors. However, Skinner and others found that some behaviors could be modified only with specific associated stimuli. For example, *taste aversion learning* quickly and effectively modifies eating behavior with an aversive gastrointestinal stimulus. Electrical shocks and loud noises are far less effective at modifying eating behaviors, presumably because these aversive stimuli do not effectively disrupt the eating reward system driving behavior.

The term *motivation* is commonly used to describe purposeful behavior in animals. Motivation does not, however, describe something tangible found in the brain. Rather, it is a term for inferences made about why we engage in behaviors. For example, *regulatory behaviors* like feeding and drinking are motivated by *homeostatic mechanisms*. Homeostatic mechanisms are activated when a physiological state is altered from a certain set point. A glucostat mechanism indicates when blood glucose is low, motivating eating behavior, or when glucose is high, causing feeding to cease. Regulatory behaviors are mediated by the hypothalamus. *Nonregulatory behaviors* include all other behavior and are mediated by a variety of forebrain structures, most prominently the frontal lobe.

The hypothalamus influences behavior through both endocrine responses and autonomic nervous system activation. The *medial forebrain bundle (MFB)* is a dopamine-containing fiber tract that makes up the major hypothalamic pathway used in motivated behavior. The hypothalamus also mediates pituitary gland responses via the *infundibulum*, a tissue stalk of fibers connecting the two structures. Endocrine responses are in turn initiated by release of pituitary hormones. The pituitary gland is actually only half endocrine gland (the anterior half). The posterior pituitary is composed of neural tissue directly influenced by hypothalamic connections. The anterior and posterior pituitary regions release different combinations of hormones affecting many different areas of the body and subsequently affecting many different behaviors. Hypothalamic function is mediated by three mechanisms. First, a *feedback mechanism* directly monitors the blood levels of hormones, decreasing and increasing hypothalamic function as hormone levels rise and fall around the homeostatic set point. Second, the hypothalamus receives direct input from the limbic system and the frontal lobe. Third, hypothalamic neurons undergo structural and biochemical changes in response to experience. Direct electrical stimulation of the hypothalamus produces a variety of behaviors depending on the location of the electrode. Three features of these behaviors provide insight into the types of behaviors controlled by the hypothalamus. First, stimulated behaviors are smooth, well-integrated, goal-directed behaviors. Second, these behaviors are related to survival (e.g., eating, drinking). Third, animals appear to find stimulation of these behaviors pleasant.

The limbic system includes several structures that comprise a primitive cortex sometimes called a limbic lobe. James Papez was among the first to speculate a contribution of the limbic lobe to emotions, noting dramatic emotional changes in people who suffered from rabies damage to neural structures in this lobe. The *hippocampus, amygdala*, and prefrontal cortex are considered limbic structures. Each of these structures has extensive neural connections to the hypothalamus. Stimulation of the amygdala evokes a fear response in animals, while lesions produce changes in feeding and hypersexuality. Abnormalities in dopamine projections from the prefrontal cortex have been implicated in the emotional blunting of schizophrenia. Damage to the frontal lobe may result in difficulty focusing on tasks, making individuals easily distractible. In this regard, the frontal lobe may be considered a structure mediating selection of behaviors.

Feeding is a regulatory behavior influenced by the digestive system, the hypothalamus, and by cognitive factors. The digestive system provides glucose for brain function. When glucose levels are reduced the brain initiates feeding behavior. When food is introduced into the lower digestive tract (beginning of the intestine) *cholecystkinin (CCK)* is released. CCK signals the hypothalamus, which in turn evokes a sensation of diminished hunger. Lesions of the lateral hypothalamus or fibers passing through this region produces *aphagia*, while lesions of the ventromedial hypothalamus produce *hyperaphagia*. These findings suggest an essential role for the hypothalamus in mediating initiation and cessation of feeding behavior. In particular, neurons in the hypothalamus that sense glucose levels (glucostatic neurons) and lipids (lipostatic neurons) may monitor blood concentrations and regulate behaviors to maintain homostatic levels of these substances. Cognitive factors such as thinking about food or associations made to food odors may also influence eating behavior. The inferior frontal cortex receives direct input from olfactory bulbs, suggesting a role for this brain region in cognitive influences in feeding.

Drinking is a regulatory behavior that may be evoked by osmotic or hypovolemic thirst. *Osmotic thirst* is stimulated when a high concentration of salt in the system draws fluids from the cell into extracellular space. Cells surrounding the third ventricle act as detectors for these osmotic changes. *Hypovolemic thirst* is stimulated when fluid volume (generally blood volume) decreases. When this happens the kidneys detect the blood pressure decrease and send a hormonal signal to the hypothalamus to increase fluid consumption. Hypovolemic thirst differs from osmotic thirst in that consumption of both water and solutes (e.g., salt) is preferred over consumption of water only.

Nonregulatory, like regulatory, motivated behaviors are strongly influenced by hormones and hypothalamic function. Sexual behavior provides a good model for assessing these influences. Gonadal hormones (i.e., androgens) may have *organizing effects*, such as influencing the anatomical makeup of structures during fetal development. Interestingly, testosterone has its masculinizing effects on neural structures only after it is converted to estradiol by intracellular aromatase. Females are protected from the masculinizing effects of their own estradiol by a liver enzyme called *alpha fetoprotein*. Neural *sexual dimorphism* is most evident in the hypothalamic region of the *medial preoptic area*, which is approximately five times larger in males than in females. Gonadal hormones also have *activational effects*, evoking behaviors such as sexual response in female rats. The *lordosis* response shown by sexually receptive female rats, for example, is mediated by the ventromedial hypothalamus but only exhibited when estrogen and progesterone levels are adequate to stimulate this region. A clear link between neuroanatomy and sexual orientation has not been established, but some evidence suggests that structural differences exist between some heterosexual and homosexual men.

Emotions are expressed through both physiological changes and motor behaviors. Like motivated behaviors, the hypothalamus is important for mediating emotional responses. In addition the amygdala and cortical regions (primarily in the frontal lobe) are also involved. Determining how emotional responses are stimulated has long been debated. The *James-Lange theory*, or *somatic marker hypothesis* (a more recent variation), suggests emotions are not set responses, but rather interpretive responses to both autonomic changes and the stimuli evoking the physical response. This theory is bolstered in part by research showing that individuals who suffer from high spinal-cord injury (and thus lose much sensation of autonomic changes) report feeling weaker emotional responses to environmental stimuli than individuals with low spinal-cord injury. The amygdala appears to play an especially important role in emotional responses to fear-provoking stimuli. When this structure is bilaterally damaged, animals exhibit a marked decrease in aggression and fear responses known as *Kluver-Bucy syndrome*.

Emphasizing the role of the frontal cortex in emotional responses, researchers cite findings from patients undergoing frontal *lobotomy*, a form of *psychosurgery*. Such surgery results in patients who exhibit decreased emotion in facial expression and decreased prosody (emotional inflection in speech). These patients also have difficulty interpreting emotions expressed by others. It is believed the cortical tissue from the frontal lobe is responsible for providing a cognitive interpretation of autonomic responses.

Knowing that brain structures underlie emotions, it is not surprising that imbalances in brain chemistry and function can result in emotional disorders. *Depression* affects nearly 10 percent of the population. There is a genetic component to depression that likely results in dysfunction of neurotransmitter transmission in structures associated with emotions. The most effective antidepressant drugs increase noradrenaline and serotonin transmission, implicating these two neurotransmitters as primarily responsible for this disorder. *Anxiety disorders* are the most prevalent of all psychiatric disorders, affecting somewhere between 15 and 30 percent of the population. The most effective *anxiolytic* drugs are the *benzodiazepines* that act as agonists on GABA receptor sites. Anxiety is a useful emotion for survival, reducing contact with feared or dangerous stimuli. Anxiety disorders are thought to be an overactivity of this normally useful emotion.

The opposite sensation from anxiety is reward. Reward is a useful emotion for inducing and maintaining contact with useful stimuli (such as food and mates). In the 1950s it was found that animals would engage in *intracranial self-stimulation* of certain brain regions. Among the most effective areas for *brain stimulation reward* is the *medial forebrain bundle*, also known as the *mesolimbic dopamine pathway*, terminating in the *nucleus accumbens*. One common feature of all the rewarding pathways for self-stimulation is the existence of dopamine-containing fibers. It is also interesting to note that recreational drugs that are addictive and/or frequently abused stimulate pathways containing dopamine fibers. It short, it appears these reward pathways evoke strong positive emotions that may be equally associated with either useful stimuli (food, mates) or addictive drugs.

## KEY TERMS

*The following is a list of important terms introduced in Chapter 11. Give the definition of each term in the space provided.*

### Evolutionary and Environmental Influences

Innate releasing mechanism (IRM)

Reinforcers

Taste aversion learning

### Types of Motivated Behavior

Motivation

Regulatory behaviors

Homeostatic mechanism

Nonregulatory behaviors

Hypothalamus

Infundibulum

Medial forebrain bundle (MFB)

Feedback mechanism

*The Limbic System*

Papez circuit

Amygdala

Frontal lobe

Prefrontal cortex

*Control of Regulatory Behaviors*

Feeding

Cholecystokinin (CCK)

Aphagia

Hyperphagia

Drinking

Osmotic thirst

Hypovolemic thirst

**Control of Nonregulatory Behavior**

Sexual behavior

Organizing action

Gonadal hormones

Activating effect

Sexual dimorphism

Alpha fetoprotein

Preoptic area

Lordosis

Medial preoptic area (POA)

Agenesis

Androgen insensitivity syndrome

Congenital adrenal hyperplasia

Androgenital syndrome

### Emotion

James-Lange theory

Somatic marker hypothesis

Kluver-Bucy syndrome

Psychosurgery

Frontal leukotomy

Depression

Anxiety disorders

Anxiolytic drugs

Benzodiazepines

Generalized anxiety disorder

Phobias

Panic disorder


### Reward

Intracranial self-stimulation


Brain stimulation reward


Mesolimbic dopamine pathway


Nucleus accumbens


Incentive


Reward


## KEY NAMES

*The following is a list of important names introduced in Chapter 11. Explain the importance of each person in the space provided.*

B. F. Skinner


John Garcia


James Papez

# PRACTICE TEST

# Multiple-Choice Questions

*Answer each of the following multiple-choice questions with the best possible answer based on information from your text.*

1. What happened in the 1950s when Hebb and colleagues allowed subjects to exist in a stimulation-free environment where they did not have to engage in any motivated behaviors?
   A. Subjects generally became very bored in less than 24 hours before asking to discontinue
   B. Subjects slept for an average of 3 days before asking to discontinue
   C. Subjects suffered severe depression for an average of 3 days before asking to discontinue
   D. Subjects suffered hallucination during an average of 3 days before asking to discontinue
   E. Subjects enjoyed themselves for an average of 7 days before the study was discontinued

2. The early "drive theory" of behavior suggested that animals engage in sex when energy stores for this behavior are high, and continued to do so until energy stores are decreased. Which of the following research discoveries rendered the drive theory obsolete?
   A. The finding that brain structure differences are associated with homosexual behavior
   B. The establishment of a relationship between hormone levels and sexual behavior
   C. The finding that lesions of the hypothalamus could disrupt sexual behavior
   D. The discovery of Kluver-Bucy syndrome following lesions of the amygdala
   E. None of the above; drive theory remains a prominent position in sexual behavior research

3. B. F. Skinner was among the earliest and most adamant proponents of the theory that motivated behaviors, including avoidance behaviors such as phobias, could be explained by which of the following?
   A. Genetics
   B. Reinforcement history
   C. Neurotransmitter imbalance
   D. Hormones
   E. Evolution

4. Which of the following would *not* be considered a behavior mediated by a homeostatic mechanism?
   A. Eating
   B. Drinking pure water
   C. Drinking water containing salts
   D. Putting on a sweater
   E. Engaging in sexual behavior

5. Which of the following is *not* implicated as a major contributor in control of motivated behaviors?
   A. Hypothalamus
   B. Pituitary gland
   C. Frontal lobe
   D. Occipital lobe
   E. The limbic system

6. Which of the following neurotransmitters is found in high concentrations in the medial forebrain bundle and considered a major chemical influencing motivated behaviors?
   A. Dopamine
   B. Acetylcholine
   C. Epinephrine
   D. Serotonin
   E. Endorphins

7. The frontal lobe is thought to play an important role in selecting behaviors to be exhibited. Damage to the frontal lobe often results in which of the following?
   A. Inability to show any emotion
   B. Inappropriate expression of emotions
   C. Chronic depression
   D. Chronic anxiety
   E. None of the above

8. Which of the following organs contributes most to maintaining homeostatic balance of blood glucose?
   A. Kidneys
   B. Liver
   C. Stomach
   D. Small intestine
   E. Large intestine

9. When would you expect blood concentrations of cholecystokinin (CCK) to rise?
   A. One hour prior to a meal
   B. At the onset of a meal
   C. Near the end of a meal
   D. One hour after a meal
   E. Approximately the middle of the night

10. Which of the following would be most likely to induce osmotic thirst?
    A. Loss of blood due to a severe knife wound
    B. Loss of blood due to a minor bloody nose
    C. Ingestion of distilled water
    D. Ingestion of a slice of watermelon
    E. Ingestion of a bag of potato chips

11. Which of the following is responsible for masculinizing sexually dimorphic neurons in the male brain during fetal development?
    A. Testosterone
    B. Estrogen
    C. Testosterone that is converted into estrogen
    D. Estrogen that is converted into testosterone
    E. None of the above, hormones are not responsible for this process

12. In what structure are the sexually dimorphic organizational effects of gonadal hormones most apparent?
    A. Hippocampus
    B. Hypothalamus
    C. Amygdala
    D. Frontal lobe
    E. Cerebellum

13. Research on hypothalamus dimorphism comparing homosexual males, heterosexual males, and females suggests that the hypothalamus of homosexual males . . .
    A.  is most similar to that of heterosexual males
    B.  is most similar to that of females
    C.  is different from both heterosexual males and females
    D.  is similar to females only in homosexual males who exhibit overt feminine behavior
    E.  is similar to females only in homosexual males who exhibit overt masculine behaviors

14. According to the James-Lange theory of emotions, your experience of emotions is based on which of the following?
    A.  Stimulation of the spinal cord
    B.  Autonomic nervous system response
    C.  Cognitive function
    D.  Cognitive interpretation of an autonomic nervous system response
    E.  An autonomic nervous system response to cognitive functioning

15. Which of the following is *not* a symptom of Kluver-Bucy syndrome?
    A.  A tendency to examine objects by mouth
    B.  An increase in homosexual behavior
    C.  Lack of fear
    D.  Aphasia marked by picky eating habits
    E.  Extreme tameness

16. Schizophrenia is thought to result in part from dysfunctional input from the frontal lobe to the hypothalamus. Which of the following is a feature shared by schizophrenics and patients who have undergone frontal lobotomy?
    A.  Lack of facial expression
    B.  Hallucinations
    C.  Delusions
    D.  Manic episode
    E.  All of the above

17. Which of the following is *not* true of the emotional disorder of depression?
    A.  There is a genetic component
    B.  Serotonin is implicated as a primary neurotransmitter in this disorder
    C.  It affects approximately 35 percent of the population
    D.  Approximately 70 percent of people reporting depression respond to drug treatment
    E.  It is among the most common psychologically disruptive disorders in the world

18. Anxiety disorders are thought to be a result of which of the following?
    A.  Abnormal dopamine-receptor response in the hypothalamus
    B.  Abnormal dopamine-receptor response in the amygdala
    C.  Abnormal GABA-receptor response in the hypothalamus
    D.  Abnormal GABA-receptor response in the amygdala
    E.  Abnormal frontal-lobe function

19. The mesolimbic region is considered a reward pathway that utilizes which of the following?
    A.  Dopamine
    B.  GABA
    C.  Serotonin
    D.  Testosterone
    E.  Estrogen

20. What is the primary difference between a phobia and a panic attack?
    A.   Panic attacks involve a clearly dreaded object or situation
    B.   Phobias involve a clearly dreaded object or situation
    C.   Panic attacks are not considered an anxiety disorder
    D.   Phobias are not considered an anxiety disorder
    E.   There is no difference between the two, they are different names for the same disorder

## Short Answer Questions

*Answer each of the following questions with a brief but complete written answer based on information from your text.*

1.  What is an innate releasing mechanism (IRM)? Give an example of an IRM in humans.

2.  Briefly describe taste aversion learning as demonstrated by John Garcia in wolves. Could taste aversion learning be established by pairing a particular food with a loud noise? Explain your answer.

3.  Explain what is meant by a homeostatic mechanism. Use eating as an example of a behavior associated with a homeostatic mechanism.

4.  Give an example of an organizational and an activation effect of gonadal hormones.

5.  Male rats with medial preoptic area (POA) lesions do not mate. Briefly describe how Barry Everett showed that this decrease in mating behavior did not indicate a loss of sex motivation in these rats.

6. Briefly describe the James-Lange theory (recently modified to the somatic marker hypothesis) of human emotional experiences.

7. Briefly explain the basis for the Kluver-Bucy syndrome and list at least three features of this syndrome.

8. As a form of psychosurgery the frontal lobotomy has a rich history. Describe the results from initial animal studies of lobotomies and give an example of why this surgery might have been performed on a human.

9. Anxiety is likely not an abnormal behavior, since it can be a very useful response under certain circumstances. Briefly explain this statement.

10. Briefly explain why a person would continue to engage in the self-destructive behavior of cigarette smoking when they know such behavior is not useful and may even be detrimental.

# Matching Questions

*Complete each of the following matching questions based on information from your text.*

1. Match the following structure to the behavioral response you would expect to see if the structure were damaged or lesioned.

   A. Amygdala             ____ Lack of prosody
   B. Lateral hypothalamus    ____ Reduced fear response
   C. Ventromedial hypothalamus    ____ Hyperphagia
   D. Frontal lobe           ____ Disruption of male sexual behavior
   E. Medial preoptic area     ____ Aphagia behavior

2. Match the following disorders to the appropriate feature or characteristic.

|   |   |   |
|---|---|---|
| | | ___ Treated with anxiolytic drugs |
| A. | Schizophrenia | ___ Reduced dopamine from frontal lobe |
| B. | Depression | ___ Disruption of serotonin and noradrenaline |
| C. | Anxiety disorder | ___ Overactivity of GABA$_A$ receptors |
| | | ___ Affects nearly 10 percent of the population |

3. Match the following physiological change with the expected behavior or sensation.

|   |   |   |
|---|---|---|
| A. | Loss of blood | ___ Satiety |
| B. | Ingestion of salt | ___ Fear response |
| C. | Release of CCK | ___ Hypovolemic thirst |
| D. | Release of estrogen | ___ Osmotic thirst |
| E. | Stimulation of amygdala | ___ Sexual receptivity |

4. Match the following anxiety disorders with their appropriate symptom or characteristic.

|   |   |   |
|---|---|---|
| | | ___ Persistent and unrealistic worries |
| A. | Generalized anxiety disorder | ___ Involve a clearly dreaded object or situation |
| B. | Panic disorder | ___ Recurrent attacks of intense terror |
| C. | Phobia | ___ Often leads to agoraphobia |
| | | ___ Most common type of anxiety disorder |

5. Label each of the following as an organization (O) or activational (A) effect of hormones.

___ Testosterone producing sexual dimorphism of preoptic area

___ Testosterone producing male sexual behavior

___ Estrogen and progesterone producing lordosis

___ Congenital adrenal hyperplasia causing an enlarged clitoris

___ Estrous cycle hormones increasing dendritic branching

# Diagrams

1.  Below is a frontal section through the hypothalamus. Indicate the approximate location of lesions that would produce the following: 1) Aphasia, 2) Hyperaphagia, 3) Disruption of lordosis response.

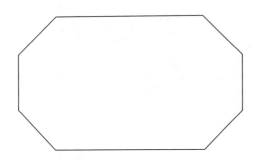

2.  Indicate which of the below neurons would be masculinized during development.

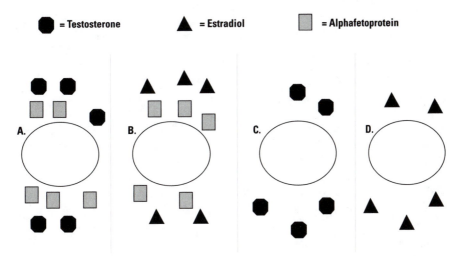

3.  Below is a diagram of a cell in homeostatic balance. Alter this diagram to indicate a state that would induce osmotic thirst.

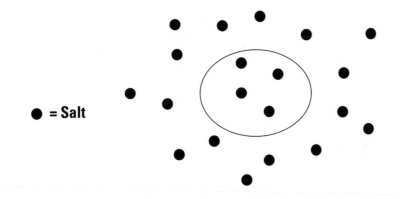

4. On the diagram below, indicate approximately how you would perform a lobotomy.

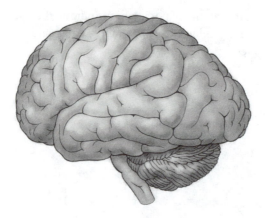

5. Below is an incomplete diagram of a pituitary gland connected to the hypothalamus. Complete the diagram by correctly subdividing the pituitary. Also indicate where hypothalamic neurons terminate in the pituitary.

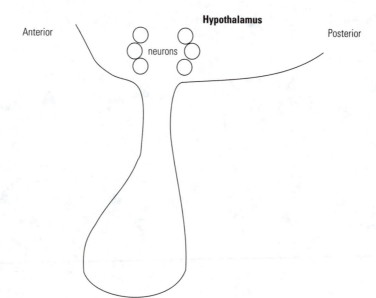

# CD-ROM Exercises

1. Visit module CNS3 of your CD to better visualize the location of the hypothalamus. Notice the central location of this structure when viewing the entire three-dimensional brain.

2. Visit module CNS2 of your CD to better conceptualize the relative size of the frontal lobe compared to the rest of the brain. Imagine where the damage would occur in this brain in a person undergoing a prefrontal lobotomy.

3. Visit module RM2 of your CD to view a video showing self-stimulation in a rat. Notice how determined the rat is to stimulate his own brain regions. Consider this video in terms of drug self-administration studies that have shown similar determination in evoking intracranial drug administration.

# The Web

*Consider using the following Web sites for additional information on some of the topics from this chapter:*

1. American Anorexia Bulimia Association, Inc.: www.aabainc.org/

2. Obesity Meds and Research News: www.obesity-news.com/

3. Anxiety Disorders Association of America: www.adaa.org/

4. Depression Resource Center: www.healingwell.com/depression/

5. Sex Differentiation Disorders: www.ohsu.edu/cliniweb/C19/C19.391.775.html

The easiest way to get to these sites is to link to them through the student Web site at www.worthpublishers.com/kolb. This site also has further study aids and practice quizzes.

# CROSSWORD PUZZLE

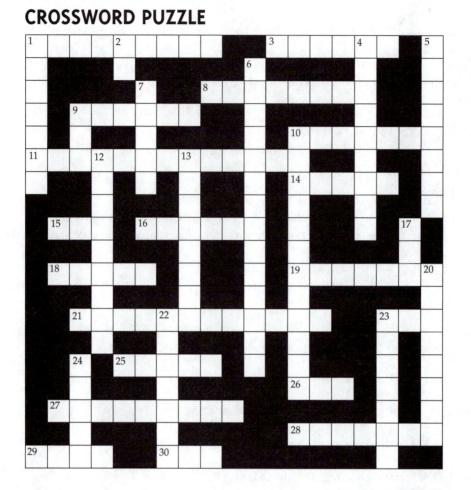

## Across

1. The "F" in MFB
3. The "M" in MFB
8. Area responsible for male sex behavior; medial _____
9. Something that encourages behavior
10. Testosterone is an example of one
11. A behavior that is not a regulatory one
14. He proposed an emotional circuit after observing people with rabies
15. Past tense of eat
16. He used taste aversion learning to keep wolves away from sheep
18. Sensation that can enhance eating behavior
19. Gland above the kidney, becomes active when you're stressed
21. A syndrome that can masculinize women
23. High level of negative emotions can make you do this
25. With 7 down, they had a theory of emotions named after them
26. An example of 11 across
27. Robinson and Berridge developed the _____ sensitization theory of drug addiction
28. Unsettling emotion, treated with 6 down when it becomes chronic
29. Lesions of the amygdala produce the Kluver-_____ syndrome
30. Cholecystokinin; abbr.

## Down

1. An example of a regulatory behavior
2. 23 down, to his friends
4. The nucleus _____ is implicated in many theories of drug addiction
5. Failure of a structure to develop
6. Class of GABA agonists; e.g., valium
7. 2nd name in 25 across theory
9. Behavioral response to a fearful stimulus
10. Primary subcortical structure associated with all types of motivated behavior
12. The "R" in IRM
13. Process of remembering a behavior
17. 8 across; abbr.
20. Surgery designed to disconnect a portion of the frontal cortex
22. Thirst induced by salt ingestion
23. #1 name in pigeon learning research, maybe all learning research
24. Disorder marked by high levels of anxiety

# 12 Why Do We Sleep?

## CHAPTER SUMMARY

Sleep appears to be a behavior that, like many other behaviors, helps animals adapt to their environment to maximize food acquisition and minimize energy loss. Humans are *Diurnal* animals, meaning we are active and gather food during daylight and we are inactive and conserve energy at night. The phenomenon of our body systems actually slowing down at night to conserve energy and then speeding up during the day is called a *biological rhythm*. One very interesting question that may be asked is where such rhythms originate. The concept of a biological clock that keeps track of time and influences biological rhythms has been a theme of philosophy and research for nearly three centuries. Only recently, however, has extensive study begun to reveal details of the biological basis for these rhythms. Among the findings was that numerous cycles or *periods* of activity exist. In addition to *circadian* (around a day) cycles, research has shown *ultradian* (smaller than a day), *infradian* (between one day and one year), and *circannual* (around a year) rhythms. Of greatest interest to neuroscientists are behaviors mediated by circadian rhythms, including our sleep–wake cycle. Studying these cycles researchers determined that circadian rhythms are not entrained to an exact 24-hour period, but rather appear to respond to light and dark cues in the environment to reset the rhythm each day. When the constant light is present, the time period generally extends beyond a 24-hour period, resulting in a *free-running rhythm* of about 25–27 hours for humans. Thus it appears that individuals have a personal rhythm period to which they would adhere without environmental light cues. However, with light cues all rhythms may be reset each day to approximately 24 hours. Such light cues are called *zeitgebers*, literally meaning "time-givers." One interesting behavioral phenomenon related to circadian rhythms is the effect of *jet lag* on travelers. Because our endogenous rhythms tend to be greater than 24 hours, travel from east to west (where daylight is gained) tends to be less disruptive than travel from west to east. In other words, west-to-east travel results in a greater discrepancy between our endogenous-rhythm period and the zeitgeber, making adjustments more difficult.

Of particular interest to researchers was the neural basis of the biological clock mediating rhythms. In the 1930s *Curt Richter* proposed that the biological clock acted as a *pacemaker* instructing other neural structures when to be active. After numerous attempts Richter determined that the *suprachiasmatic nucleus (SCN)* of the hypothalamus appears to act as the primary pacemaker for circadian rhythms. As the name suggests, this nucleus is located just dorsal from the optic chiasma and receives light input from the environment via the *retinohypothalamic pathway*. Since Richter's research, neural pacemakers have also been located in the pineal gland and in the retina. However, the SCN is still considered the primary pacemaker for mediating most circadian rhythm. Not surprising, the SCN shows greater activity during the light portion of the light–dark cycle than during the dark portion. This activity continues even when the SCN is isolated from all neural input from other brain regions. SCN function also appears to be innate since animals raised in constant darkness show rhythmic activity. In addition, transplantation of SCN neurons from one animal to another will produce rhythms in the recipient animal that are consistent with those of the donor animal.

Although the SCN is the primary pacemaker, it is not itself responsible for producing behavior. Rather, the SCN appears to influence neural systems known as "slave" oscillators to produce behaviors such as feeding, body temperature, sleeping, and so on.

Sleeping and waking are among the most intriguing and thus the most studied behaviors. For the most part, we all generally sleep for several hours during each 24-hour period. One exception is *insomniacs* who are unable to sleep regularly or for adequate periods of time. To understand sleep disorders, we must first understand normal sleep patterns. Sleep is generally studied using physiological measures from a polygraph including EEG, EMG, and EOG to monitor changes in behavior. EEG has shown a reliable pattern of changes in brain waves as a person progresses from wakefulness into sleep. This pattern includes several overlapping stages of brain activity where electrical output shows progressively greater amplitude and lower frequency of brain-wave activity. These waves are called *beta* (15–30 Hz), *alpha* (7–11 Hz), and *delta* (1–3 Hz) *rhythms* and represent progression from wakefulness to deep sleep in respective order. Interestingly, after reaching the deepest stage of slow-wave delta-rhythm sleep, a person will then begin to cycle back up beta-rhythm brain activity in a state of *REM* sleep. During a typical night's sleep a person will cycle back and forth through deep sleep to REM approximately four to six times. As the night progresses, REM sleep is extended and *NREM* sleep is reduced. There is variability in individual sleep patterns, but most people exhibit a much larger proportion of REM sleep during infancy and childhood than in later adulthood. During slow-wave NREM sleep there are a variety of biological changes. Body temperature, heart rate, blood flow all decrease, while perspiring and release of growth hormone increase. We move about quite frequently, and in some individuals sleepwalking and night terrors may occur at this time. REM sleep is even more remarkable in terms of associated behaviors. The body becomes paralyzed with the exception of slight twitches. Body-temperature regulatory systems cease functioning, allowing body temperature to rise or fall with the surrounding environment. Brain-wave activity increases and the cognitive experience of dreaming occurs.

There are many theories of why we dream, including Freud's extensive overview published in the book *Interpretation of Dreams*. Contemporary theories are generally categorized as continuity or discontinuity theories. Continuity theories propose that anxieties of the day that drive daydreaming continue into NREM and then into REM sleep, forming the basis of dreams. Discontinuity theories propose that REM dreams and the neural basis for REM sleep are not necessarily based on a continuation of ruminating over anxieties throughout the day and through NREM sleep. One such hypothesis is the *activation-synthesis hypothesis*, which suggests that the cortex is bombarded with neural signals during REM sleep and in response to these signals generates images and actions based on memory stores, often (but not always) using recent memories. The *evolutionary hypothesis of dreams* suggests that dreams often include threatening elements of our environment as an adaptive means of enhancing ability to recognize and avoid such threats when awake.

As with dreaming, there are several theories as to why we sleep. Perhaps the earliest theory is that sleep is simply a passive process of brain inactivity occurring when environmental stimuli are reduced. However, research refutes this theory, showing that total lack of environmental stimuli actually tends to reduce time spent sleeping. Another theory is that sleep is a biological adaptation that allows conservation of energy during times when food is most difficult to obtain. Sleep may also be a restorative process, during which the body replenishes depleted chemicals, enzymes, and the like used up during the wakeful period. However, some evidence suggests that total sleep deprivation, even for several days, does not appear to have lasting debilitating effects that might be expected if this theory were true. Sleep may also act to enhance memory storage, allowing the brain a period to solidify and organize experiences. Research has shown that sleep deprivation may reduce memory consolidation, and that dreams in particular may be responsible for aspects of memory storage.

The neural basis for sleep appears to be located primarily with the brainstem. The *reticular activating system* (*RAS*) includes the *reticulum*, and when activated stimulates *desynchronized* EEGs associated with wakefulness. Damage to the RAS results in a state of relatively permanent sleep commonly termed *coma*. Desynchronized EEGs are associated with acetylcholine released when alert but not moving, and serotonin released when moving. For sleep to occur, release of both of these neurotransmitters onto cortical neurons must be decreased. REM sleep appears to be mediated by a brainstem region just anterior to the cerebellum known as the peribrachial area. This structure sends cholinergic projections to the *medial pontine reticular formation* (*MPRF*) that in turn initiates PGO (pons, geniculate, occipital) waves associated with dreams.

Sleep disorders may occur during NREM and REM sleep. NREM disorders include *insomnia* (inability to sleep) and *narcolepsy* (falling asleep at inappropriate times). There are many factors that may contribute to sleep disorders. For example, approximately 35 percent of insomnia cases are associated with depression and anxiety. *Drug-dependent insomnia* results when drug-inducing sedatives create an imbalance in the normal chemical transmission associated with sleep, resulting in an inability to sleep without taking these drugs. Narcolepsy affects about 1 percent of the population and is distinguished from normal tiredness by its frequency and tendency to disrupt normal daily activities. One cause of narcolepsy is sleep apnea, an intermittent inability to breathe during periods of sleep, resulting in constant waking throughout the night. REM disorders include *sleep paralysis*, a fairly common condition in which an individual experiences paralysis normally associated with REM sleep as they are falling asleep or waking. *Cataplexy* is a rare form of sleep paralysis in which an individual loses muscle tone when fully awake, often during times of high emotional arousal. During a cataplexy episode, the individual may also experience *hypnogogic hallucinations* that are thought to result from stimulation of brain mechanisms normally activated during dreams. In contrast to sleep paralysis, *REM without atonia* is a condition in which individuals do not undergo paralysis during REM sleep. This condition can result in complex movements, often resulting in the person acting out the dream. Cataplexy and narcolepsy can be treated with amphetamines, whereas REM without atonia is treated with benzodiazepines that block REM sleep.

## KEY TERMS

*The following is a list of important terms introduced in Chapter 12. Give the definition of each term in the space provided.*

### A Clock for All Seasons

Diurnal

Biological clocks

Biological rhythms

Period

Circannual rhythms

Circa

Circadian rhythms

Ultradian rhythms

Infradian rhythms

Free-running rhythms

Zeitgebers

Entrained

Jet lag

**Neural Basis of the Biological Clock**

Pacemaker

Suprachiasmatic nucleus

Retinohypothalamic pathway

In phase

**Sleep**

Insomniac

Electroencephalograph (EEG)

Electromyograph (EMG)

Electrooculograph (EOG)

Beta rhythm

Alpha rhythm

Delta rhythms

REM

NREM

*Interpretation of Dreams*

Activation-synthesis hypothesis

Evolutionary hypothesis

Basic rest–activity cycle (BRAC)

Microsleeps

### The Neural Basis of Sleep

Desychronized EEG

Reticulum

Reticular activating system (RAS)

Coma

Peribrachial area

Medial Pontine Reticular Formation (MPRF)

Magnocellular nucleus medulla


*Sleep Disorders*

Insomnia


Narcolepsy


Drug-dependency insomnia


Sleep apnea


Sleep paralysis


Cataplexy


Hypnogogic hallucinations


REM without atonia


Seasonal affective disorder (SAD)


Restless Legs Syndrome (RLS)

## KEY NAMES

*The following is a list of important names introduced in Chapter 12. Explain the importance of each person in the space provided.*

Curt Richter

Sigmund Freud

## PRACTICE TEST

## Multiple-Choice Questions

*Answer each of the following multiple-choice questions with the best possible answer based on information from your text.*

1. Which of the following is an example of a circannual rhythm?
   A. Migratory cycles
   B. Eating behavior
   C. Sleep behavior
   D. Menstrual cycle activity
   E. All of the above

2. In humans, the free-running nature of our biological clock is not usually apparent because with each day we reset the clock using environmental cues. Without cues to reset the clock, what would be the approximate period of a circadian rhythm?
   A. 12–14 hours
   B. 16–18 hours
   C. 20–22 hours
   D. 25–27 hours
   E. 29–31 hours

3. Which of the following is an example of a zeitgeber?
   A. Food
   B. Temperature
   C. Light
   D. Sexual behavior
   E. Blood pressure

4. Within which of the following structures is the suprachiasmatic nucleus located?
   A. Hippocampus
   B. Hypothalamus
   C. Brainstem
   D. Cerebral cortex
   E. Pituitary gland

5. Which of the following is true of the suprachiasmatic nucleus?
   A. Metabolic activity is higher during the day than at night
   B. Neurons are more active during the day than at night
   C. If all pathways into and out of this structure are severed, it maintains rhythmical activity
   D. Individual cells from this structure each maintain a rhythmical activity
   E. All of the above

6. The suprachiasmatic nucleus does not actually drive behavior, but rather drives structures that in turn produce behavior. What is the term given to behavior-producing systems that are under the control of suprachiasmatic nucleus activity?
   A. Slave oscillators
   B. Entrainment systems
   C. Circadian nuclei
   D. Endocrine glands
   E. Subordinate systems

7. Among the devices used for measuring sleep activity is the polygraph. Which of the following polygraph components is used when measuring sleep behavior?
   A. Electroencephalograph
   B. Electromyograph
   C. Electrooculograph
   D. All of the above
   E. None of the above

8. Which of the following is true of EEG recordings as a person passes into progressively deeper stages of NREM sleep?
   A. Wave frequency increases, wave amplitude increases
   B. Wave frequency increases, wave amplitude decreases
   C. Wave frequency decreases, wave amplitude decreases
   D. Wave frequency decreases, wave amplitude increases
   E. Wave frequency and amplitude remain unchanged until the onset of REM sleep

9. Which of the following is *not* a characteristic of slow-wave (NREM) sleep?
   A. Increased body temperature
   B. Increased perspiration
   C. Decreased heart rate
   D. Decreased blood flow
   E. Increased growth hormone secretion

10. Which of the following is *not* a characteristic of REM sleep?
    A. Penile erection
    B. Paralysis of skeletal muscles
    C. Twitching of fingers and toes
    D. Loss of temperature regulation
    E. Dreams generally last only a few seconds

11. According to the activation-synthesis hypothesis of dreams, a dream about your professor attacking you could result from which of the following?
    A. A high level of activation of the cortex
    B. A high level of output from the brainstem
    C. A recent emotional experience
    D. A recent encounter with that professor
    E. All of the above

12. According to the evolutionary hypothesis of dreams, a dream about your professor attacking you could result in which of the following?
    A.  Insomnia
    B.  A fear of your professor
    C.  A sexual attraction to your professor
    D.  A desire to sit in the front of the classroom
    E.  A desire to spend more time with your professor

13. In 1965 a student stayed awake for 260 hours (nearly 11 days). What lasting effect did this sleep deprivation have on this student?
    A.  He now enters REM sleep much less than before the sleep deprivation
    B.  He now enters REM sleep much more than before the sleep deprivation
    C.  He now sleeps more hours per night than before the sleep deprivation
    D.  He now sleeps fewer hours per night than before the sleep deprivation
    E.  The sleep deprivation had no apparent lasting effects on the student

14. One difficulty with sleep-deprivation studies is keeping subjects from engaging in ANY sleep. For example, a person can actually engage in a few moments of sleep, becoming less responsive to external stimuli and presumably gaining some benefits of sleep, while sitting or standing. What is the term researchers have given to these brief sleep periods?
    A.  Microsleeps
    B.  Cat naps
    C.  Power naps
    D.  Daytime deltas
    E.  Afternoon alphas

15. Supporting the theory of sleep as a function of memory storage, PET scans have shown that cortical areas that become active during task-acquisition trials in subjects also become active during which of the following?
    A.  Alpha-wave activity
    B.  NREM sleep
    C.  Delta-wave activity
    D.  REM sleep
    E.  All of the above

16. In general, it could be said that the neural structures responsible for initiating sleep are centered in which of the following?
    A.  The hypothalamus
    B.  The pituitary gland
    C.  The brainstem
    D.  The cortex
    E.  The spinal cord

17. The region that appears to be responsible for sleep–wake behavior is known as the RAS. RAS is an abbreviation for which of the following?
    A.  Region Associated with Sleep
    B.  Reticular Activating System
    C.  Rest And Sleep system
    D.  Rest And Stimulation system
    E.  Region of Alertness and Sleep

18. What two neurotransmitters released in the cortex are associated with desynchronized EEG waves?
    A. Dopamine and serotonin
    B. Dopamine and norepinephrine
    C. Serotonin and norepinephrine
    D. Acetlycholine and norepinephrine
    E. Acetlycholine and serotonin

19. Which of the following is *not* true of cataplexy?
    A. It may be treated with amphetamine or Ritalin
    B. Attacks may be triggered by excitement
    C. Attacks may be accompanied by hallucinations
    D. Attacks result in a lose of all muscle tone
    E. Attacks generally occur when a person is drowsy and not alert

20. Which of the following has been used to successfully treat REM without atonia?
    A. Benzodiazepines
    B. Muscle relaxants
    C. Amphetamine
    D. Ritalin
    E. Alcohol

## Short Answer Questions

*Answer each of the following questions with a brief but complete written answer based on information from your text.*

1. Which type of travel tends to produce the more severe jet-lag symptoms, flying east to west or west to east? Briefly explain your answer.

2. The suprachiasmatic nucleus is a very descriptive name for a structure closely involved in biological rhythms. Briefly explain where this structure is located and why this location is important for circadian rhythms.

3. Briefly describe methods of experimental studies designed to show that rhythmic patterns of behavior are neither learned after birth nor entrained to the mothers rhythms during fetal development.

4. Briefly describe how the suprachiasmatic nucleus can mediate a circannual pattern of sexual behavior in a male animal. Include in your description the role of pineal gland and melatonin secretion.

5.  Sigmund Freud suggested that many (perhaps most) dreams contained sexual content. Contemporary sleep researchers suggest only about 1 percent of dreams contain such content. What do these contemporary researchers see as the primary content of most dreams?

6.  Briefly describe either the activation-synthesis hypothesis or the evolutionary hypothesis of dreams.

7.  Summarize very briefly the primary premise of each of the four following theories of sleep: 1) Sleep as a passive process; 2) Sleep as a biological adaptation; 3) Sleep as a restorative process; 4) Sleep as a means of enhancing memory storage.

8. REM sleep is thought to have some significance in human sleep behavior. This theory is strengthened by research investigating the effects of selective REM deprivation on subjects. Briefly describe two confirmed effects of REM deprivation that have been reported?

9. Briefly compare and contrast the sleep disorders of narcolepsy and cataplexy.

10. Briefly explain the relationship between narcolepsy and sleep apnea.

# Matching Questions

*Complete each of the following matching questions based on information from your text.*

1. Match the following rhythms to their appropriate time period.

   A. Circannual rhythm
   B. Circadian rhythm
   C. Ultradian rhythm
   D. Infradian rhythm

   ____ Around one year
   ____ Less than one day
   ____ Between one day and one year
   ____ Around one day

2. Match the following structures or regions to their appropriate feature or description.

   A. Suprachiasmatic nucleus
   B. Cerebral cortex
   C. RAS
   D. Median raphe
   E. Brainstem

   ____ Damage to this may result in coma
   ____ PGO spikes originate here
   ____ Considered the location of the main biological clock
   ____ EEGs are recorded from this area
   ____ Contains serotonin neurons that project to neocortex

3. Indicate whether each of the following is associated with REM or NREM sleep.

   A. _____ Delta rhythms
   B. _____ Paralysis
   C. _____ Night terrors
   D. _____ Sleepwalking
   E. _____ Loss of temperature-regulatory mechanism

4. Match the following sleep disorders with their appropriate feature of description.

   A. Sleep apnea
   B. Insomnia
   C. Drug-induced insomnia
   D. Hypnogogic hallucination
   E. Night terrors

   ____ More common in people who are overweight
   ____ Anxiety and depression account for about 35 percent of cases
   ____ Results from tolerance development
   ____ May occur during a cataplexy attack
   ____ NREM disorder seen especially in children

5. Match the following drugs to the sleep disorder for which they are prescribed as treatment.

   A. Benzodiazepines
   B. Amphetamine
   C. L-dopa
   D. Light therapy

   ____ Seasonal Affective Disorder
   ____ Cataplexy
   ____ Restless Leg Syndrome
   ____ REM without atonia
   ____ Narcolepsy

# Diagrams

1. The diagram below depicts waking periods of a normal subject over 8 days. Indicate how you would expect waking patterns to differ if this subject were deprived of light cues over that same time period (shaded bars indicate dark period, open bars indicate light period).

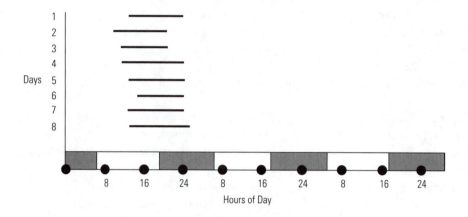

2. Which of the 3 travelers (indicated on the map below) would you expect to experience the greatest sensation of jet lag?

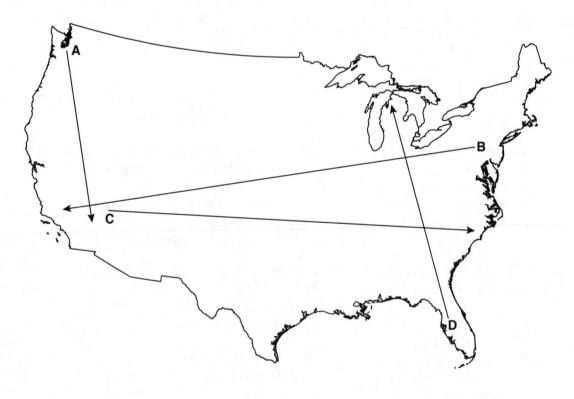

3.  The line below depicts an approximate EEG recording from a subject during Stage 1 sleep. Draw two additional lines indicating approximately what the EEG recordings would look like when the subject is in Stage 4 sleep, and when the subject is awake and alert.

Stage 1:

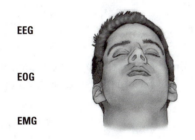

Stage 4:

Awake and Alert:

4.  Connect the electrodes to the appropriate location on the subject below.

**EEG**

**EOG**

**EMG**

5.  Draw arrows to the approximate location of the following structures associated with sleep and wakefulness: Hypothalamus, Reticular activating system, Medial pontine reticular formation.

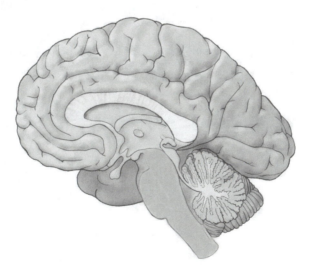

## CD-ROM Exercises

1. Visit module RM1 of your CD to review methods utilized to obtain EEG recordings. Take particular note of EEG recordings from the stages of wake and sleeping.

## The Web

*Consider using the following Web sites for additional information on some of the topics from this chapter:*

1. National Sleep Foundation: www.sleepfoundation.org/

2. Restless Legs Syndrome Foundation: www.rls.org/

3. Central Sleep Apnea Informational Page: members.aol.com/blackcover/csa.html

4. Narcolepsy Internet: www.narcolepsy.org/

5. Night Terror Resource Center: www.nightterrors.org/

   The easiest way to get to these sites is to link to them through the student Web site at www.worthpublishers.com/kolb. This site also has further study aids and practice quizzes.

# CROSSWORD PUZZLE

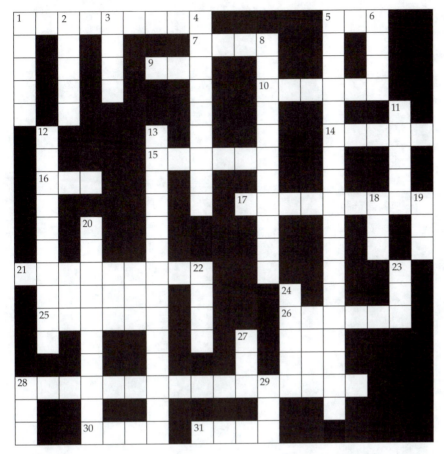

**Across**

1. Middle word in 23 down abbr., often associated with emotion
5. These really move during dreams
7. Term for sleep where dreams seldom occur
9. With 18 down, term for disruptive time-zone travel effect
10. One in the suprachiasmatic nucleus, another in the retina, with 20 down
14. It's the way 5 across moves during dreams
15. Disorders where people have difficulty breathing during sleep
16. 17 across; abbr.
17. _____ activating system is responsible for aspects of wake–sleep cycle
21. Person who unwillingly pulls all-nighters
25. 19 down without this might have you running around the bedroom at night
26. Term for the actual amount of time required to complete rhythm cycle
28. Recordings of muscles, sometimes used in sleep research
30. When these become too restless during sleep it is considered a sleep disorder syndrome
31. Common term for 8 down; cat ____

**Down**

1. Waves seen on 28 down when you begin to relax and enter sleep
2. Author of *Interpretation of Dreams*
3. ____ plexy can have you on the floor with laughter
4. When 10 across is reset by a zeitgeber it is said to be ____
5. Recordings of eyes, sometimes used in sleep research
6. 28 across; abbr.
8. Technical term for a very short sleep session
11. Latin word meaning "around"
12. Occurring at cycles of around a year
13. Types include hypnogogic or LSD–induced
18. See 9 across
19. Dream sleep; abbr.
20. There's another one in the pineal gland, see 10 across
22. State lacking consciousness, usually after severe brain damage
23. Disorder when people become depressed in the winter; abbr.
24. Causes a type of insomnia; 15 across singular
27. 5 down singular; abbr.
28. Scalp recordings of electrical activity during sleep; abbr.
29. Proper term for 30 across sleep disorder; abbr.

# 13 How Do We Learn from Experience?

## CHAPTER SUMMARY

In this chapter the concept of *brain plasticity* is emphasized as a physiological basis for learning and memory. *Learning* is defined as a process that results in a relatively permanent change in behavior, whereas *memory* is the ability to recall or recognize previous experiences. Laboratory studies of learning and memory using animals have incorporated hundreds of tasks for animals. Among the earliest studies were those conducted by *Ivan Pavlov* using *classical conditioning* to teach associations between two stimuli. More recent variations of this type of conditioning are *eye-blink conditioning* and *fear conditioning*, both of which pair a conditioned stimulus (CS) to an unconditioned response (UCR) to produce a learned conditioned response (CR). These experiments have shown that separate pathways in the cerebellum and the amygdala are associated with eye-blink response and fear response, respectively. In this regard even simple forms of learning may be mediated by different brain regions or systems.

*B. F. Skinner* expanded on earlier research conducted by *Edward Thorndike* to develop a learning paradigm now known as *operant conditioning*. Operant conditioning requires an animal to learn an association between its actions and the consequences of those actions. More recently *Richard Morris* developed a swim task for rats that required the use of visual and spatial cues to correctly complete the task. The Morris water maze tests a particular form of learning known as *visuospatial learning*.

Applying information from animal research to humans is difficult in part because much of human learning and memory is verbal. One general division of human memory seems to be the categories of *implicit* and *explicit* memory. In general terms, implicit memory refers to an unconscious memory (one that is not verbalized), whereas explicit memory refers to a conscious verbal memory. Implicit learning, also known as *procedural memory*, includes conditioned motor responses such as those involved in learning to ride a bicycle. Explicit memory, also known as *declarative memory*, includes recall of content of experiences such as remembering when you last rode a bicycle. The way in which these two types of memories are processed and stored seems to differ as well. Procedural memory utilizes a "bottom-up" processing scheme beginning, for example, with lower-order ("bottom") sensory feedback and muscular movements that are then related to, or incorporated into, higher-order cortical memories. Declarative memory utilizes a "top-down" processing scheme beginning with a higher-order ("top") cortical process of memory recall.

Distinctions can also be made between short-term and long-term memory. Short-term memory is held only for several minutes at most, and is controlled primarily by the frontal lobe. Long-term memory may hold information for a lifetime. Long-term verbal memories are controlled primarily by the temporal lobe. It should be noted, however, that even though some locations are more prevalent in learning and memory, it appears that nearly the entire nervous system can show plasticity responses with experiences.

In the 1920s Karl Lashley began a multi-decade search for the location of a neural circuitry responsible for memory. His conclusion was that when damage occurs the size of the area of damage was a greater factor in memory loss than was the location. Soon after Lashley's conclusion, a patient (H.M.) recovering from neurosurgery to reduce seizures exhibited near total loss of declarative memory as a result of the surgery. It was determined that damage to the anterior hippocampus, amygdala, and surrounding cortical structures were the cause of this memory loss. Since Lashley had produced primarily lesions of cortical regions and tested animals in procedural tasks, it was determined that his conclusion that cortical lesions had little if any effect on implicit memory was valid. Later research showed that loss of implicit memory (and subsequent disruption of procedural tasks) is produced by lesions of the basal ganglia, an area that Lashley had not examined in his lesion studies.

From the vast amount of data collected a theory of regions associated with explicit and implicit memory has begun to emerge. Explicit memory is currently believed to involve structures of medial temporal cortical regions, the frontal cortex, and closely related structures. *Alzheimer's disease* results in severe atrophy of tissue near the medial temporal region and is characterized by severe explicit-memory deficits. Similarly, *Korsakoff's syndrome* results in atrophy of the frontal lobe of most patients and is characterized by impairments of short-term explicit memory. The hippocampus likely plays an important role in visual and spatial contributions to explicit memories. Animals with hippocampal lesions are severely debilitated in visual-recognition tasks. In the same regard, animals that are particularly adept hiding and then finding food stores tend to have large, well-developed hippocampal regions. Implicit memories appear to arise from basal-ganglia function stimulated by cortical inputs. The unconscious nature of these memories is accounted for by the lack of connections from the basal ganglia back to the cortex. *Parkinson's disease* is marked by degeneration of the basal ganglia and is characterized by deficits in implicit memory.

*Emotional memory* represents a unique category of memory. This type of memory is controlled primarily by the amygdala, and when dysfunctional may result in a pathology known as panic disorder. Lesions of the amygdala abolish emotional memory with little effect on implicit or explicit memory.

*Santiago Ramón y Cajal* first suggested in the 1920s that learning was likely a function of structural changes to the neuron. However, evidence substantiating this theory has only recently been produced. Researchers now know that the shape of dendrites show a great deal of plasticity, changing morphology in response to changing experiences of the organism. Gain or loss of synapses in turn results in changes in local circuitry. Very recent research also suggests that the central nervous system is also capable of producing new neurons in response to new experiences. For example, mice housed in an enriched environment (one containing many environmental stimuli) had more hippocampal neurons than mice raised in an impoverished environment. In humans, complexity of dendritic arbors is correlated with extent of formal education. Females have more complex dendritic arbors in Wernicke's area than males, correlating with superior verbal skills.

Several factors are capable of influencing neural plasticity. For example, the number of dendritic spines is positively correlated with the circulating estrogen seen in female rats during their four-day estrous cycle. *Glucocorticoids* produced by the adrenal gland in response to stress can be neurotoxic if maintained at a high level over an extended period of time, ultimately reducing the number of neurons, especially in the hippocampus. In addition to hormones, *neurotrophic factors* may also influence neural plasticity. One of these chemicals, *nerve growth factor*, is known to stimulate dendritic growth during development. *Brain-derived neurotrophic factor (BDNF)* is released during maze solving in rats and may act in a manner similar to nerve-growth factor in adult animals. Psychoactive drugs may also produce long-term changes in structure and function of synapses. Amphetamine and cocaine can increase dendritic growth and spine density in prefrontal-cortex and nucleus-accumbens neurons, resulting in sensitization of those synapses to future administration of the drug.

Neuronal plasticity is perhaps most apparent when assessing recovery from brain damage. The "three-legged cat solution" suggests that when behavioral function is lost as a result of injury, behavioral modifications can be made to compensate (as might be seen in a cat learning to walk on three legs). Such behaviors are undoubtedly mediated by synaptic changes associated with learning new skills. The new circuit solution suggests that following neural damage, new synaptic connections may form or old synapses may become more active in an effort to mediate more behaviors with less neural tissue. This type of plasticity may be enhanced by pharmacological intervention, such as the administration of nerve growth factor shortly after the damage has occurred. There is now evidence that neuronal transplants may also be useful for reversing some deficits following brain damage. However, this procedure is currently limited to only a few types of damage, such as Parkinson's disease. Finally, research with epidermal growth factor (EGF) has shown that cells lining the ventricles may be stimulated to reproduce and migrate to some regions of the brain. This research is very recent and encouraging, however, researchers have yet to determine how to encourage newly migrated cells to establish functional connections as the next step in reversing deficits.

# KEY TERMS

*The following is a list of important terms introduced in Chapter 13. Give the definition of each term in the space provided.*

### What Is Learning and Memory

Brain plasticity

Learning

Memory

Pavlovian conditioning

Respondent conditioning

Classical conditioning

Eye-blink conditioning

Fear conditioning

Instrumental

Operant conditioning

Visuospatial learning

Learning set

Implicit memory

Explicit memory

Declarative memory

Procedural memory

*Neural Systems: Implicit/Explicit*

Alzheimer's disease

Korsakoff's syndrome

Emotional memory

*Structural Basis of Plasticity*

Glucocorticoids

Neurotrophic factors

Nerve growth factor

Drug-induced behavior sensitization

*Recovery from Brain Injury*

Three-legged cat solution

Epidermal growth factor

# KEY NAMES

*The following is a list of important names introduced in Chapter 13. Explain the importance of each person in the space provided.*

Ivan Pavlov

Edward Thorndike


B. F. Skinner


Karl Lashley


Santiago Ramón y Cajal


## PRACTICE TEST

## Multiple-Choice Questions

*Answer each of the following multiple-choice questions with the best possible answer based on information from your text.*

1.  Which of the following has been determined to be the cause of Alzheimer's disease?
    A.  Genetics
    B.  Exposure to toxins in adulthood
    C.  Exposure to toxins during fetal development
    D.  Abnormal rapid aging of neurons
    E.  The cause of Alzheimer's disease is unknown

2.  Which of the following terms refers to the type of learning studied by Ivan Pavlov?
    A.  Pavlovian conditioning
    B.  Respondent conditioning
    C.  Classical conditioning
    D.  All of the above
    E.  None of the above

3.  When fear-conditioning a rat evokes an anxiety response from a tone that has been paired to an electrical shock, the tone represents which of the following?
    A.  Conditioned response
    B.  Conditioned stimulus
    C.  Unconditioned response
    D.  Unconditioned stimulus
    E.  Could represent any of the above depending on design of the study

4. Edward Thorndike was one of the earliest researchers to examine instrumental condi-
   tioning. However, _____ is generally the researcher associated with this
   type of conditioning.
   A. Ivan Pavlov
   B. Richard Morris
   C. B. F. Skinner
   D. Karl Lashley
   E. Santiago Ramón y Cajal

5. Richard Morris developed which of the following apparatus designed to assess visu-
   ospatial learning in rats.
   A. Operant-conditioning box
   B. Radial-arm maze
   C. Water maze
   D. Fear-conditioning apparatus
   E. Eye-blink apparatus

6. An amnesic person is taught a new motor task. Three days later that person shows a
   high level of retention for the motor functions, but cannot recall ever learning the task.
   This person is showing which of the following?
   A. Explicit memory with no implicit memory
   B. Implicit memory with no explicit memory
   C. Both explicit memory and implicit memory
   D. Neither implicit nor explicit memory
   E. Amnesic patients cannot be tested for memory recall

7. The term "top-down" processing is sometimes used to describe the process used in
   declarative memory. From the term "top-down" processing, what does the word "top"
   refer to?
   A. Dendrite
   B. Axon terminal
   C. Brainstem
   D. Cortex
   E. Pituitary gland

8. Memory is often divided into short-term and long-term memory. Long-term verbal
   memories of verbal information appear to be stored in the temporal region. What
   region appears to play an important role in temporary, short-term, memories?
   A. Frontal
   B. Temporal
   C. Parietal
   D. Occipital
   E. Short-term memories are not influenced by cortical regions

9. At the age of 78, patient J.K. began to show significant deficits in implicit memory that
   were believed to result from degeneration of the basal ganglia. Which of the following
   was responsible for basal-ganglia degeneration, and ultimately memory impairments,
   seen in J.K.?
   A. Korsakoff's syndrome
   B. Alzheimer's disease
   C. Parkinson's disease
   D. Severe seizures
   E. Normal aging

10. Korsakoff's syndrome can result in severe memory deficits. Which of the following is the cause of Korsakoff's syndrome?
    A. Alcohol consumption
    B. Thiamine deficiency
    C. Aging
    D. Genetics
    E. Head trauma

11. Which of the following neurotransmitters is released in high concentration in the basal ganglia, and as such implicated in implicit memory?
    A. Serotonin
    B. Acetylcholine
    C. Dopamine
    D. Norepinephrine
    E. Epinephrine

12. What effect would you expect in an animal that had bilateral lesions of the amygdala?
    A. Loss of implicit memory
    B. Loss of explicit memory
    C. Loss of emotional memory
    D. Loss of short-term memory
    E. All of the above

13. Morphological changes in which of the following most likely represents neural changes associated with learning and memory?
    A. Glial cells
    B. Myelin sheathes
    C. The blood–brain barrier
    D. Dendritic arbors
    E. Nuclear DNA

14. Elizabeth Gould and her colleagues recently provided evidence that new neurons may form in response to memory associated with the water-maze task. In what structure did these researchers report genesis of these neurons?
    A. Frontal cortex
    B. Amygdala
    C. Hippocampus
    D. Olfactory bulb
    E. Temporal lobe

15. Researchers have long speculated that morphological changes in the brain could be correlated to learning. When Scheibel and colleagues examined Wernicke's area tissue from deceased patients, which of the following did they find?
    A. More neurons in college-educated patients than high school–educated patients
    B. More glial cells in college-educated patients than in high school–educated patients
    C. More dendritic arbors in college-educated patients than in high school–educated patients
    D. All of the above
    E. None of the above

16. Which of the following hormones has been shown to affect neural structure in adult animals?
    A.  Estrogen
    B.  Testosterone
    C.  Glucocorticoids
    D.  All of the above
    E.  None of the above

17. In animals, brain-derived neurotrophic factor (BDNF) is released and thought to promote structural changes in neurons during . . .
    A.  maze learning
    B.  REM sleep
    C.  NREM sleep
    D.  fetal development
    E.  sexual behavior

18. Robinson and Kolb have shown that when rats are sensitized to amphetamine through repeated injections, there is a subsequent . . .
    A.  decrease in release of dopamine
    B.  loss of glial cells in dopamine-rich regions
    C.  loss of neurons in dopamine-rich regions
    D.  increase in neurons in dopamine-rich regions
    E.  increase in growth of dendrites and spine density in dopamine-rich regions

19. The therapy of replacing lost neurons to promote recovery of lost behavioral function in humans with degenerative diseases has been most successful utilizing cells from which of the following?
    A.  Rats
    B.  Pigs
    C.  Monkeys
    D.  Human fetuses
    E.  None of the above

20. Epidermal growth factor (EGF) has been most successful at promoting neural growth when injected into what region?
    A.  Basal ganglia
    B.  Hippocampus
    C.  Frontal cortex
    D.  Amygdala
    E.  Ventricles

## Short Answer Questions

*Answer each of the following questions with a brief but complete written answer based on information from your text.*

1. Briefly describe what is meant by the term "brain plasticity" and explain how this term relates to learning and memory.

2. Describe in basic terms the difference between classical and operant conditioning.

3. Describe in general terms the difference between implicit and explicit memory.

4. For a large part of his career, Karl Lashley searched for a neural circuit for memory, using knife-cut lesions of the cortex in rats in an attempt to disrupt their maze-learning ability. Give at least two reasons why Lashley was unsuccessful in his attempts to disrupt memory using these methods.

5. Briefly describe the type of surgery that was conducted on patient H.M. and the result of that surgery. Include in your description three brain structures affected by the surgery.

6. In what type of animal would you expect to have a large, well-developed hippocampus? Explain your answer.

7. Briefly describe the cause of Korsakoff's syndrome, the associated memory impairment, and the affected brain region most likely responsible for the impairment.

8. In an effort to show neuroplasticity in adults, researchers have assessed brains of individuals with highly skilled motor functions (such as playing a string instrument), and brains of animals that have undergone amputation of a limb. Briefly describe how the brain responds in each of these cases and what these findings tell us about the capacity for neural reorganization in the adult brain.

9. Briefly explain what is meant by the "three-legged cat solution" when describing recovery from neural damage.

10. According to the new circuit solution of recovery from neural damage, what two forms of therapy would you suggest for a patient? Explain why such therapies are thought to be beneficial.

# Matching Questions

*Complete each of the following matching questions based on information from your text.*

1. Identify each type of learning as operant conditioning (OC) or classical conditioning (CC).

   A. ___ A dog waiting near the table to be fed food scraps
   B. ___ Ducking your head when you hear a loud noise
   C. ___ The feeling of hunger when you smell pizza
   D. ___ Studying late into the night before an exam
   E. ___ Holding the door open for someone entering a building behind you

2. Identify each of the following as more closely associated with implicit memory (IM) or explicit memory (EM).

   A. ___ Riding a bicycle
   B. ___ Childhood memories
   C. ___ Declarative memory
   D. ___ Procedural memory
   E. ___ Top-down processing
   F. ___ Bottom-up processing

3. Match each of the following neural structures or regions to the memory with which they are most closely associated.

   A. Hippocampus          ___ Visual object memory
   B. Frontal lobe          ___ Short-term memory
   C. Amygdala              ___ Emotional memory
   D. Basal ganglia         ___ Implicit memory
   E. Perirhinal cortex     ___ Object location

4. Match each of the following disorders with the appropriate symptom or characteristic.

                                        ____ Degeneration of frontal lobe

A. Parkinson's disease       ____ Loss of implicit memory

B. Alzheimer's disease       ____ Degeneration of entorhinal cortex

C. Korsakoff's syndrome     ____ Caused by a vitamin deficiency

                                          ____ Degeneration of the basal ganglia

5. Match each of the following mechanisms for promoting recovery of behavioral function with the appropriate description or feature.

                                        ____ Recommends use of speech therapy

A. Three-legged cat solution    ____ Undamaged regions will assume control of behavior

B. New circuit solution        ____ Recommends use of nerve growth factor

C. Replacing lost neurons      ____ Recommends use of epidermal growth factor (EGF)

                                        ____ Has been used in many Parkinson's patients

# Diagrams

1. In the diagram depicting a Morris water maze below, show a typical pattern of paths taken by rats to find the hidden platform when released for three trials. In this version of the task a cue on the wall is used to help the animal locate the platform.

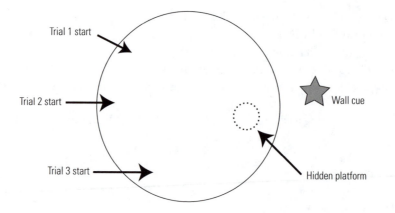

2.   On the diagram of the brain below, identify the approximate regions of the superior, middle, and temporal gyrus.

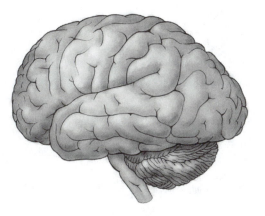

3.   On the diagram of the ventral surface of the brain below, identify the approximate location of the following structures: Amygdala, hippocampus, entorhinal cortex, parahippocampal cortex, perirhinal cortex.

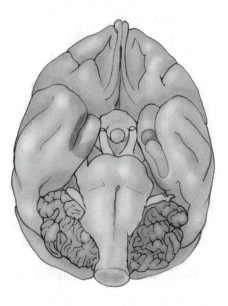

4.   Below is a depiction of a dendrite with dendritic spines during times of moderate estrogen concentration. Indicate how you would expect dendrites to change with varying levels of estrogen concentration.

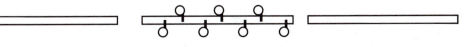

Low Concentration                    Moderate Concentration                    High Concentration

5. A normal healthy neuron is depicted in the diagram below. Indicate the type of change you would expect in that neuron with the progression of Alzheimer's disease.

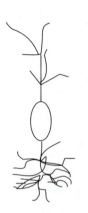

Normal Healthy Neuron　　　　Early Alzheimer's　　　　Advanced Alzheimer's

## CD-ROM Exercises

1. Visit module CNS1 of your CD to review brain structures associated with learning and memory. Take particular note of the temporal cortical region, the hippocampus and the amygdala considering their roles in memory.

## The Web

*Consider using the following Web sites for additional information on some of the topics from this chapter:*

1. Alzheimer's Association: www.alz.org/

2. Wernicke-Korsakoff Syndrome fact sheet: www.caregiver.org/factsheets/wks.html

3. Coma Recovery Association, Inc.: www.comarecovery.org/index.html

4. Nice hippocampus Web page: www.psycheducation.org/emotion/hippocampus.htm

5. The B. F. Skinner Web page: www.bfskinner.org/

The easiest way to get to these sites is to link to them through the student Web site at www.worthpublishers.com/kolb. This site also has further study aids and practice quizzes.

# CROSSWORD PUZZLE

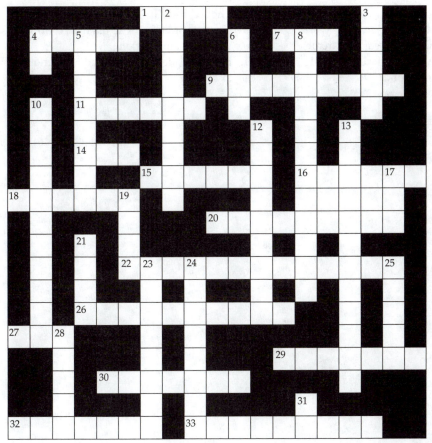

## Across

1. Drinking enough of these filled with beer over the years could lead to Korsakoff's
4. With 17 down, a type of conditioning (learning) using a puff of air
7. Drinking enough of this with tonic over the years could lead to Korsakoff's
9. Referred to by some as 12 down or 26 across
11. Recovery solution named for an animal amputee with 14 across and 28 down
14. Animal for which recovery solution in 11 across was named
15. The fellow who pioneered 9 across/12 down/26 across, Ivan to his friends
16. Primate used for some learning research
18. The "F" in NGF that promote recovery of neural function
20. One of the first to study 32 across, Ed to his friends, he used cats
22. Increased behavioral response after experiencing a stimulus, opposite of habituation
26. Least common of terms for 9 across and 12 down

27. Understanding a solution may be used for many circumstances is a learning _____
29. He followed the work of 20 across, using pigeons and rats mostly
30. NGF is one of many trophic _____
32. 29 across studied learning using this type
33. A type of learning associated with stimuli that evoke a lot of anxiety, for example

## Down

2. The "E" of EGF
3. Perhaps the first to suggest learning was associated with morphological changes, Ramón to his friends
4. 29 across, to his friends
5. Basal ganglia memory, like how to ride a bike
6. Garcia kept these from eating sheep with taste aversion learning in the last chapter
8. Another term for 32 across
10. Memory that remembers the process of learning
12. Referred to by some as 9 across and 26 across, this one was named for Ivan

13. 9, 26, 32 across, 8 & 12 down are all followed by this word
17. See 4 across
19. Common lab rodents for research
21. A type of conditioning based on extreme anxiety, usually with electrical floor grid
23. Memory that's not implicit

24. Korsakoff's technically is not a disease but rather a _____
25. The "N" in NGF
28. Number of limbs 14 across had to work with after amputation
31. Boxing result that could lead to memory loss; abbr.

# 14 How Does the Brain Think?

## CHAPTER SUMMARY

In trying to determine how the brain "thinks," it appears that many systems are likely involved. In the mammalian brain, these systems are thought to be located primarily in the neocortex. Because "thought," "emotion," "motivation," and other aspects of the human experience have no physical basis, they must be studied as *constructs*. Constructs, in simple terms, are descriptions of processes based on information or impressions gathered from observations. Psychologists often use the term *cognition* to describe thought processes. Cognition is the ability to attend to internal or external stimuli and to respond to these stimuli in a meaningful manner. Human thought is unique, in that it is closely tied to language. Although other animals have the cognitive ability to interpret vocalizations, they lack the ability to structure such vocalization into *syntax*. Syntax thus represents a particularly important element in the development of complex human thought. Syntactic language is believed to have evolved from a tendency of the human brain to order strings of events, movements, or thoughts. A lack of this general tendency to order output in nonhuman animals suggests that this may be the most critical feature in the development of complex thought. Furthermore, ordering behavior seems to be controlled by the neocortex in the frontal lobe, one of the most highly developed regions in the human brain compared to other animals. Thus, although many animals are likely capable of thought, the human brain has developed the most complex abilities for this feature.

It is difficult to determine the neural basis for thought, since it likely involves a variety of interconnected units depending on the output. However, it has been shown that even a single neuron is capable of responding to a particular stimulus. Thus, the basis for cognition is likely a convergence of many such neurons linked together as cohesive units. The process of cognition likely results as information is collected from many of these basic units of neural processing and a single higher-level structure produces a response. One of the highest-level regions of brain functioning is the *association cortex*. The association cortex receives primary input from the thalamus and other cortical regions that have already undergone a great deal of convergence and processing. The association cortex is believed to then process this higher-level information with consideration to stored knowledge about the internal and external environment. For example, visual input of an object is processed to determine what the object is and where the object is located using the association cortex in the temporal and parietal lobes, respectively.

There appears to be a correlation between fine motor control and some cognitive processes, including spatial cognition. It is believed that discrete movements are interpreted and integrated, particularly in the right parietal association cortex, to create spatial mapping. Attending to subtle cues also appears to be essential to complex cognitive function. The association cortex in the frontal and parietal lobes is particularly involved in attention. Damage to the parietal lobe of one hemisphere may result in *neglect* of one half of the body and visual field, including not dressing or grooming one half of the body and not being conscious of objects in one half of the field of vision.

Related to processes of ordering and attending to stimuli, the frontal lobe is responsible for planning behaviors. Individuals with frontal-lobe damage exhibit a great deal of difficulty organizing and planning a series of behaviors to be executed in the future (known as temporal organization). One sensitive test of frontal-lobe damage is the Wisconsin Card Sorting Task that requires a series of shifts from one sorting strategy to a new strategy.

It was shown that neurons in the frontal lobe of monkeys also have a capacity to "understand" movements of other monkeys. These cells (called *mirror cells*) became active when the subject performed a particular movement, but more interesting, these same cells became active when the subject viewed another monkey performing the same movement. These findings suggest mirror cells in the frontal association cortex are capable of recognizing external stimuli in the context of internal stimuli. In simple terms, mirror cells "understand" some aspect of the external stimuli. PET scans suggest mirror cells exist in humans as well, but are localized primarily to the left hemisphere of the frontal lobe.

The study of the human brain and behavioral function, known as neuropsychology, was long limited to assessing human behavior following damage produced by strokes, tumors, disease, and so on. Technological advances have recently begun to help us increase our understanding of brain functions associated with thought processes without reliance on brain damage. Such technology includes PET scans, as previously mentioned, along with *magnetic resonance imaging (MRI)* and *functional MRI (fMRI)*. MRI uses magnetic fields to produce a relatively high resolution image of the brain. fMRI uses this same method with the addition of locating regions of higher oxygen consumption to identify regions that become particularly active during mental tasks. *Transcranial magnetic-stimulation (TMS)* uses magnetic coils localized to regions over the skull to disrupt function of specific cortical regions. Use of these and other techniques to study cognition is often referred to as the field of *cognitive neuroscience*.

The fact that some processes of human thought appear to be dominated by a particular hemisphere is referred to as *functional asymmetry*. Functional asymmetry likely results in part from *anatomical asymmetry*, the tendency for structures to be larger in one hemisphere. One example of this is the larger volume of sensorimotor cortex representing the face in the left hemisphere of the brain. Presumably this anatomical asymmetry is directly related to the functional asymmetry of language production in this hemisphere. Analyses of functional and anatomical asymmetry have suggested that right parietal regions of association cortex control thought associated with spatial cognition and music appreciation, while the same region of the left hemisphere controls thought associated with language, reading, and arithmetic. Some individuals have had their corpus collosum cut in an effort to reduce epileptic seizures. The result of this surgery (in addition to reduction of seizures) is that the two hemispheres are unable to communicate, providing a unique opportunity for studying functional asymmetry. One interesting finding from these patients is that when an object is presented only in the left visual field (to the right hemisphere), the subject reports not seeing any object. However, when presented with the opportunity to select the object from a group of objects with the left hand (controlled by the right hemisphere), the subject will choose the correct object. It appears that the left hemisphere, having neither seen the object nor having received input from the right hemisphere about the object, responds verbally that it has seen nothing. The right hemisphere, though aware of the object, is incapable of producing language and thus does not respond to the quarry of object identification. Also interesting is the finding that although the left hemisphere appears to control comprehension of language, comprehension of Braille reading is controlled by the right hemisphere. This finding is likely due to the fact that Braille requires spatial patterning for comprehension.

In addition to hemispheric differences, there are also gender differences in cognitive organization. In general terms, females show greater proficiency in verbal tasks, whereas males show greater proficiency in spatial tasks. Differences appear to be mediated by gonadal hormones, since they are not apparent in rats that have had gonads removed at birth. In human females the increase in verbal fluency appears to coincide with the onset of puberty, suggesting an organizational effect of ovarian hormones. In addition, language disruption is more likely to occur with damage to the posterior cortex of males and the anterior cortex of females. One theory for gender differences in humans is that evolution may have favored males with spatial abilities that enhanced hunting and gathering strategies. Females, on the other hand, would benefit more from developing fine motor and communication skills that would enhance rearing offspring.

The relationship of handedness to hemispheric control of language is significant but not absolute. Virtually all right-handed individuals have left-hemisphere language centers. Approximately 70 percent of left-handed individuals also have left-hemisphere language centers. The remaining left-handed individuals are about evenly split between having right-hemisphere language centers and bilateral language centers (also called *anomalous speech representation*). The neurological reason for handedness, not being a function of hemispheric dominance, remains unknown.

Intelligence is often referred to, but is ill defined. Using all measures of intelligence to date, it has been determined that brain size correlates poorly to intelligence. Case studies of Einstein's brain have revealed some interesting findings of specific regions being larger, but these data are far from conclusive. Some researchers believe there are numerous categories of intelligence, including not only mathematical and verbal skills, but also navigation and social skills, among others. Most researchers agree that intelligence may be measured in terms of *convergent thinking* and *divergent thinking*. In general terms, convergent thinking refers to the ability to generate a single answer to a specific question (such as mathematical solutions), whereas divergent thinking requires generating numerous possible answers to a single question (such as determining all the possible ways to get a high score on your final exam). In terms of these types of intelligence, damage to the parietal lobes results in disruption of convergent thought. Divergent thought processes, on the other hand, are selectively disrupted with damage to the frontal lobes. Regardless of how intelligence is categorized or subdivided, there appear to be both genetic and environmental contributions to the neural basis for intellectual thought.

The concept of consciousness, or awareness of our mental capacities, is likely a collection of processes including sensory perception, thought, emotion, language, and so on. Research suggests that some perception occurs at a level below consciousness. Some neurological disorders also emphasize this point. Previous chapters have described blindsight, agnosias, and implicit learning in amnesia. These disorders illustrate that perception and even learning can occur without conscious knowledge. On the other hand, it appears consciousness may be stimulated without appropriate perception. This is a more difficult concept, but consider visual hallucinations as an example. In this case there is conscious perception of a nonexistent stimulus. In other words, the nervous system is responsible for both unconscious and conscious thought, and these processes (though intimately linked) are controlled separately.

# KEY TERMS

*The following is a list of important terms introduced in Chapter 14. Give the definition of each term in the space provided.*

### Characteristics of Thinking

Constructs

Syntax

### Association Cortex

Spatial cognition

Attention

Neglect

Extinction

Planning

### Studying Brain and Cognition

Neuropsychology

Magnetoencephalogram (MEG)

Magnetic resonance imaging (MRI)

Functional MRI (fMRI)

Transcranial magnetic stimulation (TMS)

Cognitive neuroscience

*Cerebral Asymmetry*

Apraxia

Split brain

*Cognitive Organization*

Anomalous speech representation

Synesthesia

*Intelligence*

Convergent thinking

Divergent thinking

Consciousness

# PRACTICE TEST

# Multiple-Choice Questions

*Answer each of the following multiple-choice questions with the best possible answer based on information from your text.*

1. In the mammalian brain, which structure is considered to hold the many systems required for higher-level thinking?
   A. Brainstem
   B. Basal ganglia
   C. Hippocampus
   D. Thalamus
   E. None of the above

2. Which of the following best describes a construct as defined in your text?
   A. An element of genetic coding required for thought
   B. An element of a neuron required for thought
   C. A system of neurons within a brain structure required for thought
   D. A brain structure required for thought
   E. A mental process that cannot be seen but inferred to exist as a basis for thought

3. More important for human thought than words is the process of being able to string together words into grammar. What is another term for this process?
   A. Ambulating
   B. Syntax
   C. Cognition
   D. Constructing
   E. Language

4. The process of stringing together words to create language is likely one of the most prevalent features of advanced thought in humans. Language, however, is not the only example of our tendency to combine behaviors into complex outputs. Which of the following represents another example of this ability?
   A. Composing music
   B. Creating rules for games
   C. Choreographing dances
   D. Producing movies
   E. All of the above

5. Information sent to the association cortex may be thought of as which of the following?
   A. Direct from sensory systems
   B. Direct from motor systems
   C. Highly fragmented
   D. Highly processed by other brain structures
   E. Having little consequence on thought

6.  Attention is essential for proper cognitive functioning. What happens in individuals who suffer damage to parietal association cortex in one hemisphere that disrupts attention.
    A.  They may exhibit unilateral neglect
    B.  They may fail to dress one side of their body
    C.  They may not see objects presented in half of their visual field
    D.  They may fail to respond to commands to move the limbs on one side of the body
    E.  All of the above

7.  The Wisconsin Card Sorting Task is an excellent screening tool for damage to which of the following regions?
    A.  Parietal lobe damage
    B.  Frontal lobe damage
    C.  Spinal damage
    D.  Visual inattention
    E.  Hippocampal damage

8.  Although mirror neurons have been found in both monkeys and humans, one fundamental difference between the two is that these neurons are . . .
    A.  larger in humans
    B.  smaller in humans
    C.  localized to the left hemisphere in humans
    D.  localized to the right hemisphere in humans
    E.  found in all lobes of the brain in humans

9.  MRI has become a very useful research tool for those studying cognition in the human brain. What does MRI stand for?
    A.  Metabolic Resistance Imaging
    B.  Metabolic Resolution Imaging
    C.  Metabolic Reaction Imaging
    D.  Metabolic Resonance Imaging
    E.  None of the above

10. MRI techniques are especially useful when assessing increased metabolism in regions that become active during particular behaviors. Which of the following alters properties of the blood allowing the MRI to indicate increased metabolism?
    A.  Change in oxygen content
    B.  Change in hydrogen content
    C.  Change in carbon dioxide content
    D.  Change in temperature
    E.  Change in pressure

11. What is the primary use for the technique of transcranial magnetic stimulation (TMS)?
    A.  It is used to activate deep brain structures
    B.  It is used to activate structures in the cortex
    C.  It is used to disrupt function of deep brain structures
    D.  It is used to disrupt function of structures in the cortex
    E.  None of the above

12. The most likely reason that the sensorimotor cortex representing the face in the left hemisphere is larger than the same region in the right hemisphere is that it is responsible for . . .
    A. language interpretation
    B. language production
    C. expression of emotions
    D. spatial representation
    E. All of the above

13. Which of the following statements is true of hemispheric asymmetry?
    A. It is apparent only in humans
    B. It is apparent only in humans and some higher-order primates
    C. It is apparent only in humans and all other primates
    D. It is apparent in most animals with the exception of birds
    E. It is apparent in most animals including many species of birds

14. According to research results from the Kimura lab, which ear should you turn toward your professor during a lecture and which ear should you turn toward the jukebox at the bar?
    A. Right ear toward professor, left ear toward jukebox
    B. Left ear toward professor, right ear toward jukebox
    C. Left ear toward both professor and jukebox
    D. Right ear toward both professor and jukebox
    E. Kimura found no difference in ear preference for language and music

15. Split-brain individuals provide a unique opportunity to assess independent functioning of the two hemispheres. What is the name of the structure that is severed to produce these individuals?
    A. Thalamus
    B. Hypothalamus
    C. Basal ganglia
    D. Frontal cortex
    E. None of the above

16. Which of the following appears to be the most likely contributing factor to development of superior verbal fluency in females when compared to males?
    A. Lack of testosterone during fetal development
    B. Presence of estrogen during fetal development
    C. Influence of estrogen at puberty
    D. Social influences during childhood
    E. None of the above

17. A person with anomalous speech representation . . .
    A. has a speech center in the left hemisphere
    B. has a speech center in the right hemisphere
    C. is more likely to be left-handed than right-handed
    D. all of the above
    E. none of the above

18. In the 1920s, Charles Spearman proposed that differences in brain architecture could result in the capacity for high or low "g" intelligence. What does the "g" stand for?
    A. General
    B. Gonadal
    C. Geographical
    D. Group
    E. Geometric

19. Hebb proposed that all individuals have two forms of intelligence. Intelligence A is innate potential. Intelligence B is intelligence that may be influenced by which of the following?
    A. Disease
    B. Injury
    C. Experience
    D. Exposure to toxins
    E. All of the above

20. Regarding consciousness, it is possible to perceive stimuli without being consciously aware of that perception. In this text you have read about several disorders with symptoms that include lack of conscious awareness of stimuli. Which of the following is *not* an appropriate example of a disorder that results in this phenomenon?
    A. Blindsight
    B. Form agnosia
    C. Implicit learning in amnesia
    D. Visual neglect
    E. Phantom-limb pain

## Short Answer Questions

*Answer each of the following questions with a brief but complete written answer based on information from your text.*

1. Briefly explain what the term *cognition* means and how cognition relates to thought.

2.  Much of the information in this chapter suggests that stringing together sequences of behaviors is a high-level approach to thinking. Give a brief example of how successfully stringing together behavioral output could be advantageous to survival of an animal.

3.  The frontal lobe is thought to be essential for temporal organization of behavior. Briefly explain what is meant by temporal organization, including a simple example.

4.  Briefly explain when "mirror neurons" fire and the proposed function of these cells.

5.  Describe the basic difference in research methods used in the field of neuropsychology compared to the field of cognitive neuroscience.

6.  Briefly explain what is meant by the terms *anatomical asymmetry* and *functional asymmetry*. Give a simple example of each.

7.  If a split-brain person were exposed to a coffee mug in their left visual field and then asked to identify the object, they would reply that they had not seen an object. However, if allowed to select the object they had just seen from a group of objects, they would accurately choose the coffee mug. Briefly explain the neurological basis for this phenomenon.

8. Briefly describe the phenomenon of synesthesia.

9. Briefly explain what is meant by convergent thinking and divergent thinking. Give a brief example of each.

10. Given the example of professional athletes being capable of responding to a ball moving too fast for conscious tracking and perception, it is accurate to say that humans are capable of thinking at an unconscious level. Give an example of a neurological disorder in which unconscious learning or perception occurs as a result of the disorder. Briefly describe the unconscious process seen in the disorder.

# Matching Questions

*Complete each of the following matching questions based on information from your text.*

1. Match the following techniques with the appropriate description or feature.

   A. MRI
   B. fMRI
   C. SQUID
   D. TMS

   ___ Creates images showing blood-flow changes in the brain
   ___ Used to disrupt regional blood flow and associated behaviors
   ___ Used to record magnetic fields and produce MEG
   ___ Utilizes magnetic fields and radio pulses to produce brain images

2. Match the following brain regions with the most appropriate cognitive function.

   A. Left hemisphere
   B. Right hemisphere
   C. Frontal lobe

   ___ Map reading
   ___ Language production
   ___ Temporal planning
   ___ Music appreciation
   ___ Language comprehension

3. Identify each of the following as being associated with convergent thinking (CT) or divergent thinking (DT).

   ___ Disrupted particularly by frontal-lobe damage
   ___ Measured with traditional intelligence tests
   ___ Solving arithmetic problems or defining words
   ___ Used to generate numerous answers for a single question
   ___ Disruption is often associated with apraxia or aphasia

4. Match the following neurological phenomena with the appropriate feature or description.

   A. Split brain
   B. Apraxia
   C. Frontal-lobe damage
   D. Synesthesia
   E. Neglect

   ___ Ignoring sensory information, usually on one side of the body
   ___ Inability to make voluntary movements
   ___ Causes difficulty with the Wisconsin Card Sorting task
   ___ Caused by damage to the corpus callosum
   ___ Joining sensory experiences across sensory modalities

5. Match each of the following terms with their appropriate description or definition.

   A. Construct
   B. Syntax
   C. Spatial cognition
   D. Extinction
   E. Planning

   ___ Pattern or structure of word order in a phrase
   ___ The temporal organization of behavior
   ___ Idea resulting from a set of impressions
   ___ A form of neglect
   ___ Term for a wide range of mental abilities

# Diagrams

1. Label the following regions of the primary association cortex on the diagram below: Primary motor, Primary sensory, Primary visual, Primary auditory.

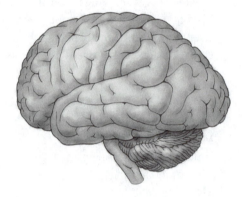

2. Below are diagrams of two individuals, each with a severed corpus callosum. Indicate the appropriate neural pathway taken by incoming visual information for each individual. Also indicate which individual will respond correctly when asked to name the object flashed on the screen in front of them.

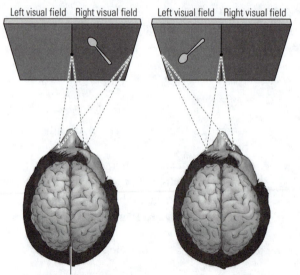

3.  Which of the following best represents a comparison of neurons from the prefrontal region between male and female rats that had their gonads or ovaries removed at birth?

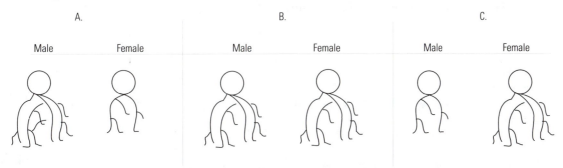

4.  Which of the following would have the most difficulty with the task of drawing the figure below?
    A.  Split-brain person using left hand.
    B.  Split-brain person using right hand.
    C.  Person with intact brain using right hand.
    D.  Person with intact brain using left hand.

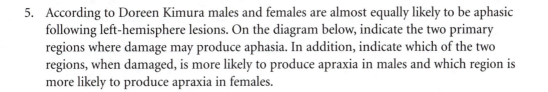

5.  According to Doreen Kimura males and females are almost equally likely to be aphasic following left-hemisphere lesions. On the diagram below, indicate the two primary regions where damage may produce aphasia. In addition, indicate which of the two regions, when damaged, is more likely to produce apraxia in males and which region is more likely to produce apraxia in females.

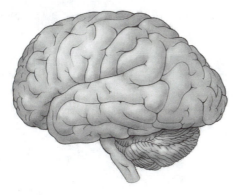

# CD-ROM Exercises

1.  Visit module CNS2 of your CD to review lobes of the cortex. Note that somatosensory cortex and motor cortex are adjacent regions. Also note the central location of the thalamus.

2.  Visit modules RM8 and RM9 of your CD to review the methods of PET and MRI. Note the differences in these techniques and try to imagine the advantages of one technique over the other in diagnosing the source of brain dysfunction.

3. Visit module CNS1 of your CD to review information on regions of the brain associated with language. Note the asymmetry of language centers. Also note connections between language structure required for this intricate behavior.

## The Web

*Consider using the following Web sites for additional information on some of the topics from this chapter:*

1. Cognitive Neuroscience Society: www.dartmouth.edu/~cns/

2. Nice split-brain site link: www.macalester.edu/~psych/whathap/UBNRP/UBNRP.html

3. Synesthesia and the synesthesic experience:
   web.mit.edu/synesthesia/www/synesthesia.html

4. Psychiatric Neuroimaging Group: pni.unibe.ch/

5. Apraxia Kids: www.apraxia-kids.org/

   The easiest way to get to these sites is to link to them through the student Web site at www.worthpublishers.com. This site also has further study aids and practice quizzes.

# CROSSWORD PUZZLE

**Across**

1. Common lab animal used for research
3. Study of the neural basis of 29 across is often called cognitive _____
7. Frontal association cortex is particularly necessary for this aspect of thought
10. Instead of doing this puzzle, I bet you'd rather be on laying beach getting one of these
12. What a lab rat does when it's tired of standing
14. Most emotions are expressed in this region
15. 2nd of 3 words in magnetic technique
16. Magnetoencephalogram; abbr.
17. Inability to make voluntary movements, when not paralyzed that is.
19. Like music, the right hemisphere also appreciates this stimulus
21. Technique from 16 & 32 across; abbr.
23. An idea resulting from a set of impressions
25. Common term for result of cutting the corpus callosum with 31 down
26. Prefix meaning "three"

29. Word used to describe the process required for thought
30. Medial forebrain bundle; abbr.
32. 3rd of 3 words in magnetic technique
34. Frontal association cortex is particularly necessary for this aspect of thought too.
35. A condition where a person ignores sensory information.

**Down**

1. After this semester you could probably use a little R&R (_____ and relaxation)
2. First word in 8 down abbr.
4. To examine again, as in giving a cognitive task a second time
5. Type of thinking used to define terms or solve math problems
6. Long-term unconscious state where higher level thought and function does not occur
8. Technique where magnet is placed next to skull to disrupt neural processes; abbr.
9. Fancy term for hearing colors
11. Term for patterns and structure used for words in human language

13. If you have a question _____ your professor for help
16. Impulses used for 8 down and 21 across
18. Mental construct that is hard to determine, though the IQ test tries.
20. Word added to the beginning of 21 across when used for real-time research
22. Term for 35 across when it occurs simultaneously with a competing stimuli

23. Word for outer brain layer, with association
24. Active word form for "thought"
27. Factor that will eventually slow the thought process in us all
28. 20 down and 21 across; abbr.
31. See 25 across for first word
33. Choking reflex that does not require thought

# What Have We Learned and What Is Its Value?

## CHAPTER SUMMARY

In this final chapter we review the concepts of *brain* and *behavior* as they were presented throughout the text. To begin, we learned that the brain has evolved as an organ that creates a representation of the external world and produces behavior in response to the world. The success of the human species suggests that the brain has evolved into a highly functional organ. In examining the anatomy and physiology of the brain, we learned that the neuron is the basic unit of all function, and that the synapse is the key site of communication between neurons. The synapse also appears to be the key site of learning and memory. Regarding development of the nervous system, we learned that both genetics and experience contribute to structure and function of the system. Furthermore, the state of *consciousness* emerges as a means of organizing information entering the brain, *knowledge* created by the brain, and behavior produced by the brain. Examining specific behavioral functions, it became apparent that localized regions of the brain control specific functions. Part of this organization is the subdivision of sensory information into pathways used for producing action (e.g., movement) and for producing knowledge (e.g., object recognition). In most respects, the brain is symmetrical, with similar structures controlling similar functions in both hemispheres. In some cases, however, aspects of behavior may actually be localized to a specific hemisphere, a phenomenon known as functional asymmetry.

The physiological basis for all neural function is a combination of excitation and inhibition. Neurons may excite or inhibit other neurons. Structures may excite or inhibit other structures. Brain regions may excite or inhibit particular behaviors. Adding to the nearly infinite possibilities of brain development and function, we learned about plasticity in the nervous system. Plasticity refers to the finding that brain structure and function may be influenced through fetal development, and throughout life, by both internal and external experiences. Although behavior produced by the brain is thought of as a means of enhancing survival, we learned that animals may engage in behavior for numerous other reasons. In fact, behavior sometimes appears to result simply as a means of producing stimulation for the brain. Abnormalities in brain structure and function may result in abnormal behavior. Such brain abnormalities may be structural, biochemical, or functional. The results of abnormalities may range from minor (minor movement or memory impairment) to fatal (degenerative brain diseases). Taken together this information shows that the study of brain and behavior cannot be considered a single discipline; rather, this very broad area of study is *multidisciplinary*, encompassing many theories, techniques, and fields of study.

One of the most intriguing areas of research is assessing disorders of brain and behavior. This area is particularly interesting because of the difficulty in identifying causes of, and developing treatments for, these disorders. As an example of a treatable disease, *phenylketonuria (PKU)* has a known genetic basis that results in a deficiency, but can be circumvented by dietary restrictions during a critical period of neural development. Most disorders, however, are far less well understood. Even those disorders for which treatments are now readily prescribed (e.g., antidepressants, antipsychotics, anxiolytics) are not necessarily well understood. As a result, many pharmacological treatments affect numerous neural systems in addition to the system they are intended to stabilize, often resulting in incomplete treatment and side effects.

The first step in effective *treatment* is the ability to *identify* and *classify* disorders. The *ICD-10* and *DSM-4* are examples of texts designed to help unify diagnosis among researchers and physicians. These documents, however, are subject to ever-changing criteria resulting from advances in research or even changes in social perspective on behavior. Furthermore, although these diagnostic manuals may identify characteristics of disorders, they contribute less significantly to understanding causes of abnormal behavior. Lack of a clear understanding of causes is due in large part to the range of possible contributing sources. These sources include abnormal anatomy, chemistry, physiology, and genetics. Any combination of these sources may also interact with the environment, creating a very wide range of potential contributing factors.

*Schizophrenia* and *affective disorders* provide two examples of behavioral disorders with a range of potential causes. Because evidence suggests significantly different factors may contribute to schizophrenia, this disorder has been subdivided into two major categories. Type I schizophrenia, marked by positive symptoms such as agitated movements and hallucinations, is thought to result primarily from dopamine dysfunction. Type II schizophrenia, marked by negative symptoms such as poor cognition and lack of response to antipsychotic drugs, is thought to result from brain abnormalities, including cortical atrophy. Some researchers believe that type II schizophrenia may simply be a more extreme form of type I. In addition, researchers have recently identified a variety of neurotransmitter abnormalities (in addition to dopamine) that may contribute to the disorder.

*Affective disorders*, such as *depression*, *mania*, and *bipolar disorder*, also appear to have numerous potential causes. For example, although low concentrations of serotonin and norepinephrine have been implicated in depression, when these neurotransmitters are lowered in normal individuals they do not report depression symptoms. It is also unclear why immediate elevation of these transmitters does not reduce symptoms in depressed individuals. These findings clearly suggest that the neuropathology of schizophrenia and affective disorders may include many factors.

Treatments for neurological disorders can be broadly *categorized* into three separate areas. *Neurosurgical treatment* involves physical manipulation of brain structures, usually in the form of brain or spinal surgery. Neurosurgery represents the most invasive form of treatment and is generally reserved for relatively severe dysfunction that is not treatable by other means. Although most useful for removing foreign matter (i.e., tumors), this form of treatment has also been successful in reducing some symptoms of neurological disease, such as seizures or tremor associated with Parkinson's disease. *Pharmacological treatments* involve use of drugs to alter synaptic functioning. Far less invasive than neurosurgery, this has become the treatment of choice for a variety of behavioral disorders. However, lack of drug specificity and resulting side effects make this course of treatment far from perfect. *Behavioral treatment* represents the third and least invasive category of treatment. Although generally thought of in terms of physical therapy, recent research suggests that cognitive and emotional therapies may be useful as well. Some forms of emotional therapy have roots in *psychotherapy*, pioneered by Freud. In general terms, Freud felt that emotional balance was best gained through the process of psychotherapy. In some regards, this theory appears to be validated by the findings that some forms of physical therapy are enhanced when combined with psychological therapy.

## KEY TERMS

*The following is a list of important terms introduced in Chapter 15. Give the definition of each term in the space provided.*

### Concepts of Brain and Behavior

Brain

Behavior

Knowledge

Categorize

Consciousness

Multidisciplinary

### Disorders of Brain and Behavior

Phenylketonuria (PKU)

Identify

Classify

International Classification of Disease (ICD)

Diagnostic and Statistical Manual (DSM)

Treatments

Neurosurgical treatment

Pharmacological treatment

Behavioral treatment

Anxiolytics

Valium

Atypical drugs

Prozac

Psychotherapy

Cognitive therapy

# PRACTICE TEST

# Multiple-Choice Questions

*Answer each of the following multiple-choice questions with the best possible answer based on information from your text.*

1. Which of the following animals is capable of using sensory perception to create the most "correct" representation of the external world?
   A. Bats
   B. Dogs
   C. Chimpanzees
   D. Humans
   E. None of the above

2. Which of the following is the most accurate statement regarding the anatomy of neurons across species?
   A. Neurons are most complex in mammals.
   B. Neurons are most complex in birds.
   C. Neurons are most complex in large animals.
   D. Neurons are remarkably similar across species.
   E. Neurons are remarkably different across species.

3. Events as dissimilar as learning and drug addiction actually share which common feature?
   A. They are both associated with changes in receptor or synaptic number.
   B. They both occur in all humans at some time throughout life.
   C. They both occur in all species of animals at some time throughout life.
   D. Only primates have a neural system capable of these two behaviors.
   E. Only humans have a neural system capable of these two behaviors.

4. Although the developmental stages are initiated by genetic instructions, the details of development may be strongly influenced by which of the following?
   A. Hormones
   B. Disease
   C. Injury
   D. Experiences
   E. All of the above

5. An interaction between genes and the environment on nervous system structure and function occurs . . .
   A. in the first trimester of fetal development
   B. throughout fetal development
   C. throughout fetal development and infancy
   D. until puberty
   E. throughout life

6. Which of the following is not true of consciousness or the conscious thought process?
   A. It provides an adaptive advantage when a large amount of information is processed.
   B. It helps to decide behavior in some situations.
   C. In some cases it appears to use pathways separate from unconscious thought.
   D. It is generally processed more rapidly than unconscious thought.
   E. Humans are capable of both conscious and unconscious thought processes.

7. Among the primary difficulties of localizing behaviors to brain structures is . . .
   A. difficulty defining some behaviors
   B. the fact that some behaviors consist of more than one specific aspect of that behavior
   C. that research has shown that more than one structure may mediate a single behavior
   D. that even extensive lesions may not eliminate all aspects of a particular behavior
   E. all of the above

8. In a more abstract sense of brain function than that proposed in the Law of Bell and Magendie, it could be said that each sensory modality has a separate system for action and . . .
   A. reaction
   B. nonaction
   C. reflex
   D. knowledge
   E. all of the above

9. Regarding the emphasis put on lateralization, it is worth noting that _____ functions are undertaken by both sides of the brain.
   A. no
   B. only one or two
   C. few
   D. many
   E. all

10. Which of the following is the most accurate statement regarding cell inhibition?
    A. Cell inhibition may only increase a behavior.
    B. Cell inhibition may only decrease a behavior.
    C. Cell inhibition may increase or decrease a behavior.
    D. Cell inhibition does not influence behavior.
    E. Cell inhibition increases behavior in all animals except humans.

11. Behaviors such as the tremor associated with Parkinson's disease or the hallucinations associated with schizophrenia are most likely due to _____ input.
    A. excessive excitatory
    B. loss of excitatory
    C. formation of new excitatory
    D. loss of inhibitory
    E. loss of both excitatory and inhibitory

12. Brain plasticity is seen in neurons constantly changing in response to experience. This plasticity is best reflected in our ability to do which of the following?
    A. Increase monosynaptic reflexes
    B. Increase spinal reflexes
    C. Increase emotional expression
    D. Increase movement
    E. Increase learning and memory

13. Neural plasticity is restricted in part by sensory boundaries. In simple terms this means that loss of visual system input may not be assumed by which of the following?
    A. Auditory system
    B. Somatosensory system
    C. Gustatory (taste) system
    D. Olfaction (smell) system
    E. Any of the above

14. In which case might the forebrain override a lower brain drive to engage in feeding behavior?
    A. If the food were located in a particularly dangerous place
    B. If the animal were overweight
    C. If the food were not sweet
    D. If no water were available with the food
    E. If there was only a very small portion of food available

15. For which of the following disorders have researchers developed the most effective treatment?
    A. Depression
    B. Schizophrenia
    C. Bipolar disorder
    D. Mania
    E. PKU

16. Which of the following has been implicated as a contributing factor in the development of schizophrenia?
    A. Dopaminergic dysfunction
    B. Frontal cortex atrophy
    C. Glutamate abnormalities
    D. GABA abnormalities
    E. All of the above

17. Which of the following is categorized as an affective disorder?
    A. Depression
    B. Mania
    C. Bipolar disorder
    D. All of the above
    E. None of the above

18. The American Psychiatric Association developed which of the following as a guide for diagnosing psychiatric disorders?
    A. Diagnostic and Statistical Manual (DSM)
    B. Physician Desk Reference (PDR)
    C. Minnesota Multiphasic Personality Inventory (MMPI)
    D. International Classification of Disease (ICD)
    E. All of the above

19. Fetal cell implants had limited success as a neurosurgical treatment to reverse symptoms of degenerative diseases. However, new hopes have arisen from recent results of brain implants of cells taken from which of the following sources?
    A.  Pigs
    B.  Monkeys
    C.  Adrenal gland tissue
    D.  Bone marrow
    E.  Tumor cell lines

20. Aspects of psychotherapy pioneered by Freud still have a use in behavioral therapy today. Which type of disturbances are most responsive to this type of therapy?
    A.  Cognitive
    B.  Language
    C.  Emotional
    D.  Memory
    E.  None of the above

## Short Answer Questions

*Answer each of the following questions with a brief but complete written answer based on information from your text.*

1.  "Development is not governed by a strict genetic code." Briefly explain this statement taken from your text.

2.  "A fundamental difficulty in localizing functions begins with the problem of defining what a function might be." Choose a behavior and briefly explain this statement in the context of that behavior.

3. One significant problem with identifying behavioral disorders is the tendency to selectively notice and report symptoms. As an example, explain how selective reporting might occur when someone believes a patient has Alzheimer's disease.

4. According to your text, the brain is plastic in two fundamental ways. Briefly describe these two types of plasticity.

5. Patients with Parkinson's disease typically do not show any behavioral symptoms until well over half of their nigrostriatal dopamine neurons have degenerated. Why are symptoms not evident sooner, say after 25 percent degeneration, in these patients?

6. In this chapter you read that just because a drug produces improvement in symptoms, this does not mean that the drug is acting on a central biochemical aspect of pathology. Explain this statement, considering a drug that is capable of reducing tremor in Parkinson's disease.

7. In an earlier version of the DMS classification scheme of psychiatric disorders, homosexuality was listed. Explain why homosexuality is not listed in the most recent edition of the DMS.

8. Explain how a lesion or a stimulating brain electrode might be used as a neurosurgical treatment for a human brain disorder. Use Parkinson's disease for your example.

9.  Explain the term *magic bullet* as it is used in the study of pharmacological treatments for brain damage. Is L-dopa a magic bullet for Parkinson's disease? Explain your answer.

10. Although this text has emphasized biological aspects of behavior, therapies such as psychotherapy pioneered by Freud are still used effectively in treating some aspects of brain damage. Give an example of the type of behavioral deficit due to brain damage that might be effectively treated by psychotherapy.

# Matching Questions

*Complete each of the following matching questions based on information from your text.*

1.  The basis for PKU has been well established across many disciplines. As such this disorder may be effectively treated. Match the following disciplines with their respective findings of PKU.

    A.  Genetics          ____ Impairment in hydroxylation of phenylalanine to tyrosine
    B.  Biochemistry      ____ IQ score of less than 50, in 95 percent of patients
    C.  Histology         ____ Decreased neuron size, dendritic length, and spine density
    D.  Neurology         ____ Mental retardation, abnormal EEG
    E.  Behavior          ____ Inborn error of metabolism due to defective recessive gene

2. Match the following disorders to the most appropriate behavioral feature.

   A. Depression             ___ Hallucinations and agitated movements
   B. Bipolar disorder      ___ Severe behavioral deficits
   C. Mania                 ___ Characterized by excessive euphoria
   D. Schizophrenia type I    ___ Dysfunction of norepinephrine and serotonin
   E. Schizophrenia type II   ___ Little is known about underlying neurobiology

3. Match the following disorders to the appropriate cause or description.

   A. Tay-Sach's disease     ___ Poor nutrition
   B. Schizophrenia         ___ Infection
   C. Encephalitis           ___ Hormonal anomaly
   D. Korsakoff's disease    ___ Genetic error
   E. Androgenital syndrome   ___ Developmental anomaly

4. Match the following treatment categories with the appropriate term or description.

                              ___ L-dopa
   A. Neurosurgical        ___ Brain lesions
   B. Pharmacological     ___ Psychotherapy
   C. Behavioral           ___ Least invasive
                              ___ Most invasive

5. Match the following drug class to the appropriate feature or description.

                              ___ Anxiolytic
   A. Phenothiazines      ___ Treatment for a serious motor disorder
   B. Valium              ___ Antianxiety drug
   C. L-dopa            ___ Antipsychotic drug
                              ___ Treatment for Parkinson's disease
                              ___ Treatment for schizophrenia

# The Web

*Consider using the following Web sites for additional information on some of the topics from this chapter:*

1. National Alliance for Research on Schizophrenia and Depression: www.mhsource.com/narsad

2. National PKU News: http://205.178.182.34/

3. Manic-Depressive and Depressive Association of Boston: www.mddaboston.org/

4. Functional and Stereotactic Neurosurgery: neurosurgery.mgh.harvard.edu/fnctnlhp.htm

5. Society for Neuroscience: www.sfn.org

The easiest way to get to these sites is to link to them through the student Web site at www.worthpublishers.com/kolb. This site also has further study aids and practice quizzes.

# CROSSWORD PUZZLE

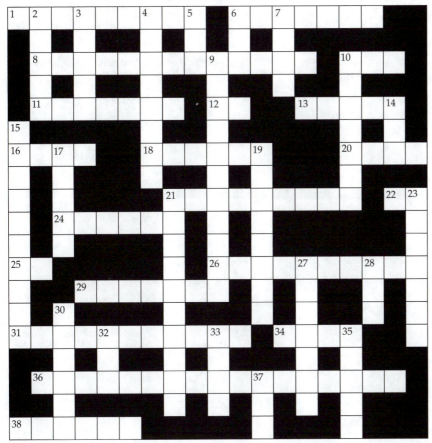

## Across

1. Brains use input to create _____ about the world
6. Term given to a system that is capable of changing
8. The synapse is the key site for _____ between neurons
10. Initials of the author of this study guide
11. This is the primary input used for 1 across
12. Genetic make-up of 3 down
13. Founder of psychotherapy
16. Pavlov, to his friends
18. These are often removed using neurosurgical techniques
20. Parkinson's may cause rigidity in legs and _____
21. Functional _____ refers to behaviors being controlled by one or the other hemisphere
22. Term for taking too much of a drug; abbr.
24. 29 across; singular
25. 4th-year student (hopefully); abbr.
26. Language developed, in part, to help do this with information needed for 1 across
29. Basic unit of the brain (along with glial cells, that is)
31. 14 down and 28 down were designed for this purpose, regarding mental disorders
34. Source for spices, teas, and some pharmacological treatments
36. Encompassing more than one discipline, as in the study of brain and behavior
38. Most popular antianxiety drug of the 1970s

## Down

2. Body parts where brains connect to spinal cords
3. Human adult female
4. Where terminals most often form synapses
5. And so on, and so on; abbr.
6. Brain scanning technique mentioned often in this text
7. The terminal represents the end of this structure
9. Name for class of drugs that reduce anxiety
10. Least invasive type is behavioral
14. Guide that identifies mental disorders, now in its 4th edition; abbr.
15. Word for first letter in 14 down

17. 7 down, plural
19. Meaning "of the same size and shape," as in the brain hemispheres
21. 38 across in one; 9 down singular
23. Parkinson's is one example
27. Basis for some diseases, such as 37 down
28. Guide less well known than 14 down; abbr.
30. Word for the third letter in 14 down

32. Best day of the week for a college student; abbr.
33. Opposite of naughty
35. The organ you've studied throughout this text
37. Disease that causes mental retardation if not treated; abbr.

# Answers

## Chapter 1: What Are the Origins of Brain and Behavior?

**Multiple-Choice Questions**

1. D (p. 3)
2. A (p. 3)
3. B (p. 3)
4. E (p. 4)
5. D (p. 6)
6. C (p. 7)
7. B (p. 8)

8. C (p. 9)
9. C (p. 9)
10. C (p. 10)
11. A (p. 10)
12. E (p. 12)
13. E (p. 15)
14. A (p. 18)

15. C (p. 22)
16. C (p. 23)
17. D (p. 23)
18. D (p. 27)
19. A (p. 29)
20. D (p. 31)

**Short Answer Questions**

1. (p. 5)
2. (p. 7)
3. (p. 9)
4. (p. 10)

5. (p. 12)
6. (p. 19)
7. (p. 25)
8. (p. 27)

9. (p. 29)
10. (p. 32)

**Matching**

1.

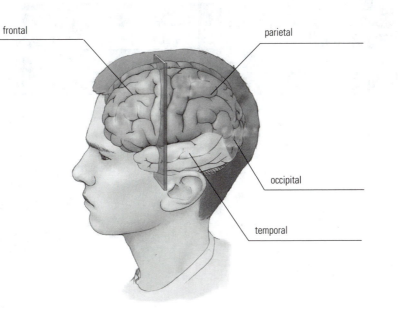

frontal
parietal
occipital
temporal

2. _E_ materialism  
   _D_ animal instincts  
   _C_ dualism  
   _A_ genes  
   _B_ mentalism  

4. _1_ Rat  
   _5_ Homo sapiens  
   _2_ Elephant  
   _3_ Chimpanzee  
   _4_ Dolphin  

3. _D_ Most recently evolved species  
   _C_ Co-existed with early modern-day humans  
   _A_ First to walk upright  
   _B_ Known for their use of tools  

## Crossword Puzzle

```
¹B E ²H A V I O R     ³N A T U R A L ⁴A L
R     E               ⁵C             P
A   ⁶M O T O R         U     ⁷H   ⁸G E N E
I     I               L       O     Y
N     S               ⁹T E M P O R A L   I
¹⁰S A P I E ¹¹N S       U     I         I
    H       E         R       N       ¹²F
¹³G E N E S   T       ¹⁴H E M I S ¹⁵P H E R E
Y       R             D       E       O
R       E   ¹⁶S ¹⁷C N S         R       N
U   ¹⁸P S Y C H E     H         I       T
S           G         ¹⁹O C ²⁰C I P I T A L
            M         R   O   H       L
²¹P R I ²²M A T E     D   O   R
N       E   ²³N E A N D E R T ²⁴H A ²⁵L S
S       N   T     T           A   O   O
        D ²⁶C E R E B ²⁷E L L U M     O   B
²⁸C O R T E X   D     S   Q       O   E
        L
```

# Chapter 2: How Is the Brain Organized?

## Multiple-Choice Questions

1. A (p. 41)
2. C (p. 41)
3. B (p. 41)
4. C (p. 43)
5. C (p. 44)
6. C (p. 47)
7. B (p. 50)

8. E (p. 50)
9. E (p. 51)
10. E (p. 53)
11. B (p. 53)
12. C (p. 54)
13. B (p. 55)
14. E (p. 55)

15. E (p. 57)
16. C (p. 59)
17. A (p. 60)
18. B (p. 62)
19. E (p. 68)
20. B (P. 68)

## Short Answer Questions

1. (p. 40)
2. (p. 44)
3. (p. 53)
4. (p. 54)

5. (p. 55)
6. (p. 59)
7. (p. 62)
8. (p. 68)

9. (p. 70)
10. (p. 72)

## Matching

1. _A_ Anterior
   _B_ Posterior
   _F_ Ventral
   _C_ Medial
   _E_ Superior
   _F_ Inferior
   _B_ Caudal
   _A_ Rostral

2. _B_ Peripheral nervous system (PNS)
   _C_ Spinal nervous system
   _A_ Central nervous system (CNS)
   _B_ Internal nervous system

3. _D_ Hypothalamus
   _B_ Ventricles
   _E_ Neocortex
   _C_ Cerebellum
   _A_ Corpus Callosum

4. _1_ Cortex
   _3_ Midbrain
   _2_ Diencephalon
   _4_ Hindbrain

5. _C_ Basal ganglia
   _E_ May affect many regions of the brain
   _D_ Pia mater and Arachnoid layer
   _A_ Limbic system
   _B_ Facial nerves

## Diagrams

1.

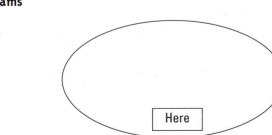

Here

2.

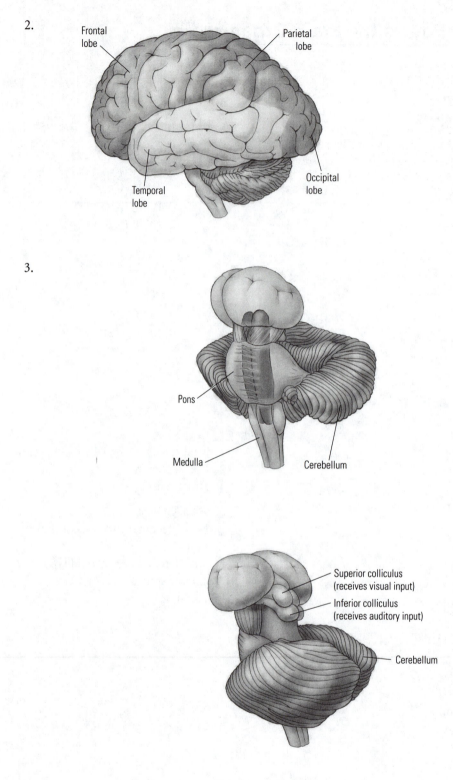

Frontal lobe

Parietal lobe

Occipital lobe

Temporal lobe

3.

Pons

Medulla

Cerebellum

Superior colliculus (receives visual input)

Inferior colliculus (receives auditory input)

Cerebellum

4.

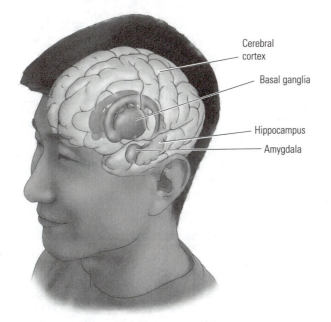

Cerebral cortex

Basal ganglia

Hippocampus

Amygdala

5.

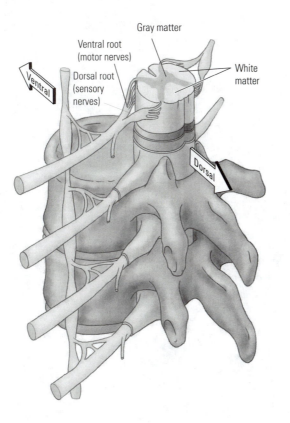

Gray matter

Ventral root
(motor nerves)

Dorsal root
(sensory
nerves)

White
matter

Ventral

Dorsal

6.

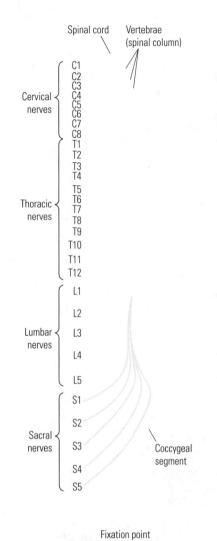

Spinal cord  Vertebrae (spinal column)

Cervical nerves { C1 C2 C3 C4 C5 C6 C7 C8

Thoracic nerves { T1 T2 T3 T4 T5 T6 T7 T8 T9 T10 T11 T12

Lumbar nerves { L1 L2 L3 L4 L5

Sacral nerves { S1 S2 S3 S4 S5

Coccygeal segment

7.

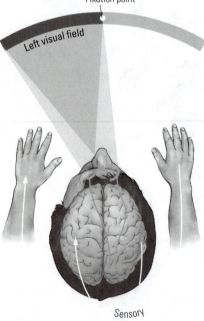

Fixation point

Left visual field

Sensory

Motor

## Crossword Puzzle

Completed answer grid (clue number shown with first letter):

**Across**

- 2. NEOCORTEX
- 6. AMYGDALA
- 8. GLOBUS
- 11. GYRI
- 12. HEMISPHERES
- 14. CAUDATE
- 19. LOBE
- 21. SUBCORTICAL
- 22. BASAL
- 23. CORPUS
- 27. HINDBRAIN
- 28. AXONS
- 29. CONTRALATERAL
- 31. SUBSTANTIA
- 32. DORSAL

**Down**

- 1. LIMBIC
- 3. COLLICULUS
- 4. GANGLIA
- 5. P
- 7. D
- 9. SAGITTAL
- 13. P
- 15. R
- 16. S
- 17. F
- 18. H
- 20. VENTRICLE
- 24. S
- 25. C
- 26. F
- 30. P

# Chapter 3: What Are the Units of Brain Function?

## Multiple-Choice Questions

1. E (p. 79)
2. C (p. 80)
3. D (p. 80)
4. A (p. 82)
5. E (p. 84)
6. D (p. 85)
7. B (p. 87)

8. D (p. 88)
9. C (p. 88)
10. E (p. 92)
11. D (p. 96)
12. E (p. 97)
13. C (p. 98)
14. B (p. 98)

15. E (p. 100)
16. B (p. 102)
17. E (p. 103)
18. D (p. 104)
19. D (p. 105)
20. D (p. 106)

## Short Answer Questions

1. (p. 82)
2. (p. 83)
3. (p. 87)
4. (p. 87)

5. (p. 88)
6. (p. 89)
7. (p. 92)
8. (p. 98)

9. (p. 101)
10. (p. 106)

## Matching

1.  C  soma
    A  terminal
    D  axon
    B  dendrite

2.  F  single short axon and single short
       dendrite
    E  dendrite connected directly to axon

 D  many dendrites extend directly
    from soma
 B  long axon with two sets of dendrites
    extend from soma
 C  many dendritic branches form a fan
    shape
 A  extensive dendrites, large soma,
    long axon to muscle

3.

 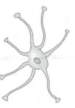   

Ependymal cell   Astroglia (Astrocyte)   Microglial cell   Oligodendroglial cell   Schwann cell

4. _A_ cell membrane
   _C_ endoplasmic reticulum
   _B_ nucleus
   _E_ microtubules
   _D_ Golgi bodies
   _G_ lysosmes
   _F_ mitochondria

5. _B_ caused by recessive allele
   _A_ caused by dominant allele
   _D_ no known genetic contribution
   _C_ caused by additional chromosome

## Diagrams

1.

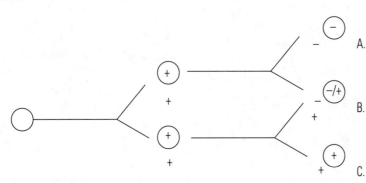

2.

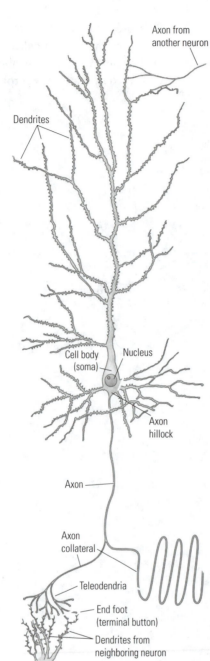

Axon from another neuron

Dendrites

Cell body (soma)    Nucleus

Axon hillock

Axon

Axon collateral

Teleodendria

End foot (terminal button)

Dendrites from neighboring neuron

3.

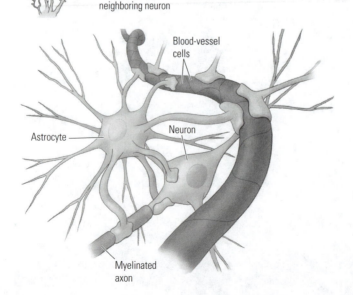

Blood-vessel cells

Astrocyte

Neuron

Myelinated axon

4.

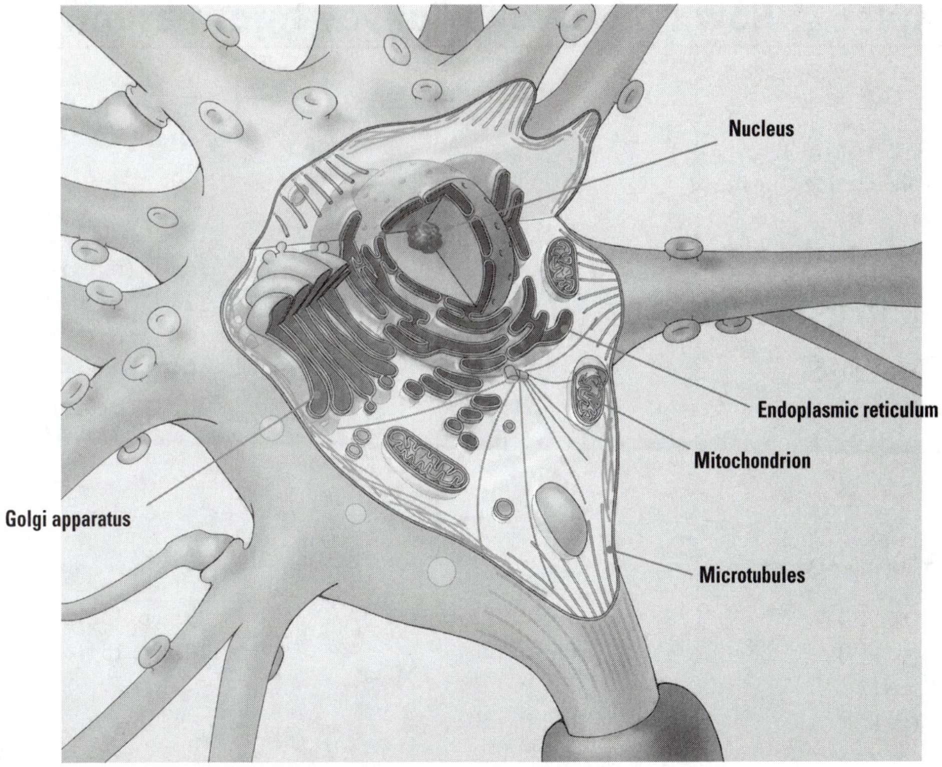
Nucleus
Endoplasmic reticulum
Mitochondrion
Golgi apparatus
Microtubules

5.

| HN + NN | HN + HN | HH + NN | TN + NN | TN + TN | TT + NN |
|---|---|---|---|---|---|
| .5 | .75 | 1.0 | 0.0 | .25 | 0.0 |

## Crossword Puzzle

| | | | | | | | | | | | | | | | | | | |
|---|---|---|---|---|---|---|---|---|---|---|---|---|---|---|---|---|---|---|
| | 1 M | U | L | T | I | 2 P | L | E | | | 3 A | 4 P | | | | | | 5 D |
| | O | | | | | U | | | | | | H | | 6 O | | 7 B | | N |
| | L | | 8 H | O | R | M | O | N | E | | 9 C | E | L | L | | 10 R | N | A |
| 11 S | E | X | | | | P | | | | | | N | | I | | A | | |
| | C | | | 12 M | | | | | | | | O | | 13 G | L | I | A | L |
| 14 H | U | N | T | I | N | 15 G | T | O | N | S | | T | | O | | N | | |
| | L | | | C | | E | | | | | 16 X | Y | | D | | | | 17 I |
| 18 M | E | 19 M | B | R | A | N | E | | 20 S | | | P | | 21 E | N | 22 D | | N |
| R | | E | | O | | E | | | O | | | E | | N | | O | | T |
| N | | N | | T | | | | | M | | 23 P | | | D | | M | | E |
| A | | D | | U | | | | 24 B | A | R | R | I | E | R | | I | | R |
| | 25 W | E | B | B | | | 26 R | | | | O | | | O | | N | | N |
| | | L | | U | | | I | | 27 R | E | T | R | O | G | R | A | D | E |
| | | | | L | | | B | | | | O | | | L | | N | | U |
| 28 D | | | 29 N | E | U | R | O | T | R | 30 A | N | S | M | I | T | T | E | R |
| O | | | O | | | | S | | | X | | | | A | | | | O |
| 31 W | I | L | D | | 32 A | T | O | M | | O | | | | | | 33 I | O | N |
| N | | | E | | | | M | | | 34 N | 35 E | U | R | O | N | | | |
| | | | | 36 G | A | T | E | | | | R | | | | | | | |

# Chapter 4: How Do Neurons Convey Information?

## Multiple-Choice Questions

1. C (p. 116)
2. C (p. 116)
3. B (p. 117)
4. A (p. 118)
5. E (p. 118)
6. E (p. 121)
7. A (p. 121)

8. D (p. 124)
9. E (p. 125)
10. A (p. 125)
11. C (p. 126)
12. C (p. 128)
13. B (p. 129)
14. C (p. 132)

15. A (p. 132)
16. D (p. 133)
17. E (p. 135)
18. D (p. 137)
19. C (p. 141)
20. C (p. 143)

## Short Answer Questions

1. (p. 116)
2. (p. 119)
3. (p. 121)
4. (p. 122)

5. (p. 125)
6. (p. 125)
7. (p. 127)
8. (p. 130)

9. (p. 132)
10. (p. 134)

## Matching

1.  + Postassium
    + Sodium
    + Calcium
    − Chloride
    − Intracellular proteins

2.  I Large negatively charged protein molecules
    I Higher concentration of potassium ions
    E Higher concentration of sodium ions
    I Negative charge
    E Higher concentration of chloride ions

3.  IS Initation of the action potential
    EP Hyperpolarization
    IS Depolarization
    EP Refractory period

4.  B Insensitivity to the chemical messages
    B Autoimmune disorder
    C Produces abnormal EEG
    A Causes degeneration of motor neurons
    C Neurons fire synchronously

5.  B First recording technique developed
    A Activity heard as a beep or pop
    B Records alpha rhythms in relaxed subject
    C Records brain response, discrete stimulus
    C Reports N and P waves

## Diagrams

1.

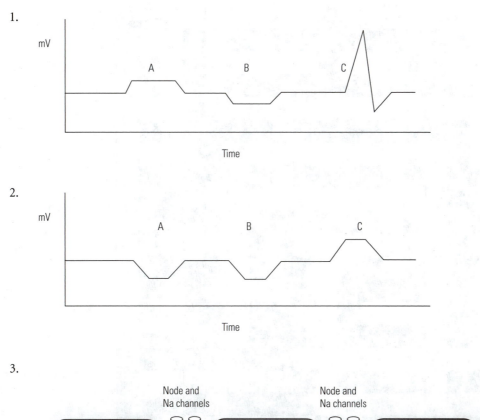

2.

3.

Node and
Na channels

Node and
Na channels

4.  Neuron B

5.

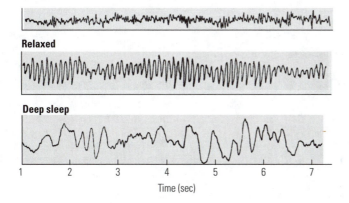

**Alert**

**Relaxed**

**Deep sleep**

Time (sec)

## Crossword Puzzle

| | | | | | | | | | | | | | | | |
|---|---|---|---|---|---|---|---|---|---|---|---|---|---|---|---|
| ¹T | H | ²R | E | S | H | O | L | D | | ³S | C | H | W | ⁴A | ⁵N |
| | | A | | | | | | | | | | | | L | ⁶E | N | ⁷D |
| ⁸N | O | N | E | | ⁹E | E | G | | ¹⁰C | L | A | M | P | G | | E |
| | | V | | | L | | | | | | H | | A | | | P |
| ¹¹O | L | I | G | O | D | E | N | D | R | O | ¹²G | L | I | A | | ¹³T | W | O |
| S | | E | | | | C | | | | | I | | | T | | I | | L |
| C | | R | | ¹⁴P | O | T | E | N | T | I | A | L | ¹⁵S | | | ¹⁶V | I | A |
| I | | | | O | | R | | | | N | | | E | | | E | | R |
| ¹⁷L | A | W | | ¹⁸S | T | I | M | U | L | ¹⁹A | T | I | N | G | | | | I |
| L | | | | T | | C | | | | L | | | S | | | | | Z |
| ²⁰O | N | E | | ²¹S | P | A | T | I | ²²A | L | | | ²³I | P | S | P | | A |
| S | | | | Y | | L | | | B | | | | T | | | | | T |
| C | | ²⁴P | | N | | | | | S | | ²⁵G | L | I | A | | ²⁶E | | I |
| O | | U | | ²⁷A | X | O | N | | O | | | | V | | | R | | O |
| P | | M | | P | | | | | L | | | ²⁸E | ²⁹P | S | P | | | N |
| E | | ³⁰P | O | T | A | S | S | I | U | M | | | A | | | | |
| | | I | | | | | | T | | ³¹R | E | S | T | I | N | G |
| ³²E | L | E | C | T | R | O | D | E | | | | C | | | | |
| | | | | | | ³³R | H | Y | T | H | M | S | | | | |

# Chapter 5: How Do Neurons Communicate?

## Multiple-Choice Questions

1. B (p. 153)
2. B (p. 154)
3. D (p. 157)
4. E (p. 159)
5. D (p. 160)
6. A (p. 162)
7. B (p. 162)

8. C (p. 163)
9. C (p. 164)
10. A (p. 165)
11. C (p. 165)
12. B (p. 166)
13. D (p. 167)
14. E (p. 167)

15. E (p. 171)
16. C (p. 174)
17. C (p. 178)
18. D (p. 179)
19. A (p. 176)
20. D (p. 182)

## Short Answer Questions

1. (p. 158)
2. (p. 160)
3. (p. 160)
4. (p. 163)

5. (p. 167)
6. (p. 169)
7. (p. 170)
8. (p. 172)

9. (p. 178)
10. (p. 176)

## Matching

1.  B  Main excitatory transmitter
    A  Found at neuromuscular junction
    C  Main inhibitory transmitter
    E  Synthesized as a gas
    D  Used for pain reduction

2.  D, B  Depression
    A, B  Schizophrenia
    A     Drug abuse
    A     Parkinson's disease
    C     Alzheimer's disease
    D     Manic behavior

3.  C  identified in California in the 1980s
    B  result of severe influenza
    A  idiopathic
    C  result of MPTP
    A  disease of aging

4.  I  Binding site attached directly to
       membrane pore
    M  Changes cell activity through a
       series of steps
    M  Associated with G-proteins
    I  Mediates rapid changes in mem-
       brane voltage
    I  Structurally similar to voltage-sen-
       sitive channel
    M  Often utilizes second messenger
       systems

5.  P  Rest and digest
    S  Heart rate increase
    P  Cholinergic neurons
    S  Adrenergic neurons
    S  Fight or flight

**Diagrams**

1.

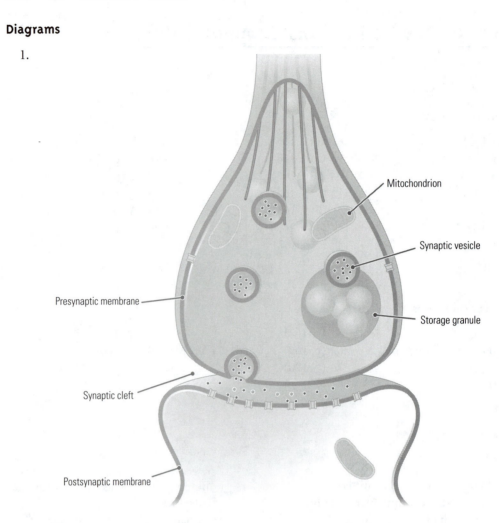

Mitochondrion

Synaptic vesicle

Presynaptic membrane

Storage granule

Synaptic cleft

Postsynaptic membrane

2.

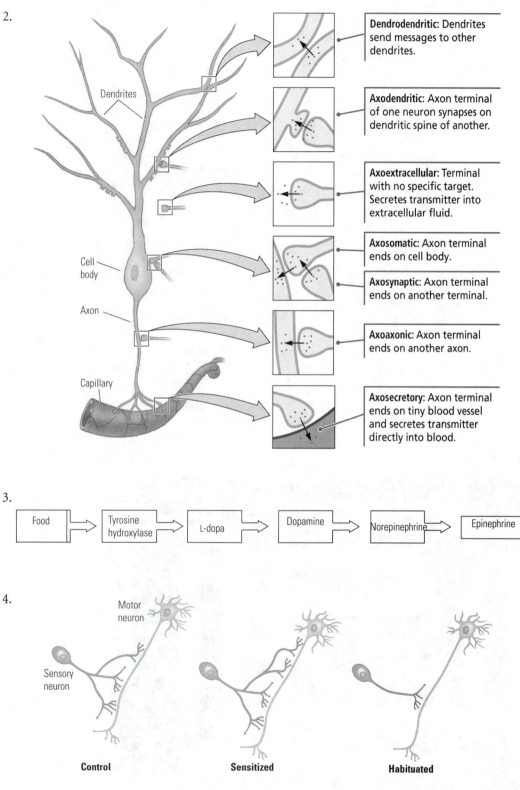

**Dendrodendritic:** Dendrites send messages to other dendrites.

**Axodendritic:** Axon terminal of one neuron synapses on dendritic spine of another.

**Axoextracellular:** Terminal with no specific target. Secretes transmitter into extracellular fluid.

**Axosomatic:** Axon terminal ends on cell body.

**Axosynaptic:** Axon terminal ends on another terminal.

**Axoaxonic:** Axon terminal ends on another axon.

**Axosecretory:** Axon terminal ends on tiny blood vessel and secretes transmitter directly into blood.

Dendrites

Cell body

Axon

Capillary

3.

Food → Tyrosine hydroxylase → L-dopa → Dopamine → Norepinephrine → Epinephrine

4.

Motor neuron

Sensory neuron

**Control**　　　**Sensitized**　　　**Habituated**

5.

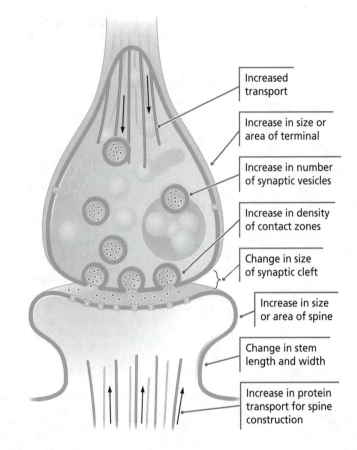

Increased transport

Increase in size or area of terminal

Increase in number of synaptic vesicles

Increase in density of contact zones

Change in size of synaptic cleft

Increase in size or area of spine

Change in stem length and width

Increase in protein transport for spine construction

## Crossword Puzzle

| | | | | | | | | 1 B | | 2 D | | | 3 L | E | U | | 4 E |
|---|---|---|---|---|---|---|---|---|---|---|---|---|---|---|---|---|---|
| | | 5 C | A | R | B | O | 6 N | E | | T | | | T | | | | N |
| 7 R | | A | | | | | E | T | | P | | 8 S | E | 9 C | O | N | D |
| 10 E | R | | | 11 G | L | U | T | A | M | A | T | E | | H | | | O |
| T | | 12 T | | | R | | | M | | N | | E | | E | | | R |
| R | | R | 13 E | N | D | O | R | P | H | I | N | S | | M | | | P |
| O | | E | P | | T | | | N | | S | | I | | I | | | H |
| G | | M | | | R | | 14 C | L | E | F | T | | | C | | | I |
| R | | O | 15 G | A | B | A | O | | | T | | I | | A | | | N |
| A | | R | | | N | | | 16 N | | I | | Z | | L | | | |
| 17 D | Y | S | K | I | N | E | S | I | 18 A | A | | A | | | | | |
| E | | | | | A | | | C | A | C | | T | | | | | |
| | | 19 N | O | R | E | P | I | N | E | P | H | R | I | N | E | 20 S | |
| | | O | | | T | | T | | | O | | | | 21 M | E | T | |
| | 22 H | A | B | I | T | U | A | T | 23 I | O | N | | | | | O | |
| | | E | | | | | T | | X | | | | | | | R | |
| 24 T | R | 25 A | N | 26 S | P | O | R | T | E | R | | I | | 27 G | A | M | M | A |
| W | | C | | U | | S | | | D | | | | | | | G | |
| O | 28 H | E | B | B | | 29 E | P | I | N | E | P | H | R | I | N | E | |

# Chapter 6: How Do Drugs and Hormones Influer
# Behavior?

## Multiple-Choice Questions

1. E (p. 192)
2. A (p. 193)
3. B (p. 193)
4. C (p. 196)
5. C (p. 198)
6. D (p. 199)
7. C (p. 201)

8. D (p. 203)
9. E (p. 204)
10. A (p. 207)
11. B (p. 208)
12. A (p. 209)
13. C (p. 210)
14. B (p. 212)

15. E (p. 2
16. B (p. 2
17. B (p. 210)
18. D (p. 220)
19. B (p. 227)
20. E (p. 230)

## Short Answer Questions

1. (p. 194)
2. (p. 204)
3. (p. 207)
4. (p. 209)

5. (p. 213)
6. (p. 216)
7. (p. 217)
8. (p. 220)

9. (p. 221)
10. (p. 229)

## Matching

1. _5_ Oral (eaten)
   _4_ Topical (applied to the surface of the skin or mucus)
   _2_ Intravenous (injected into a vein)
   _1_ Intracranial (injected into the brain)
   _3_ Inhalation (smoking)

2. <u>agonists</u>    block presynaptic reuptake of neurotransmitter from synapse
   <u>agonists</u>    block enzyme that breaks down neurotransmitter
   <u>antagonists</u> block postsynaptic receptor site
   <u>antagonists</u> block release of neurotransmitter from presynaptic terminal
   <u>agonists</u>    increase effectiveness of neurotransmission
   <u>antagonists</u> decrease effectiveness of neurotransmission

3. _B_ Block dopamine receptor sites
   _A_ Affects GABA$_A$ receptor
   _E_ Increases cyclic AMP
   _D_ Among the most potent analgesics
   _C_ Contributed to development of Prozac

4. _E_ Fermented and distilled
   _C_ Coca plant
   _B_ Hemp plant
   _D_ Poppy seeds
   _A_ Peyote cactus sugars

5. _C_ More common in women than ain men
   _A_ Poor nutrition may increase symptoms
   _A_ Associated with underdeveloped brain
   _C_ Sometimes treated with electroconvulsive therapy
   _B_ May be co-diagnosed with schizophrenia

**agrams**

1.

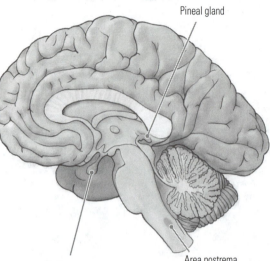

Pineal gland

Area postrema

Pituitary

2.

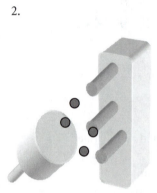 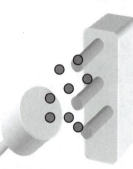 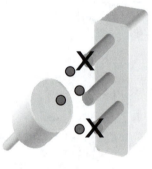

**Normal**

**Cocaine**
(Increased Dopamine)

**Neuroleptic**
(Receptor blockade)

3.

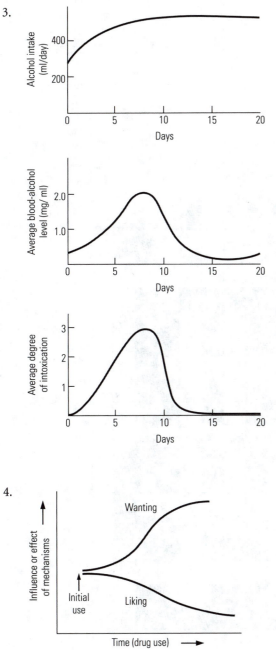

4.

5.

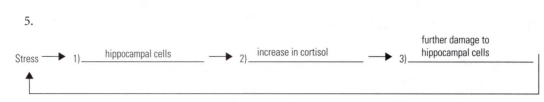

## Crossword Puzzle

| 1 H | O | 2 M | E | O | S | T | A | 3 S | I | S | | | 4 G | | 5 B | B | B |
|---|---|---|---|---|---|---|---|---|---|---|---|---|---|---|---|---|---|
| | | E | | | | | | E | | | 6 M | D | M | A | R | | |
| | | D | | 7 H | 8 L | S | D | D | | | | | B | | A | | |
| 9 S | P | I | D | E | R | | 10 A | M | 11 P | H | E | T | A | M | I | N | 12 E |
| | | A | | R | | | T | | O | | | | N | | | | M |
| | 13 E | N | D | O | R | P | H | I | N | S | | 14 M | | 15 S | | | I |
| 16 C | | I | | | | | V | | T | | | E | | E | | | N |
| U | | 17 A | N | T | I | D | E | P | R | E | S | S | A | N | T | | E |
| R | | S | | | | S | | E | | | O | S | | S | | | N |
| 18 A | B | U | S | E | R | | | M | | L | | I | | | | | C |
| R | | O | | 19 A | N | 20 T | I | A | 21 N | X | I | E | T | Y | | | E |
| E | | C | | | | D | R | | A | | M | | I | | | | |
| | | 22 W | I | T | H | D | R | A | W | A | L | | B | | Z | | |
| 23 A | | A | | I | | N | | 24 O | X | I | D | A | S | E | | | |
| C | | T | | | C | | S | | X | | | C | | T | | | |
| 25 T | O | X | I | N | | T | | P | | O | | | | I | | 26 A | |
| I | | V | | | | I | | O | | 27 N | A | R | C | O | T | I | C |
| V | | 28 E | N | D | O | C | R | I | N | E | | | N | | | I | |
| E | | | | | | T | | | | | | | | | | D | |

# Chapter 7: How Does the Brain Develop?

## Multiple-Choice Questions

1. D (p. 238)
2. E (p. 238)
3. E (p. 240)
4. B (p. 243)
5. C (p. 245)
6. D (p. 246)
7. B (p. 247)

8. D (p. 247)
9. B (p. 249)
10. E (p. 249)
11. D (p. 253)
12. A (p. 255)
13. B (p. 256)
14. E (p. 260)

15. D (p. 262)
16. E (p. 265)
17. E (p. 268)
18. D (p. 268)
19. A (p. 270)
20. B (p. 272)

## Short Answer Questions

1. (p. 238)
2. (p. 246)
3. (p. 250)
4. (p. 251)

5. (p. 258)
6. (p. 260)
7. (p. 262)
8. (p. 264)

9. (p. 270)
10. (p. 273)

## Matching

1. _4_ Progenitor cells
   _1_ Neural groove
   _3_ Neural stem cells
   _5_ Neuroblasts and glioblasts
   _2_ Neural tube

2. _A_ Stimulates production of progenitor cells
   _D_ Guide growth cones to the cell
   _C_ Guide cell migration from neural tube
   _B_ Stimulates production of neuro-blasts
   _E_ Provide adhesive surface for guiding cells

3. _C_ Axonal projections
   _B_ Dendritic branching
   _D_ Programmed cell death
   _A_ Cell proliferation
   _E_ Process of eliminating neurons

4. _D_ Formal operational
   _A_ Sensorimotor
   _B_ Concrete operational
   _C_ Preoperational

5. _A_ Lazy eye syndrome
   _C_ Serious motor problems
   _B_ Abnormal intellect and social behaviors
   _E_ Mental retardation
   _D_ Fatal soon after birth

## Diagrams

1.

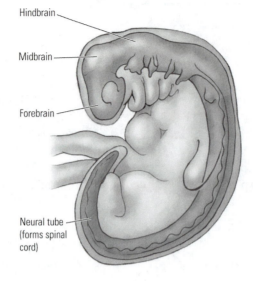

Hindbrain

Midbrain

Forebrain

Neural tube (forms spinal cord)

2.

Neuron A

Neuron B

Neuron C

3.

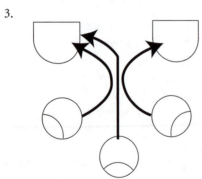

OR

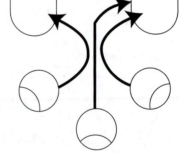

4.

Mentally Retarded

Normal

5. C

## Crossword Puzzle

**Across**

1. PERIOD
4. PLASTICITY
6. SPURTS
8. ANENCEPHALY
11. CAMS
12. NEO
13. BIFIDA
15. NEUROGENESIS
16. TUBE
18. FILOPODIUM
20. RUBELLA
21. GROWTH
23. IMPRINTING
25. TROPIC
28. HARLOW
29. STEM
30. GLIA

**Down**

Completed answer grid including: EKTA, RAA, DOW, SELL, DYNE, PHENYLKETONURIA, ENDRB, HALY, PIAG, NEATT, MICI, ROR, WRA, TORI, CARON, NETRINS, RUBELLA, PRODIAI, GRATION, HARLOW, STEM, CAM.

# Chapter 8: How Do We See the World?

## Multiple-Choice Questions

1. E (p. 279)
2. E (p. 281)
3. D (p. 281)
4. E (p. 282)
5. E (p. 286)
6. D (p. 287)
7. D (p. 288)

8. A (p. 288)
9. C (p. 291)
10. E (p. 300)
11. B (p. 301)
12. D (p. 302)
13. C (p. 306)
14. D (p. 308)

15. C (p. 310)
16. A (p. 311)
17. E (p. 314)
18. C (p. 278)
19. D (p. 283)
20. B (p. 313)

## Short Answer Questions

1. (p. 279)
2. (p. 281)
3. (p. 286)
4. (p. 298)

5. (p. 298)
6. (p. 302)
7. (p. 306)
8. (p. 306)

9. (p. 311)
10. (p. 283)

## Matching

1. __D__ Contains photoreceptors
   __B__ Directs image onto the fovea
   __C__ Controls amount of light entering
   __E__ Contains blood vessels entering eye
   __A__ Outer covering of eye

2. __R__ used primarily for night vision
   __C__ used for color vision
   __C__ highest density found in the fovea
   __C__ used for acute vision
   __R__ long and slender in shape
   __R__ most of the receptors in the eye are this type

3. __M__ receive input primarily from rods
   __M__ found in the periphery of the retina
   __P__ are sensitive to color
   __P__ are the smaller of the two ganglion cells
   __M__ are more sensitive to light

4. __E__ Deficit in reaching using visual guidance
   __A__ Usually compensated for by nystagmus
   __B__ Caused by complete lesion of one optic tract
   __C__ More common in males than females
   __D__ Inability to recognize objects

5. __2__ Optic chiasm
   __4__ Occipital lobe
   __3__ Lateral geniculate nucleus
   __1__ Fovea
   __5__ Temporal lobe

## Diagrams

1.

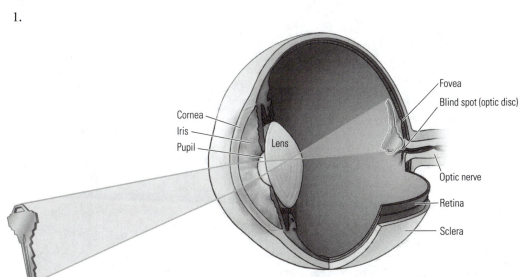

2.

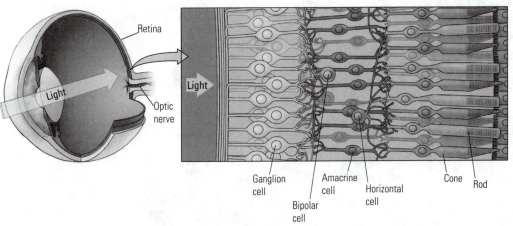

3.

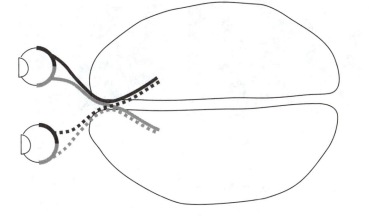

4.  A = Green

B = Red

5.

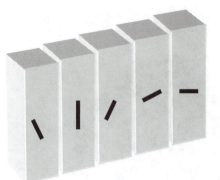

## Crossword Puzzle

| ¹P | | ²C | O | ³M | P | L | E | X | | | ⁴L | A | ⁵T | E | R | ⁶A | L | L |
|----|----|----|----|----|----|----|----|----|----|----|----|----|----|----|----|----|----|----|
| U | | | | A | | | ⁷B | | | | | | R | | | M | | |
| ⁸P | R | I | M | A | R | Y | | ⁹O | P | T | I | C | | | | A | | |
| I | | | | V | | | | N | | P | | | C | | | C | | |
| L | | ¹⁰T | H | E | O | R | I | ¹¹E | S | O | | | ¹²H | E | A | R | | |
| S | | E | | C | | | | I | | L | | | R | | | I | | |
| | | A | | E | | | | M | | A | | | O | | | N | | |
| ¹³D | O | R | S | A | L | | ¹⁴H | Y | P | E | R | ¹⁵C | O | M | P | ¹⁶L | E | X |
| | | L | | L | | | | L | | | | O | | A | | E | | |
| ¹⁷G | ¹⁸E | ¹⁹N | I | C | U | L | A | T | E | | ²⁰R | E | T | I | N | A | ²¹S | |
| | Y | N | | L | | | | | | | N | | I | | S | | U | |
| | ²²E | X | T | R | A | ²³S | T | ²⁴R | I | A | T | E | C | | | | P | |
| ²⁵S | | E | | R | | H | | R | | A | | | | | | | E | |
| T | | R | | | | E | | I | | ²⁶R | | ²⁷C | O | L | ²⁸O | R | | |
| ²⁹R | G | Y | B | | ³⁰B | L | O | B | S | O | | O | | | G | | I | O |
| I | | L | | | L | | R | | | D | | R | | | N | | O | R |
| A | | O | | | I | | Y | | ³¹S | P | O | T | | | | | R | |
| T | | B | | | N | | | | | E | | | | | | | | |
| ³²E | Y | E | S | | ³³D | I | S | C | | ³⁴A | T | A | X | I | A | | | |

# Chapter 9: How Do We Hear, Speak, and Make Music?

**Multiple-Choice Questions**

1. C (p. 319)
2. A (p. 320)
3. D (p. 321)
4. C (p. 322)
5. D (p. 323)
6. E (p. 325)
7. E (p. 327)

8. B (p. 328)
9. A (p. 330)
10. E (p. 330)
11. B (p. 330)
12. C (p. 332)
13. C (p. 334)
14. A (p. 334)

15. B (p. 336)
16. E (p. 338)
17. C (p. 339)
18. A (p. 346)
19. E (p. 348)
20. E (p. 350)

**Short Answer**

1. (p. 324)
2. (p. 328)
3. (p. 333)
4. (p. 334)

5. (p. 336)
6. (p. 337)
7. (p. 338)
8. (p. 338)

9. (p. 348)
10. (p. 351)

**Matching**

1. _B_ Measured in decibels
   _E_ Primarily right hemisphere
   _A_ Measured in hertz
   _C_ Time difference between ears
   _D_ Posterior temporal lobe

2. _2_ Ganglion cells
   _5_ Inferior coliculus
   _1_ Bipolar cells
   _3_ Cochlear nucleus
   _4_ Superior olive

3.

4. _A_ Cortex
   _D_ Hindbrain
   _E_ Cochlea
   _B_ Thalamus
   _C_ Midbrain

5. _B_ From straight right
   _A_ From ahead
   _C_ From behind
   _D_ From the left

## Diagrams

1.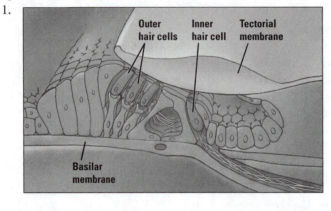

2. A. Tuba
   B. Trumpet
   C. Flute

3. B

4.

5.

|  | C. |  | A. |  | B. |  | D. |  |  |  |
|---|---|---|---|---|---|---|---|---|---|---|
| 0 | 20 | 40 | 60 | 80 | 100 | 120 | 140 | 160 | 180 | 200 |

## Crossword Puzzle

| 1 D | E | 2 C | I | 3 B | E | L |  | 4 D |  |  |  |  |  |  | 5 P |  |  |
|---|---|---|---|---|---|---|---|---|---|---|---|---|---|---|---|---|---|
|  |  | R |  | R |  | 6 F | R | E | Q | U | E | N | C | I | E | S |  |
| 7 P | R | O | S | O | D | Y |  | U |  |  |  |  |  |  | N |  |  |
| E |  | W |  | C |  | 8 I | M | 9 P | L | A | N | T | S |  | F |  | 10 B |
| R |  | A |  |  |  |  |  | I |  |  |  |  |  |  | I |  | I |
| 11 F | O | R | K | S |  | 12 W | E | R | N | I | C | K | E | 13 E | 14 E | A | R |
| E |  |  |  |  |  | N |  |  |  |  | M |  |  | L |  | D |  |
| 15 C | O | C | H | L | E | A |  | 17 A | M | 18 P | L | I | T | U | D | E | 19 E |
| T |  | A |  |  |  |  |  | O |  | S |  |  |  |  | X |  |  |
|  | 20 A | 21 M | E | M | 22 B | R | 23 A | N | E | S |  |  | 24 P | E | T |  |  |
| P |  | M |  |  | R |  | U |  | I |  |  |  | E |  |  |  |  |
| H | 25 E | C | H | O | L | O | C | A | T | I | O | N |  | R |  |  |  |
| 26 H | A | I | R |  | C |  | L |  | R |  | N |  | 27 S | O | N | G |  |
| S |  | 28 N | O |  | A |  | E |  | O |  |  |  | A |  |  |  |  |
| I |  | O |  | 29 L | O | U | D | N | E | S | 30 S |  | L |  |  |  |  |
| 31 A | N | V | I | L |  |  | S |  |  |  | O |  |  |  |  |  |  |
|  |  | S |  | 32 A |  |  |  |  |  |  | U |  |  |  |  |  |  |
| 33 O | L | I | V | E | 34 G | A | N | G | L | I | O | N |  |  |  |  |  |
|  |  |  |  | E |  |  |  |  |  | 35 D | E | A | F |  |  |  |  |

# Chapter 10: How Does the Brain Produce Movement?

**Multiple choice**

1. E (p. 356)
2. B (p. 356)
3. D (p. 357)
4. B (p. 358)
5. E (p. 360)
6. C (p. 361)
7. A (p. 363)

8. A (p. 366)
9. D (p. 367)
10. C (p. 367)
11. A (p. 370)
12. E (p. 374)
13. B (p. 375)
14. D (p. 380)

15. E (p. 383)
16. C (p. 386)
17. E (p. 387)
18. B (p. 388)
19. B (p. 392)
20. A (p. 362)

**Short Answer**

1. (p. 336)
2. (p. 373)
3. (p. 375)
4. (p. 379)

5. (p. 381)
6. (p. 383)
7. (p. 387)
8. (p. 390)

9. (p. 393)
10. (p. 376)

**Matching**

1. _A_ "Volume control" for movement
   _B_ Planning movement
   _D_ Monosynaptic reflexes
   _C_ Executing movement
   _E_ Regulating posture

2. _B_ Somatosensory cortex
   _A_ Brainstem
   _E_ Spinal cord
   _D_ Cerebellum
   _C_ Basal ganglia

3. _B_ Utilizes free nerve endings that release chemicals
   _C_ Encapsulated nerve endings monitoring tendons
   _B_ Utilizes small unmyelinated fiber
   _A_ Responds best to pressure
   _C_ Processes information on body position

4. _2_ Dorsal column nuclei
   _4_ Ventrolateral thalamus
   _1_ Muscle stretch receptors
   _3_ Medial lemniscus
   _5_ Somatosensory cortex

5. _E_ May send excitatory or inhibitory signals
   _B_ Senses changes in 3 planes of different orientations
   _D_ Small crystals of calcium carbonate
   _C_ Fluid filling the semicircular canals
   _A_ Consists of the ultricle and saccule

## Diagrams

1.

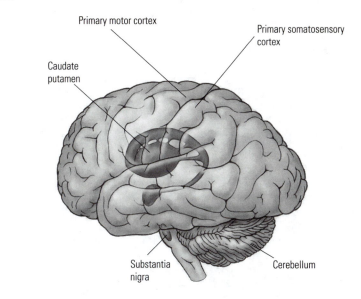

Primary motor cortex

Primary somatosensory
cortex

Caudate
putamen

Substantia
nigra

Cerebellum

2.

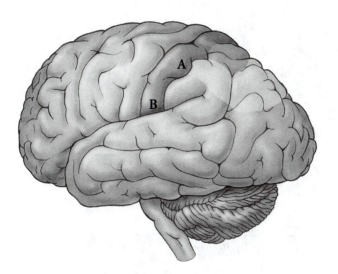

3.

4.

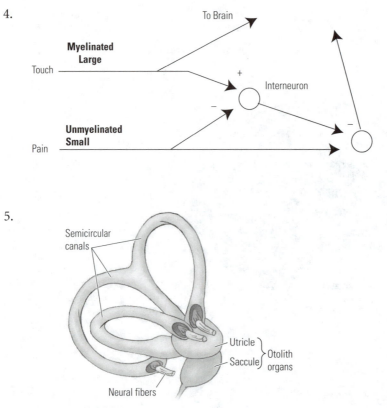

5.

## Crossword Puzzle

| | | | | | | | | | | | | | | | | |
|---|---|---|---|---|---|---|---|---|---|---|---|---|---|---|---|---|
| ¹S | | | | ²E | ³N | D | O | L | Y | M | P | H | ⁴H | | ⁵C |
| Y | | ⁶A | ⁷C | E | O | | | | | | | | Y | | A |
| S | | | O | | ⁸R | O | O | T | | | ⁹P | A | I | N | N |
| ¹⁰T | O | U | R | E | T | T | E | S | | | E | | | | A |
| E | | | T | | S | | | A | ¹¹O | ¹²U | T | R | I | C | L | E |
| ¹³M | E | D | I | A | L | | | L | T | K | | | | S |
| | | | C | | | ¹⁴G | | ¹⁵O | T | O | L | I | T | H | |
| ¹⁶M | O | T | O | R | | A | | C | | N | | | | | |
| | | | S | | ¹⁷V | E | N | T | R | O | L | A | T | E | R | A | L |
| | | | P | | E | | G | | N | | | T | | | ¹⁸P |
| ¹⁹H | ²⁰D | I | S | S | O | L | U | T | I | O | N | | I | | A |
| A | N | | T | | I | | | A | | | ²¹C | A | N | A | L |
| ²²P | Y | R | A | M | I | D | A | L | | | | | S |
| S | | | L | | B | | ²³L | | ²⁴C | | ²⁵H | A | I | R | Y |
| I | | | B | | A | | A | | O | | H | | | |
| ²⁶S | P | ²⁷I | N | A | L | | ²⁸H | O | R | N | ²⁹S | R | | ³⁰F |
| | | I | | | B | | L | | D | ³¹K | I | N | E | T | I | C |
| ³²S | Y | N | E | R | G | I | E | S | | | I | | | N |
| | | E | | | Y | | ³³P | E | N | F | I | E | L | D |

# Chapter 11: What Causes Behavior?

## Multiple Choice

1. A (p. 400)
2. B (p. 402)
3. B (p. 407)
4. E (p. 410)
5. D (p. 412)
6. A (p. 414)
7. B (p. 421)

8. B (p. 422)
9. C (p. 423)
10. E (p. 425)
11. C (p. 426)
12. B (p. 427)
13. C (p. 430)
14. D (p. 433)

15. D (p. 434)
16. A (p. 435)
17. C (p. 436)
18. D (p. 437)
19. A (p. 439)
20. B (p. 438)

## Short Answer

1. (p. 405)
2. (p. 408)
3. (p. 411)
4. (p. 427)

5. (p. 429)
6. (p. 433)
7. (p. 434)
8. (p. 435)

9. (p. 437)
10. (p. 439)

## Matching

1. __D__ Lack of prosody
   __A__ Reduced fear response
   __C__ Hyperphagia
   __E__ Disruption of male sexual behavior
   __B__ Aphagia behavior

2. __C__ Treated with anxiolytic drugs
   __A__ Reduced dopamine from frontal lobe
   __B__ Disruption of serotonin and noradrenaline
   __C__ Overactivity of GABA$_A$ receptors
   __B__ Affects nearly 10 percent of the population

3. __C__ Satiety
   __E__ Fear response
   __A__ Hypovolemic thirst
   __B__ Osmotic thirst
   __D__ Sexual receptivity

4. __A__ Persistent and unrealistic worries
   __C__ Involve a clearly dreaded object or situation
   __B__ Recurrent attacks of intense terror
   __B__ Often leads to agoraphobia
   __C__ Most common type of anxiety disorder

5. __O__ Testosterone producing sexual dimorphism of preoptic area
   __A__ Testosterone producing male sexual behavior
   __A__ Estrogen and progesterone producing lordosis
   __O__ Congenital adrenal hyperplasia causing an enlarged clitoris
   __A__ Estrous cycle hormones increasing dendritic branching

## Diagrams

1.

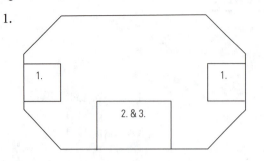

2. Neurons A, C, & D would be masculinized.

3. Add extracellular salt.

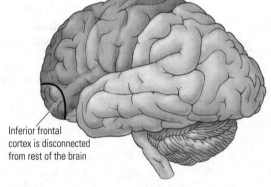

4.

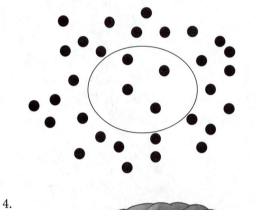

Inferior frontal
cortex is disconnected
from rest of the brain

5. All cells project to posterior pituitary

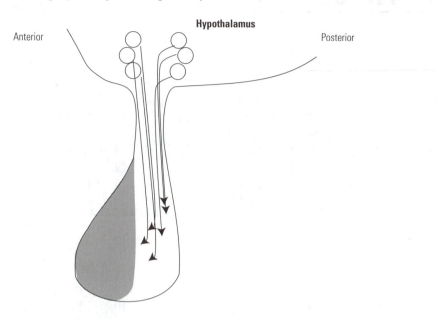

## Crossword Puzzle

| 1 F | O | R | 2 E | B | R | A | I | N | | 3 M | E | D | 4 I | A | L | 5 A |
| E | | | B | | F | | | 6 B | | | | | C | | | G |
| E | | | F | 7 L | | 8 P | R | E | O | P | T | I | C | | | E |
| D | 9 R | E | W | A | R | D | | N | | | | U | | | | N |
| I | U | | N | | | Z | | 10 H | O | R | M | O | N | E | | S |
| 11 N | O | 12 N | R | E | G | 13 U | L | A | T | O | R | Y | | B | | I |
| G | | E | | E | | E | | D | 14 P | A | P | E | Z | | | S |
| | | L | | A | | A | | I | O | | N | | | | | |
| 15 A | T | E | | 16 G | A | R | C | I | A | | S | | 17 P | | |
| | | A | | N | | Z | | E | T | | | | O | | |
| 18 T | A | S | T | E | | I | | P | H | 19 A | D | R | E | N | A | 20 L |
| | | I | | N | | N | | | L | | | | | | | O |
| 21 A | N | D | R | 22 O | G | E | N | I | T | A | L | | 23 S | O | B |
| | | G | | S | | N | | M | | | | K | | O |
| 24 P | 25 J | A | M | E | S | | E | U | | | I | | T |
| A | | O | | | 26 S | E | X | N | | O |
| 27 I | N | C | E | N | T | I | V | E | | N | | M |
| I | | | I | | 28 A | N | X | I | E | T | Y |
| 29 B | U | C | Y | 30 C | C | K | | | R | | |

# Chapter 12: Why Do We Sleep?

## Multiple Choice
1. A (p. 449)
2. D (p. 450)
3. C (p. 451)
4. B (p. 454)
5. E (p. 456)
6. A (p. 457)
7. D (p. 460)
8. D (p. 460)
9. A (p. 463)
10. E (p. 464)
11. E (p. 468)
12. B (p. 468)
13. E (p. 473)
14. A (p. 473)
15. D (p. 474)
16. C (p. 476)
17. B (p. 476)
18. E (p. 477)
19. E (p. 481)
20. A (p. 484)

## Short Answer
1. (p. 453)
2. (p. 454)
3. (p. 456)
4. (p. 458)
5. (p. 467)
6. (p. 468)
7. (p. 470)
8. (p. 473)
9. (p. 481)
10. (p. 481)

## Matching
1. A Around one year
   C Less than one day
   D Between one day and one year
   B Around one day

2. C Damage to this may result in coma
   E PGO spikes originate here
   A Considered the location of the main biological clock
   B EEGs are recorded from this area
   D Contains serotonin neurons that project to neocortex

3. NREM Delta rhythms
   REM Paralysis
   NREM Night terrors
   NREM Sleepwalking
   REM Loss of temperature-regulatory mechanism

4. A More common in people who are overweight
   B Anxiety and depression account for about 35 percent of cases
   C Results from tolerance development
   D May occur during a cataplexy attack
   E NREM disorder seen especially in children

5. D Seasonal Affective Disorder
   B Cataplexy
   C Restless Leg Syndrome
   A REM without atonia
   B Narcolepsy

## Diagrams

1. Days

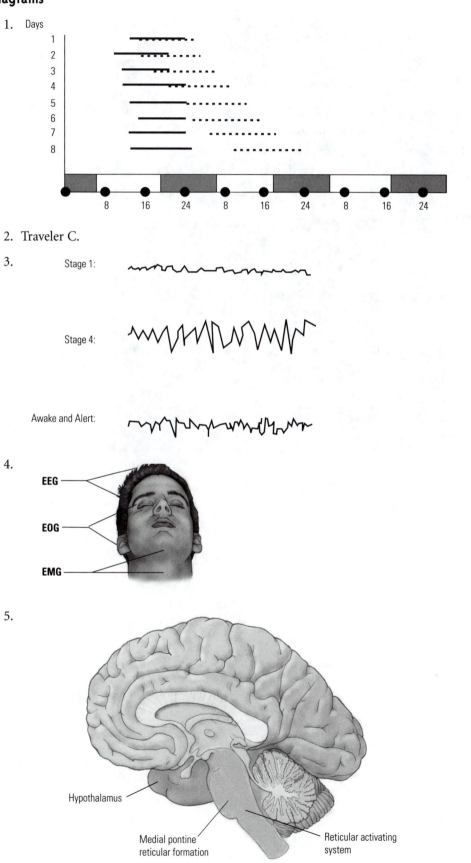

2. Traveler C.

3.  Stage 1:

    Stage 4:

    Awake and Alert:

4.  EEG

    EOG

    EMG

5.  Hypothalamus

    Medial pontine
    reticular formation

    Reticular activating
    system

## Crossword Puzzle

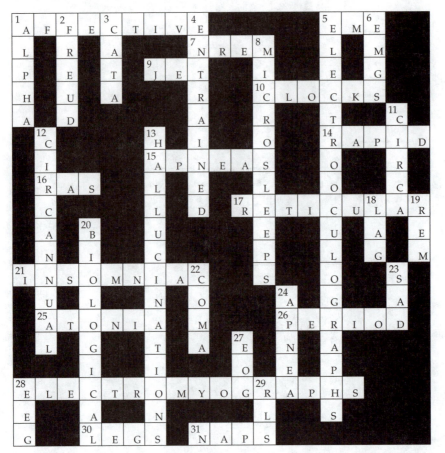

# Chapter 13: How Do We Learn From Experience?

**Multiple Choice**
1. E (p. 504)
2. D (p. 491)
3. B (p. 492)
4. C (p. 492)
5. C (p. 493)
6. B (p. 495)
7. D (p. 497)
8. A (p. 498)
9. C (p. 500)
10. B (p. 506)
11. C (p. 508)
12. C (p. 510)
13. D (p. 512)
14. C (p. 514)
15. C (p. 517)
16. D (p. 519)
17. A (p. 520)
18. E (p. 521)
19. D (p. 523)
20. E (p. 525)

**Short Answer**
1. (p. 489)
2. (p. 491)
3. (p. 496)
4. (p. 499)
5. (p. 499)
6. (p. 505)
7. (p. 506)
8. (p. 516)
9. (p. 522)
10. (p. 523)

**Matching**
1. OC A dog waiting near the table to be fed food scraps
   CC Ducking your head when you hear a loud noise
   CC The feeling of hunger when you smell pizza
   OC Studying late into the night before an exam
   OC Holding the door open for someone entering a building behind you

2. IM Riding a bicycle
   EM Childhood memories
   EM Declarative memory
   IM Procedural memory
   EM Top-down processing
   IM Bottom-up processing

3. E Visual object memory
   B Short-term memory
   C Emotional memory
   D Implicit memory
   A Object location

4. C Degeneration of frontal lobe
   A Loss of implicit memory
   B Degeneration of entorhinal cortex
   C Caused by a vitamin deficiency
   A Degeneration of the basal ganglia

5. B Recommends use of speech therapy
   A Undamaged regions will assume control of behavior
   B Recommends use of nerve growth factor
   C Recommends use of epidermal growth factor (EGF)
   C Has been used in many Parkinson's patients

## Diagrams

1.

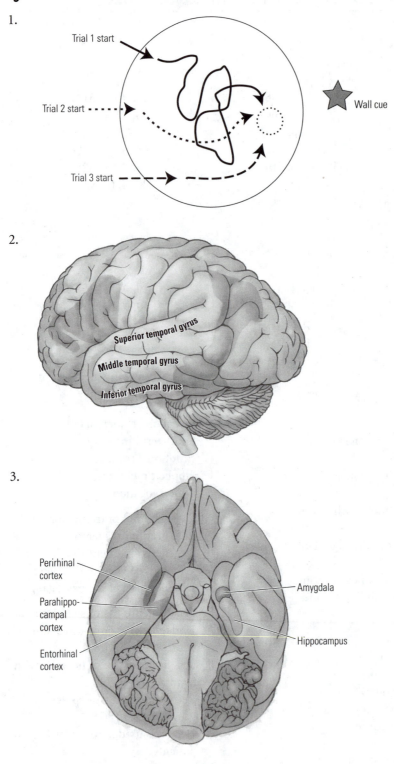

Trial 1 start

Trial 2 start

Trial 3 start

Wall cue

2.

Superior temporal gyrus

Middle temporal gyrus

Inferior temporal gyrus

3.

Perirhinal cortex

Parahippo-campal cortex

Entorhinal cortex

Amygdala

Hippocampus

4.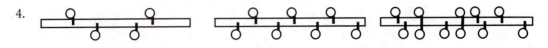

Low Concentration          Moderate Concentration          High Concentration

5.

Normal Healthy Neuron

Early Alzheimer's

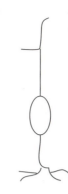
Advanced Alzheimer's

## Crossword Puzzle

|   |   |   | ¹K | ²E | G | S |   |   |   |   |   | ³C |   |   |
|---|---|---|---|---|---|---|---|---|---|---|---|---|---|---|
| ⁴B | L | ⁵L | I | N | K |   |   | ⁶W |   | ⁷G | ⁸I | N | A |   |
| F |   | M |   | P |   |   |   | O |   | N |   | A | J |   |
|   |   | P |   | I |   | ⁹C | L | A | S | S | I | C | A | L |
| ¹⁰D | ¹¹L | E | G | G | E | D |   | F |   | T |   | L |   |   |
| E | I |   | R |   | ¹²P |   | A | R | ¹³C | O |   |   |   |
| C | ¹⁴C | A | T |   | R |   | A |   | U | ¹⁵P | A | V | L | O | V |
| L | I |   | ¹⁵P | A | V | L | O | V | ¹⁶M | O | N | K | ¹⁷E | Y |
| ¹⁸F | A | C | T | O | ¹⁹R |   | L |   |   | L | E | D |   | Y |

# Chapter 14: How Does the Brain Think?

## Multiple Choice

| | | |
|---|---|---|
| 1. E (p. 530) | 8. C (p. 541) | 15. E (p. 552) |
| 2. E (p. 530) | 9. E (p. 544) | 16. C (p. 558) |
| 3. B (p. 531) | 10. A (p. 545) | 17. D (p. 563) |
| 4. E (p. 532) | 11. C (p. 546) | 18. A (p. 565) |
| 5. D (p. 535) | 12. B (p. 549) | 19. E (p. 567) |
| 6. E (p. 538) | 13. E (p. 550) | 20. E (p. 570) |
| 7. B (p. 540) | 14. A (p. 551) | |

## Short Answer

| | | |
|---|---|---|
| 1. (p. 531) | 5. (p. 542) | 9. (p. 567) |
| 2. (p. 532) | 6. (p. 549) | 10. (p. 570) |
| 3. (p. 540) | 7. (p. 553) | |
| 4. (p. 541) | 8. (p. 564) | |

## Matching

1. _B_ Creates images showing blood-flow changes in the brain
   _D_ Used to disrupt regional blood flow and associated behaviors
   _C_ Used to record magnetic fields and produce MEG
   _A_ Utilizes magnetic fields and radio pulses to produce brain images

2. _B_ Map reading
   _A_ Language production
   _C_ Temporal planning
   _B_ Music appreciation
   _A_ Language comprehension

3. _DT_ Disrupted particularly by frontal-lobe damage
   _CT_ Measured with traditional intelligence tests
   _CT_ Solving arithmetic problems or defining words
   _DT_ Used to generate numerous answers for a single question
   _CT_ Disruption is often associated with apraxia or aphasia

4. _E_ Ignoring sensory information, usually on one side of the body
   _B_ Inability to make voluntary movements
   _C_ Causes difficulty with the Wisconsin Card Sorting task
   _A_ Caused by damage to the corpus callosum
   _D_ Joining sensory experiences across sensory modalities

5. _B_ Pattern or structure of word order in a phrase
   _E_ The temporal organization of behavior
   _A_ Idea resulting from a set of impressions
   _D_ A form of neglect
   _C_ Term for a wide range of mental abilities

## Diagrams

1.

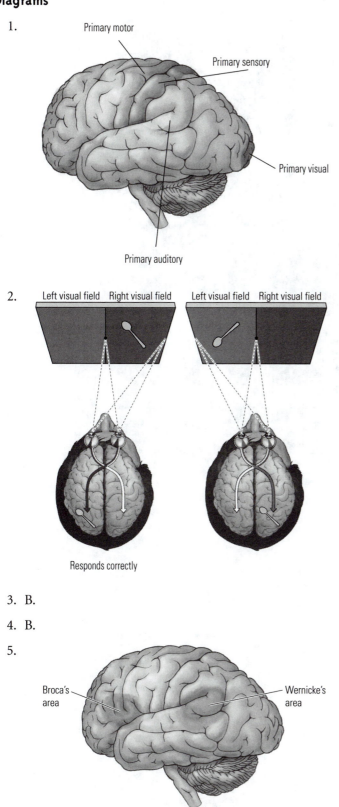

5.

Evidence for intrahemispheric differences in cortical organization of males and females. Apraxia is associated with frontal damage to the left hemisphere in women and with posterior damage in men. Aphasia occurs most often when damage is to the front of the brain in women but in the rear of the brain in men.

3. B.

4. B.

## Crossword Puzzle

Across:

1. RAT
3. NEUROSCIENCE
7. ATTENTION
10. TAN
12. SITS
14. FACE
15. RESONANCE
16. MEG
17. APRAXIA
21. MRI
23. CONSTRUCTS
25. SPLIT
26. TRI
29. COGNITION
32. IMAGING
34. PLANNING
35. NEGLECT

Down:

1. RESTAN
2. ARRAMS
5. ROOVEE
6. NOMMA
9. SYNNESSIA
11. SYY
13. AK
18. INE
19. ART
20. F
22. EXINC
24. THII
27. ATTLLGE
28. F
30. MR
31. BRT
33. GOA

# Chapter 15: What Have We Learned and What Is Its Value?

**Multiple Choice**
1. E (p. 575)
2. D (p. 576)
3. A (p. 577)
4. E (p. 578)
5. E (p. 578)
6. D (p. 578)
7. E (p. 579)
8. D (p. 581)
9. D (p. 581)
10. C (p. 582)
11. D (p. 582)
12. E (p. 583)
13. E (p. 583)
14. A (p. 584)
15. E (p. 588)
16. E (p. 594)
17. D (p. 595)
18. A (p. 590)
19. D (p. 597)
20. C (p. 599)

**Short Answer**
1. (p. 578)
2. (p. 579)
3. (p. 588)
4. (p. 583)
5. (p. 589)
6. (p. 589)
7. (p. 591)
8. (p. 597)
9. (p. 598)
10. (p. 599)

**Matching**

1.
   B Impairment in hydroxylation of phenylalanine to tyrosine
   E IQ score of less than 50, in 95 percent of patients
   C Decreased neuron size, dendritic length, and spine density
   D Mental retardation, abnormal EEG
   A Inborn error of metabolism due to defective recessive gene

2.
   D Hallucinations and agitated movements
   E Severe behavioral deficits
   C Characterized by excessive euphoria
   A Dysfunction of norepinephrine and serotonin
   B Little is known about underlying neurobiology

3.
   D Poor nutrition
   C Infection
   E Hormonal anomaly
   A Genetic error
   B Developmental anomaly

4.
   B L-dopa
   A Brain lesions
   C Psychotherapy
   C Least invasive
   A Most invasive

5.
   B Anxiolytic
   C Treatment for a serious motor disorder
   B Antianxiety drug
   A Antipsychotic drug
   C Treatment for Parkinson's disease
   A Treatment for schizophrenia

## Crossword Puzzle

|   |   |   |   |   |   |   |   |   |   |   |   |   |
|---|---|---|---|---|---|---|---|---|---|---|---|---|
| ¹K | ²N | ³O | W | ⁴L | E | D | ⁵G | E |  | ⁶P | L | ⁷A | S | T | I | C |
|  | E |  | O |  | E |  | T |  | E |  |  | X |  |
| ⁸C | O | M | M | U | N | I | C | ⁹A | T | I | O | N |  | ¹⁰T | J | B |
|  | K |  | A |  | D |  |  | N |  |  | N |  |  | H |  |
| ¹¹S | E | N | S | O | R | Y |  | ¹²X | X |  | ¹³F | R | E | U | ¹⁴D |
| ¹⁵D |  |  |  | I |  |  | I |  |  | R |  |  | S |
| ¹⁶I | V | ¹⁷A | N |  | ¹⁸T | U | M | O | R | ¹⁹S |  | ²⁰A | R | M | S |
| A |  | X |  |  | E |  | L |  | Y |  | P |  |  |
| G |  | O |  | ²¹A | S | Y | M | M | E | T | R | Y |  | ²²O | ²³D |
| N |  | ²⁴N | E | U | R | O | N |  | T |  | M |  | I |
| O |  | S |  | X |  |  | I |  | E |  |  | S |
| ²⁵S | R |  |  | I |  | ²⁶C | A | T | ²⁷E | G | O | R | ²⁸I | Z | E |
| T |  | ²⁹N | E | U | R | O | N | S |  | R |  | E |  | C |  | A |
| I |  | ³⁰M |  |  | L |  |  | Y |  | N |  |  | D |  | S |
| ³¹C | L | A | ³²S | S | I | F | ³³Y | I | N | G |  | ³⁴H | E | ³⁵R |  | E |
|  |  | N |  | A |  | T |  | I |  |  | T |  | B |
| ³⁶M | U | L | T | I | D | I | S | C | I | P | ³⁷L | I | N | A | R | Y |
|  | A |  |  | C |  | E |  | K |  | C |  | I |
| ³⁸V | A | L | I | U | M |  |  | U |  |  | N |